Mike Pilant   hb/o.p.

(412)-963-9465   pb 'p at
$ 62.40

as is

$7\frac{00}{110}$

JS3

7½

Barrios in Arms

Revolution in Santo Domingo

BARRIOS IN ARMS

Revolution in Santo Domingo

José A. Moreno

University of
Pittsburgh Press

SBN 8229-3186-9

Library of Congress Catalog Card Number 68-12723
Manufactured in the United States of America

To the Constitutionalist Commandos

Contents

Illustrations

Tables and Figures

Acknowledgments

✍ Many people, in the Dominican Republic and in the United States, have contributed in different ways to bring this study to completion—a work the author himself thought unfeasible less than two years ago. First of all, let me express my gratitude to Father Tomás Marrero and to Manuel Ortega, with whom I worked during the four months of the revolution. Their courage, dedication, and generosity stimulated me greatly in carrying out the role I was called upon to play during that violent time. Mention of all the people of San Miguel is also in order; they made it possible for me to begin to understand what the whole revolution was about. It is impossible to pay tribute to all Dominican leaders, both rebel and loyalist, who furnished me with information I requested. I can only say that once I had indicated to them the scientific purpose of my study, I was given generous cooperation. Still, I should like to pay tribute to two of my informants who are now dead: Ramón Mejía del Castillo (Pichirilo), one of the most colorful figures of the revolution, and Dr. Julio Cuello, Chief Justice of the Supreme Court, who played an important but unsuccessful role in the process of negotiations.

Invaluable help was given to me by all those persons who allowed me to use their private files to verify verbal information with historical documents that otherwise would have been impossible to obtain. Their names cannot be disclosed because most of the documents are either personal or have not been released for publication by their authors. One person I can mention, and do so with pleasure, is Dr. José A. Caro, Rector of the new university, Pedro Henríquez Ureña, who went out of his way many times to arrange meetings and interviews with people I could never have reached without his help.

There are also a number of people in this country to whom I am deeply indebted. First of all, my gratitude goes to Professor Frank W. Young of Cornell University, who often helped me overcome many obstacles during the years this study was conducted and written, and to Professors Robin M. Williams, Jr., and William F. Whyte, who were always a source of encouragement and who helped greatly to clarify a number of issues with their comments and criticism. Professor Rose K. Goldsen is to be credited with insights that—I hope—have been incorporated into the study. Professor Tom Davis and the Committee for Latin American Studies of Cornell University made possible this study by financing some stages of the present research. The Department of Rural Sociology also helped to finance some of the expenses.

I am also indebted to my wife Johanna for her patience and encouragement during the time I spent writing and revising the manuscript.

Barrios in Arms

Revolution in Santo Domingo

SANTO DOMINGO

Rebel Zone—shaded area

1 Presidential Palace
2 Copello Building
3 Independencia Park
4 Ozama Fortress
5 U.S. Checkpoints
6 Banks
7 Hospitals

Chapter 1

Participant Observation in a Revolution

I have always regretted that I was away in Europe when the Cuban revolution started. I was born in a working class family in the Cuba of dictator Gerardo Machado in 1928. I lived through the revolutionary attempts of the 1930's and through the first dictatorship of Batista. In my teens, I attended school in Havana with Fidel Castro and other boys who were later active in the struggle against Batista. Before Batista staged his second coup in 1952, I went to Europe where I spent the next eight years. I visited Cuba again in 1955 and 1956, but when Castro landed in Oriente in November 1956 I was back in Europe studying theology in the Jesuit-sponsored Heythrop College, Oxford. As soon as I finished my studies in Oxford and was ordained, I returned to Cuba to observe the changes taking place after the coming to power of my generation. I actually travelled to the sierras where Castro had started his guerrilla war against Batista three years earlier and where now the first steps of the agrarian reform were being implemented. I rode on horseback for days and had a look at the life of the peasants who had so deeply impressed the middle-class guerrillas who fought the revolution from their hills.[1]

For a comprehensive discussion of the method of participant observation, see Severyn T. Bruyn, *The Human Perspective in Sociology: The Methodology of Participant Observation* (Englewood Cliffs, N.J., 1966), pp. 1–22.

1. See Ernesto Che Guevara, *Relatos de la guerra revolucionaria* (Buenos Aires, 1965). See also Harry Eckstein, *Internal War* (Glencoe, Ill., 1964); Chalmers Johnson, *Revolutionary Change* (Boston, 1966); James C. Davis, "Toward a Theory of Revolution," *American Sociological Review,* 27 (Feb. 1962), pp. 5–19.

3

After three months in Cuba I went to Canada and then to the United States to continue my studies, this time in sociology at Cornell University, which eventually took me to Santo Domingo. I arrived there early in the fall of 1964 to do field work for my doctoral dissertation. My intention was to do an empirical study of medium-sized formal organizations to test several hypotheses on the existence of structural anomie in such organizations. By the spring of 1965, I had reviewed the literature[2] and become familiar with some problems of Dominican society through participation in the activities of the Center of Social Research set up by the Jesuit Order in Santo Domingo.[3]

When the revolution broke out, I realized that it was senseless to continue my empirical study. All the organizations I had planned to study were caught up in the turmoil of revolution, and the social upheaval of that period would certainly distort the results of any research. In all honesty, however, I cannot say that this was my primary reason for stopping my work and becoming involved in the events taking place around me.

Now in 1965 I had the opportunity to observe and perhaps participate in the events of a new revolution. I was not going to miss this second chance. It was not only scientific curiosity that drew me into an active role in these events; I felt an obligation to the community to help wherever possible to solve the national crisis. I decided first to help organize the hospitals in the north of the city where the inhabitants were hardest hit by the fighting. Later I helped to organize a community in the heart of the rebel zone. As a priest I enjoyed a certain religious immunity to travel freely across the lines through sniper fire. As time passed, I

2. I had made contact with Professor Leo Srole in order to adapt his anomie scale to organizations. See Leo Srole, "Social Integration and Certain Corollaries: An Exploratory Study," *American Sociological Review,* 21 (Dec. 1956), pp. 709–16.

3. My job in the Center for seven months before the outbreak of the revolution had placed me in a particularly sensitive position. I was able to observe closely what was happening at various levels of the social structure—the government, the church, the military, the middle class, and the labor organizations. I am profoundly indebted to the Jesuit Order for placing me in the position which I occupied all through the period of the revolution. The fact that after the revolution I requested from Rome release from my obligations to the ministry and to the Jesuit Order does not bear on the present research, since that step was taken for entirely personal reasons.

found myself more and more involved in the events and increasingly playing a leadership role in the community within the structure of a society in the process of revolution.

I began to feel a strong solidarity with the doctors and nurses in the hospitals and later with the hungry people of the barrio,[4] with the boys who were fighting in the commandos, and with the rebel leaders as we worked together to solve health and food problems. But it was not only a humanitarian attitude that drew me to the commando posts or to the trenches to listen to the sentries' conversations during the long nights. At first it was curiosity to know what was really happening; later I realized that I was the only trained sociologist in the rebel zone and that events were occurring around me which I had a responsibility to the profession to describe and analyze.[5]

My scientific interest in observing the behavior and organizations of the rebels doubled when I realized that because of my leadership role, I began to be accepted not only as one of the community but also as one with the rebels. With Spanish my mother tongue, I had no difficulty identifying with Dominicans. And the fact that I had chosen to move into the rebel zone to live with the rebels after they were surrounded by the U.S. Marines indicated my affinity to the rebel cause. However, it was obvious to me that, because of the role I was playing, I could not take any political or military stand. In my public performance I had to maintain neutrality to be able to travel through the lines and to get help needed from national and international agencies. I carefully avoided writing in the press, speaking on the radio, or attending political or military rallies. I knew only too well that a single newspaper comment could hamper the work I had undertaken. In my own mind, however, I noticed that I grew increasingly close to the rebels. When I had to admonish the rebels for something I considered wrong, I would say, "*We* are not in a revolution to get away with this." Or "It is a shame *we* do this in our zone." Moreover, when someone in the loyalist zone criticized the rebels for being

4. The *barrio* may best be defined as a community within a larger community. Its inhabitants are governed by distinct neighborhood rules of behavior and local loyalties. In short, a *barrio* is a ghetto without the latter's racial overtones.

5. My work was greatly stimulated by two visits of sociologist Rose K. Goldsen to the rebel zone.

"tigres" or "communists," during the rest of the conversation I would find myself using the word "we" when referring to the rebels.[6]

For four months I lived with the rebels, sharing their feelings, anxieties, prejudices, fears, and desires. I tried to empathize with them, to grasp the ideological and psychological processes occurring within them—processes from which I felt alienated because I had not suffered what they had suffered: hunger, injustice, oppression, insecurity, and destitution. I soon found that my role was more a participant than an observer.[7] However, the more I participated, the more I could observe. Participation reached a point that left no time to take notes; but having a descriptive or "photographic" memory, I hoped that I would soon have time to write down the major experiences. Some details would certainly be forgotten, but the variety of situations would compensate for loss of minor details.

In getting a close look at the revolution as it developed, it was necessary for me[8] to concur with the rebels in their sentiments, to participate actively in the revolutionary process as it evolved, to take a leadership role in meeting their current needs, and to maintain a minimum degree of detachment.

When the revolution ended in September 1965, I decided to return to Cornell to record my observations and to gain distance and perspective necessary if I were to describe my experiences with any objectivity. In addition, other projects connected with my research had begun to take so much of my time and energy that it became necessary for me to get away so that I could write. I also needed time to put together as many pieces of the story as I could collect. I spent the next six months writing down all that I could remember of my experiences in the Dominican revolution.

Sometimes I talked into a tape recorder; at other times I wrote as many observations as I could remember on a given subject. I kept feeding the

6. "The participant observer . . . considers the interpretations of his subjects to have first importance, and initially the observer may not want to understand these interpretations objectively; he may want to understand them subjectively through his own involvement with the culture before he can understand them from any other point of view." Severyn T. Bruyn, *The Human Perspective in Sociology: The Methodology of Participant Observation* (Englewood Cliffs, N.J., 1966), p. 12.

7. See Buford H. Junker, *Field Work: An Introduction to the Social Sciences* (Chicago, 1960), pp. 35–38.

8. See Bruyn, *Human Perspective*, pp. 13–22.

information into a series of files with such titles as "The life of the commandos," "Ideologies," "The community," "The individual," and "Integration." Occasionally I found that one topic brought a string of observations about another, and I would classify them in their own file. Sometimes a single observation that had caught my attention when it happened raised certain questions.[9] Naturally, the raw material in the files consisted of qualitative data of many different kinds.

I also began to study the written documents I had brought from Santo Domingo. The first documents were the issues of the two main Dominican newspapers, *El Caribe* and *El Listín Diario.* I had managed to secure the last four issues of these newspapers—April 25 to April 28, 1965— which dealt almost exclusively with the outbreak of the revolution. Since they are independent newspapers, they are perhaps the most important public documents of what happened during the first four days of the revolution. The second set of documents is the entire collection of the two rebel newspapers, *Patria* and *La Nación,* which were published in the rebel zone daily throughout the revolution.[10] They sold quickly throughout the city since they were the only printed news in Santo Domingo, with the exception of a conservative tabloid of small circulation. By reading this collection of newspapers I was able to verify dates of some of my observations, and to reconstruct the rebel version of the negotiations. By analyzing the news I could estimate the morale of the rebel group at different times and study ideological tendencies within the rebel organization.

Finally, I had managed to collect many single copies of bulletins and tabloids published during the revolution by all kinds of ideological groups. I had also obtained copies of practically all the publications issued in Santo Domingo and in this country on the Dominican crisis. By

9. "Such observations compel us to look for explanations, to explore the consequences, to try to fit them into our scheme of knowledge." Allen H. Barton and Paul Lazarsfeld, "Some Functions of Qualitative Analysis in Social Research," in S. M. Lipset and N. J. Smelser, eds., *Sociology: Progress of a Decade* (Englewood Cliffs, N.J., 1961), p. 97.

10. *La Nación* started publication on May 6 and *Patria* on May 14. Both newspapers maintained an outstanding record of publication, despite the fact that at some points, due to the attacks of the enemy, there were no telephones and no electricity to run the presses. Both continued to be published until months after the inauguration of the provisional government. *Patria* was eventually suppressed by U.S. troops.

reading this information, I broadened the framework of my personal observations and encountered some problems which I have attempted to answer in this study. After an intensive review of the literature, I decided I was ready to go back to the field.

The work I had done as a participant observer during the revolution focused my attention on a relatively small area of the rebel zone and on relatively few people. In discussions with people outside Santo Domingo, most of the questions asked me were naturally about the rebel leader Caamaño, the negotiations, the U.S. intervention, and other general topics. I often found myself wondering about certain issues relevant to my study which I seemed unable to comment on. From these discussions I realized that I had to present my research not only as an experiment in community development, but as part of the far larger context of the revolutionary process. However, I did not have the information required for such study. I knew most of the rebel leaders, but the knowledge obtained on the basis of these acquaintances could hardly be counted as firsthand information relevant to understanding the revolution.

It occurred to me that my own observations would benefit by being combined with the observations of several other leaders. A wealth of information which had not appeared in the press could be obtained only by personal interviews with the men who caused the events or were present when they happened. In the spring of 1966 I returned to the field to collect more information on the revolution. By then some loyalist and rebel leaders were in exile or in diplomatic posts abroad. To interview them, I traveled to Canada, Miami, Puerto Rico, and Santo Domingo. In all I spent eight weeks personally interviewing men who had taken active roles in the crisis. Approximately three hundred hours were spent in these interviews. (The complete list of people I interviewed is given in Appendix 4.)

Because I was aware that my work as participant observer had linked me emotionally and ideologically to the rebel group, I decided to build as broad a picture as possible of the crisis, by meeting and interviewing the leaders of both factions, civilians, and military. The job was further complicated because it was just two months before the elections and many leaders were involved in the campaign.[11] Also, it was difficult to

11. The presidential elections were being organized by the Provisional Government of Héctor García-Godoy and were to be held on June 1, 1966. On several

locate some of the rebel leaders who were already living in the underground; some loyalists had unlisted telephones; others did not want to
talk to "the press."

Once the first contacts were made, I had no difficulty arranging the
interviews. The rebels knew me and were quite willing to see me again.
To the loyalist and other leaders I explained the scientific purpose of the
study and no one refused to cooperate. Sometimes an interview with one
person would facilitate the next interview—friends knew unlisted telephones or summer resorts or would invite me to meet their acquaintances
informally. The interviews were conducted as casually as possible. I
assured my informants on both sides that my goal was a thorough and
unbiased understanding of the events and that I would not publish any
information which could be harmful to an informant if he could be traced
as its only possible source.[12]

I attempted to learn more about the revolution in terms of historical
facts, to know more about the men involved—their attitudes, ideologies,
prejudices, and opinions—and their positions in the Dominican social
structure, and to verify the accuracy of information I had compiled
during the revolution.

I asked open-ended questions,[13] letting the interviewee proceed at his
own pace, and interrupted with specific questions only at what seemed
good stopping points. In this way I was able to glean details I had not
previously encountered and to cross-check information disseminated by
journalists and U.S. officials and information I had received from the
other interviews. To do this, an indirect method of questioning was
required. For example, suggestions were made in the press and by U.S.
officials that Caamaño was only a front-man for the leftists "who were
really in command of the situation as early as April 27." I set out to verify
or disclaim this assertion. I could not ask a direct question, because I did

---

occasions during this period I visited Juan Bosch in his heavily guarded headquarters on the outskirts of the city from which he conducted his presidential
campaign. Threats against his life had curbed his mobility and his actual cam-
paigning was reduced to little more than a daily radio program prerecorded in
his headquarters.

12. Only one person refused to answer the straight questions I put to him. He
was very kind, but he seemed to be overly concerned about what other people
thought of him.

13. Barton and Lazarsfeld, "Some Functions of Qualitative Analysis," p. 111.

not want to distort the answer. So I asked indirectly and casually: "Did you see Caamaño on this occasion? What was he doing?" In this way I was able to trace the origins of Caamaño's leadership to the original organization of the rebels.

Likewise I was able to check the veracity of my interviewees. Perhaps the most interesting case was the verification of a story told by PRD Secretary General A. Martínez Francisco. According to him, he was kidnapped by a loyalist army officer and a CIA agent and taken to San Isidro where he was forced to read an appeal to the rebels to give up the fight. Martínez told me that when he was in San Isidro, the Papal Nuncio arrived from Puerto Rico and was asked to make an appeal for peace. I was able to check this information with the Papal Nuncio, and I could verify that he had seen Señor Martínez in San Isidro upon his arrival.[14] In my interview with Señor Martínez he mentioned the name of the loyalist officer who together with a CIA agent had kidnapped him. Some weeks later I went to interview this officer who was then playing an important role in the government. I found him very cooperative and willing to furnish a good deal of information. While he was telling the story of his participation in the crisis, he did not mention the incident with Martínez. I thought that this would be an excellent occasion to verify whether Martínez had told the truth or to what degree the officer was willing to give me accurate information. So I asked him point blank "On April 28th in the morning, did you take part in any operation to help the loyalists?" I noticed that my question shook him a little. But he looked me in the eye and said, "Yes, on that morning I was ordered to take Señor Martínez from the Mexican Embassy to San Isidro." I said, "Did you go alone or was there anybody with you?" He said, "An agent of the CIA went with me to do it."[15]

In the course of these interviews, I was able also to locate documents of historical evidence. Leaders from both sides allowed me access to their files—to read, make notes, and photostat all but top-secret papers.

I also spent many hours talking with boys from the commandos in the barrios, in the streets, and in their homes. From them I obtained further

14. (Msgr.) Emmanuele Clarizio, "Cronología de las gestiones para conseguir el cese de fuego" (Santo Domingo, 1965), mimeographed.

15. From private interview in my files.

information about the origins, organization, relationships, and conflicts among the different commandos.

In analyzing all the data I had gathered my primary challenge was that of quantity. Since I had not gone to the Dominican Republic with a specific theoretical frame to collect data upon, but had rather chanced upon the revolution and submerged myself as a participant-observer, the data I had collected touched on almost every aspect of Dominican life. Immersed as I was in the process of the revolution, I could not have foreseen which customs, norms, values, and institutions were to be affected by the revolution and which would resist its impact. Therefore I had collected much information which later did not prove relevant to the limitations of this study. This information I hope to publish in the historical section of a larger study.

The present study focuses on the sociological analysis of some characteristics and patterns of behavior of the rebels and their organizations.

In the course of putting together the mosaic of events that took place from April to September, I began to realize that events of sociological importance had developed along three different levels of organization: the political, the paramilitary, and the civic. The political process encompassed political developments that brought about and resulted from the revolution, including the efforts of the opposition to halt it. The paramilitary process was created by the participation of the civilian population in the armed struggle. Finally, the civic process was comprised of a series of functions played by groups of civilians in an attempt to cope with the problems created by the armed struggle. On each of these levels people interacted, action occurred, processes developed, and organizations emerged under circumstances that made it possible to call this series of events a revolution. These three levels were so tightly interconnected that it is difficult to discuss one without making reference to the others. In chapters 3, 4, and 5, these levels of events are discussed in an attempt to provide the reader with a historical background for the sociological analysis which comprises the main body of this work.

My analysis of the data I had gathered follows some of the methods suggested by Barton and Lazarsfeld:[16] analysis based on single observa-

16. Barton and Lazarsfeld, "Some Functions of Qualitative Analysis," pp. 95–122.

tions that raised pertinent questions or problems (such as the discovery that most of my food distributors were middle-class of Lebanese origin; see p. 77) or observations that served as indicators of a certain variable within the revolutionary social structure (such as the suggestion that a comandante's prestige could be measured by the frequency with which he participated in specialized tasks outside his own commando; see p. 60). I then began the construction of descriptive systems, devising preliminary classifications, putting ordered categories on a continuum, and creating systematic typologies.

It is obvious that in a study of this nature the use of statistics has not been possible. There is no doubt, however, that some of the operations dealing with qualitative data can stimulate and focus some kind of quantitative research along the dimensions or categories suggested in this study. Moreover, I believe that even at this stage the use of some "quasi-statistics"[17] is warranted. "Quasi-statistics" are not necessarily a step toward a quantitative study, but they may serve as a substitute for actual statistics in the case of research in which the complexity of the situation does not allow for regular statistical investigations. In such situations an able observer can approximate the results of statistical investigation while avoiding its expenses and practical difficulties.[18]

"Quasi-statistics" are used in this study in statements such as "most rebels scored high in alienation" when compared with the loyalists. Naturally, I do not have any statistical scale along which I can measure the degree of alienation in rebels and loyalists. In my interviews with groups of military men, professionals, and politicians, however, I found that those who sided with the rebels stressed in different ways the meaninglessness of their roles in Dominican society, while others did not.[19] At other times, I have used some "quasi-correlations," as in the description of the emergence of leadership in different organizations as having a catalytic effect upon other groups within the organization.[20]

This study has evident shortcomings. It has been undertaken to create

---

17. "Statements based on a body of observations which are not formally tabulated and analyzed statistically may be termed quasi-statistics." Ibid., p. 112.
18. Ibid., p. 113.
19. See Chapter 6.
20. See Chapter 10.

a preliminary approximation of what a more systematic qualitative study might be. If other such case studies are undertaken on other revolutions, it may be possible in the near future to produce comparative research on such a complex and important topic as the restructuring of a society undergoing a revolutionary process.

Chapter 2

Background of the Revolution

Late in the evening of May 30, 1961, a few miles west of the Dominican capital, Rafael Leonidas Trujillo was ambushed and shot to death by a group of five men who had been his friends. Three of the assassins were later executed after being brutally tortured on the orders of the dictator's surviving son, Ramfis Trujillo. The other two escaped death, one hiding in a friend's house, the second taking temporary refuge in the American Embassy.

The dictatorship of Trujillo, which has been described as a personalistic tyranny,[1] started in 1930 as an indirect effect of the intervention of the U.S. troops. Trujillo's training by the U.S. Marines enabled him to become chief of the National Guard, the corps created by the Marines to replace the old military structure. As commander in chief of the Guard, Trujillo became the power behind the throne during the presidency of Horacio Vázquez (1924–1930). A coup d'etat in February of 1930 ended Vázquez's leadership, and in August of that year Trujillo appointed himself president of the Dominican Republic. In the 30 years that followed, Trujillo ruled the country with an iron fist. He was the president and the chief of the armed forces; he owned almost 80 percent of the land, 45 percent of the sources of production, and the banks, services, and utilities. Further, Trujillo gave himself the titles of El Jefe, Generalissimo, Father of the Land, and Benefactor of the Country. He created

1. Jesús de Galíndez, *La era de Trujillo* (Buenos Aires, 1962), p. 180.

a new aristocracy, a class that accepted him as the Father of the Land and managed to make social and political progress under him. This new aristocracy included members of the Trujillo family[2] whom the dictator had strategically placed in high government positions, representatives of the old Dominican aristocracy now serving Trujillo in high government jobs or in diplomatic posts abroad, most of the generals and high ranking military officers, and some elements of the clergy. To be a member of the Trujillista class did not mean that one committed crimes; many of these men and women were honest and peaceful citizens. It did mean, however, that they could not interfere with, much less criticize, anything done by El Jefe or by any of his henchmen.

While Trujillo and his family, and to a lesser degree the members of the Trujillista oligarchy, had everything they needed, the Dominican masses had practically nothing. No reliable census figures are available for these years, but unemployment has been estimated as high as 30 percent of the labor force. Another 35 percent has been considered under-employed.[3] Illiteracy may have been 70 percent. Furthermore, there were no labor unions, no political parties, and no free press, radio, or television.

The national university was tightly run by political appointees, and students could not organize demonstrations or student unions. The Catholic Church was submissive to the dictator, from whom officially and privately it received many favors. Trujillo also was on good terms with the American Embassy and was praised publicly by U.S. officials.

Trujillo tolerated no public opposition. Although elections were held every five years, there was only one party and only one candidate. Trujillo always won. It was compulsory to vote; those who did not were jailed. During this tyranny of thirty-one years, there were several attempts to overthrow Trujillo, but all ended in failure and mass repression of the organizers. Additional coups were launched by exile groups from Cuba and Venezuela, the best known of which was the Cayo Confites expedition in 1947. Organized in Cuba by a young exile named Juan Bosch,

2. Ibid., pp. 189–95.
3. J. Bosch, *Partido Revolucionario Dominicano: tesis sindical* (Santo Domingo, 1966). J. I. Jiménez Grullón claims that unemployment was as high as 50 per cent of the total labor force (*La República Dominicana: una ficción* [Mérida, Venezuela, 1965], pp. 204–05).

this attempt was thwarted by U.S. pressures on the Cuban government of Grau San Martín.[4] On June 14, 1959, another important effort was initiated by a group of Dominican exiles who landed in Constanza. Trujillo captured the rebels and executed them. However, a few months later university students and young professionals founded an underground organization under the name of the June 14th Movement (1J4).

After Trujillo's death, his family, particularly his older son Ramfis, kept control of the armed forces and of the country at large. International pressures from President Kennedy and the Organization of American States, and internal opposition organized by the June 14th Movement and the newly founded nonpolitical civilian group Unión Cívica Nacional (UCN) grew steadily. A few months later the Trujillo family emptied the national treasury and went into exile. Joaquín Balaguer, Trujillo's hand-picked president, decided to form the Council of State on January 1, 1962, to rule the nation under his own chairmanship. Six other members, including the two survivors of the group who had killed Trujillo, were selected from the different political groups as members of the council. But two weeks later, the two middle-class organizations, the June 14th Movement and the UCN, brought about the resignation of Balaguer, because of his intimate collaboration with the old dictator. The presidency of the Council of State then was occupied by Rafael F. Bonnelly. Bonnelly had been minister of the interior under Trujillo, and had cooperated with him,[5] but before Trujillo's death he had joined the UCN.

One of the political exiles who returned to Santo Domingo after the death of Trujillo was Juan Bosch, the leader of the Dominican Revolutionary Party (PRD). After twenty-five years in exile in Cuba, Venezuela, and Costa Rica, Juan Bosch had become—with Rómulo Betancourt, Pepe Figueres, and Muñoz Marín—one of the most outspoken leaders of the so-called democratic left in Latin America. While in exile, Bosch and others had organized the PRD, a political organization based on the same ideology as the Cuban Revolutionary Party (Auténtico), the Acción Democrática of Venezuela, and the Popular Party of

4. CEFA, *Libro blanco de las fuerzas armadas y de la policía nacional de la República Dominicana* (Santo Domingo, 1964), pp. 420, 455–64. See also de Galíndez, *La era de Trujillo,* p. 75.

5. J. Bosch, *Crisis de la democracia de América en la República Dominicana* (Mexico City, 1964), pp. 71–73. See also de Galíndez, *La era de Trujillo,* p. 87.

Puerto Rico. These parties appealed to the large, dispossessed masses with promises of greater participation in the economic and social life of the country, greater freedom from internal dictatorships, and independence for the country as a whole from imperialistic international powers.

When, in October 1961, Bosch arrived from exile in Santo Domingo, both he and his PRD were entirely unknown in the political arena. The UCN and the June 14th Movement had managed to capture the spirit of the forces opposed to the Trujillo family and had forced Balaguer out of power. Actually the UCN had become the party in power after Balaguer was ousted. However, the two parties soon divided. The Unión Cívica became the party of the extreme right, although until 1962 it had harbored some members of the Communist Party. The June 14th Movement became the extreme left, although most of its members were from the upper middle class. Although the political campaigns of the UCN were based on the need to eradicate "Trujilloism" in the country, most of their leaders—as members of the upper or middle class—had been tightly connected with Trujillo and his family. It was a period of bickering and wrangling about which individuals had cooperated most with Trujillo. The fact was that practically everyone in the country had been linked with the dictator in some way.

Under Bosch, the PRD sought to assert itself by taking an entirely different line. It discussed problems at a national level and debated about the means available to solve them, not about the vices or virtues of individuals. The PRD addressed its appeal to the masses which, Bosch insisted, had never been considered in Dominican politics.[6] His appeal advocated structural reforms in the whole social system.

Free elections in the Dominican Republic were an unprecedented event in the life of most Dominicans. From 1848 to 1962 there had been thirty-two presidential elections, of which only four were free, and of these only two were conducted by direct popular vote. The political atmosphere was charged with great expectations. An electorate of fewer than a million and a quarter people were offered five presidential candidates and twenty-six political parties. Elections, supervised by the OAS, were held on December 20, 1962. From a total of 1,054,944 votes cast, Bosch received 628,044; his opponent from the UCN drew 317,327. The PRD elected 22 senators and 52 deputies; the UCN, 4 senators and

6. Bosch, *Crisis,* pp. 80–81.

13 deputies. The few remaining senators and deputies were elected from among the other twenty-four parties. Juan Bosch had been freely elected by an overwhelming majority of Dominicans.

The first task before the new government was revision of the constitution. The National Assembly met for four months, and on April 29, sixty days after Bosch had been inaugurated, it proclaimed a new constitution. The Constitution of 1963 was basically similar to many other Latin American constitutions; it especially resembled the Cuban constitution drawn up in 1940 under Batista and under the influence of the Auténtico Party with which Juan Bosch had become familiar while in Cuba.

As the new constitution was implemented, the government became the target of increasing accusations. On May 14, 1963,[7] in a public letter addressed to the president, the leader of the opposition UCN, Dr. Viriato Fiallo, summarized these accusations. Dr. Fiallo suggested that the "committees for the protection of the forest and sugar cane fields" were not necessary since the armed forces could take care of those, and he pointed out that in other countries such committees were known as milicias. He criticized the government for supporting an official monopoly of mass media, for awarding jobs only to members of the party in power,[8] and for placing communists in key government positions and letting them use schools and government buildings for their political indoctrination. He concluded his letter by demanding a clear and definite statement on Bosch's position toward the communist ideology.

Still, other critics of Bosch were more biased and vitriolic than Dr. Fiallo. Bosch was accused in the press, over radio and television of the following charges:[9]

1. Embezzlement of 70 million dollars in a contract with the Overseas Construction Ltd.
2. Signing secret agreements with the communists, handing the university over to them, and giving them key positions in his administration.

---

7. CEFA, *Libro blanco,* pp. 147–53. Bosch explained in his book how these accusations were entirely without foundation and yet they helped to create a false atmosphere that the communists were taking over his government. See *Crisis,* p. 128.

8. Political patronage from those in government is still an endemic practice in most of Latin America.

9. CEFA, *Libro blanco,* pp. 54–64, 286–88.

3. Violating the constitution by changing the structure of the cabinet, undermining the autonomy of the university, and interfering with the judiciary.
4. Organizing a coup against his own government to let the communists take over.
5. Creating an armed conflict with Haiti to divert public attention from domestic problems.

By July 1963, the opposition to the government was trying to create the impression of massive reaction of the populace against the policies of the government. Huge rallies of "Christian reaffirmation" were organized all over the country. Truckloads of peasants were brought from the provinces into the capital to show support for action against the communists. (The practice of transporting peasants to the city for demonstrations had been initiated by Trujillo when he had become concerned with national and international public opinion.)

Also in July, the Dominican Congress modified the Law of Public Confiscations, originally passed under the Council of State to expropriate property owned by the Trujillo family and other Trujillistas. The Congress designated itself, and not the judiciary, as the only tribunal for this procedure. When the UCN was in power, the law had been enforced by the Council of State. However, with the PRD in power, the UCN was threatened by a somewhat stricter application of the law than before. The law had been praised by the poor city dwellers and by the peasants, but denounced by organizations of industrialists, entrepreneurs, and landowners.[10] It is interesting to note that these organizations denounced the law using an argument that was to be widely applied by all opponents of the government until the downfall of Bosch. They argued that the Dominican Republic could not become a "second Cuba."[11]

The Dominican armed forces, which had been notorious for their cooperation with Trujillo and for their interference in politics since his death, had been surprisingly quiet since the election of Bosch. However, on July 16, Bosch appeared on television to tell the country that the military had put pressure on him.[12] Rumors spread throughout the country. An

10. Ibid., pp. 163–65, 266, and 271.
11. The idea of a "second Cuba" is a recurrent theme that was present in the minds of many both in Santo Domingo and in the U.S. from 1963 to 1965, and undoubtedly is still present today. See CEFA, *Libro blanco,* pp. 163–65.
12. *El Caribe,* July 17, 1963.

Juan Bosch with civilian and military rebel leaders giving his first public address after his return to Santo Domingo in September 1965

attempted coup failed, as did a general strike announced by business and shop owners.

Shortly afterward, another general strike was called by the business and shop owners. Scheduled for September 20, 1963, the strike was to protest "international communism and the complacent attitude of the government toward communist groups in the country."[13] Four radio stations were ordered off the air by the government because of their support of the illegal strike and for inciting rebellion. Nor was Bosch successful in handling the left. On the same day that he closed the radio stations, the June 14th Movement published a communiqué blaming the government and the PRD for not taking the steps necessary to curtail the activities of those plotting against the constitution.[14]

Early on the morning of September 25, a coup against Bosch's government was successful. The communiqué announcing the coup was signed

13. *Prensa Libre,* September 20, 1966, p. 1.
14. CEFA, *Libro blanco,* p. 301.

by ten generals and fifteen colonels. It blamed the government for not taking a firm stand on the issue of communism,[15] despite the clear warning given to it by the military that the issue of communism had brought the country to the brink of civil war. It indicated that the new government would respect the rights of individuals and associations, especially the right to private property and free enterprise, so that commerce, industry, and banks, free from fears of confiscation, could contribute to the development of the country.[16]

A few days after the coup, Juan Bosch, who had been under arrest, left the country in a navy frigate for the West Indies. From there he went to Puerto Rico where he was to stay for the next two years. The first and only attempt at democracy in the history of the country thus ended after seven months.

15. On the issue of being "hard" or "soft" on communism, see Daniel Bell, *The Radical Right* (New York, 1964), pp. 67–68.

16. CEFA, *Libro blanco,* pp. 90–91.

Chapter 3

The Political Organization

✍ The organization of the revolution goes back to 1963 when Juan Bosch, the constitutional president freely elected by balloting supervised by the OAS, was ousted by a group of ten generals and fifteen colonels of the armed forces who alleged that Bosch was a threat to Dominican security because he was weak in curbing the communists.[1] The democratic experiment of Bosch's government had lasted exactly seven months. Although organized opposition to the military *golpe* (coup) failed to materialize,[2] some civilian and military leaders soon started to organize a countercoup. Most important among them were Dr. Rafael Molina Ureña, Speaker of the House under Bosch, and Rafael Fernández Domínguez, a young army colonel.

The organization of a countercoup had a double goal: to restore the 1963 Constitution and to return Bosch to power. Molina Ureña was the leader of the civilian groups organized among the ranks of Bosch's PRD, which had polled 59.9 percent of the votes in 1962. He soon found support for his idea of "return to Bosch and the Constitution through revolution" among liberal elements of the PRD, which included men such

1. CEFA, *Libro blanco de las fuerzas armadas y de la policía nacional de la República Dominicana* (Santo Domingo, 1964), pp. 90–95.
2. The only exception was a group of middle-class students of the June 14th Movement who went to the mountains with their leader, Dr. Manolo Tavárez Justo. This small group was soon exterminated by the army.

22

as Peña Gómez, Manuel Espinal, Lembert Peguero, and Antonio Guzmán. By the fall of 1964 Molina Ureña had also succeeded in organizing in Santo Domingo and Santiago some groups of professionals and intellectuals in support of the revolution. Instrumental also in organizing these groups were Antonio Guzmán and Leopoldo Espaillat Nanita. These groups were highly significant to the organization of the revolution, because they included not only members of Bosch's party, but dissenters from the conservative UCN, among them former deputies Arévalo Cedeño Valdés, Aníbal Campagna, and Jottín Cury, all of whom were to play important roles in the 1965 revolution. Dissenters from other conservative parties, such as Dr. Pedro Casals, former secretary of finances in the government of the Triumvirate,[3] and Virgilio Mainardi Reyna, former governor of Santiago, also joined these groups. The significance of these groups lay in two different factors: they were made up of upper and middle class professionals,[4] and some of their members were dissenters from political parties which had opposed Bosch in 1962.

The development of the revolution also made some inroads into organized labor, particularly after the strike of May 1964. Such labor groups as ASOCHOIN, FOUPSA, and POASI were receptive to the revolutionary ideology advocated by PRD labor leaders such as Miguel Soto, Pedro J. Evangelista, and Marcos Vargas.

In January 1965 in Puerto Rico the leaders of the PRD signed the Pacto de Río Piedras with the leaders of the Social Christian Party (PRSC). Both parties thus agreed formally "to build a common front to reestablish constitutional order and to act together if faced with any event

3. The Triumvirate was the ruling body set up by the *golpistas* who overthrew Bosch. Its original members were Emilio de los Santos, Ramón Tapia, and Manuel Tavares. In December 1963, de los Santos resigned and was replaced by Donald Reid Cabral, who soon became president of the body. His position as maximum leader was enhanced in 1964 when Tapia was replaced by Ramón Cáceres—a "silent partner"—and Tavares resigned without being replaced.

4. In the fall of 1964, Juan Bosch wrote and published a book, *Crisis de la democracia de América en la República Dominicana* (Mexico City, 1964), which soon became a best seller in his country. In his book Bosch bitterly accused "all organizations of upper and middle class extraction, with the exception of political organizations involving the youth, of being openly favorable or at least indifferent" to his ousting. (My translation.) From these groups, he concluded, "Dominican democracy can expect nothing" (p. 212). Ironically enough, the book was used by these groups of professionals as an outline for their discussions.

that might bring a democratic solution to the problems of the country."[5] It should be pointed out that even as it was willing to cement this alliance with the Social Christians and dissenters from other conservative parties, Bosch's PRD never sought the support of the three Marxist parties operating in the country. On some occasions it even flatly refused their help.[6]

Because Bosch had been deposed by a small group of generals and colonels, he blamed the failure of democratic government in the Dominican Republic on a relatively small group of high-ranking officers supported by the middle class and the Church. He took pains to exonerate junior officers and the rank and file from any responsibility for his downfall.[7] Bosch had evidence of their nonparticipation in the fact that Colonel Fernández Domínguez had approached him shortly after his ouster with a plan to restore him to power. Fernández was a young officer with an outstanding record as a professional military man who advocated the professionalization of the armed forces.[8] He had been instrumental early in 1962 in curbing the dictatorial ambitions of General Rodríguez Echevarría, helping to crush a palace revolt the latter had launched against the legitimate Council of State. In 1963

5. From a photostatic copy of the original document in my files. The Pacto between the PRD and PRSC was not a secret agreement, but was highly publicized in Santo Domingo. Its publicity was calculated to create favorable public opinion for the return to constitutional order. The same impression was created by the publication on February 27, 1965, of a communiqué with 2,000 signatures of professionals requesting the return of the country to a constitutional situation. (See *El Listín Diario,* February 27, 1965.) Dr. Espaillat Nanita was instrumental in the publication of this document.

6. While the middle-class conservative UCN maintained an alliance with the PSP and the June 14th Movement before 1962, the PRD never agreed to ally itself with either of them. In 1962 the Marxist parties were opposed to the electoral process by which Bosch was elected. In 1963 the June 14th Movement accused Bosch of being "tolerant with the enemies of the fatherland" (CEFA, *Libro blanco,* p. 301), although the Movement was constant in its support of a constitutional regime. In 1966 Bosch declined to accept the electoral support offered to him by the June 14th Movement in the June elections. (See *El Caribe,* April 20, 1966.) No evidence is available which indicates that any agreement was ever reached between Bosch and the Marxist parties. (See Theodore Draper, "A Case of Defamation: U.S. Intelligence vs. Juan Bosch," *The New Republic,* 154 (Feb. 26, 1966), pp. 15–18.

7. Bosch, *Crisis,* pp. 202, 212, 214.

8. See John J. Johnson, *The Military and Society in Latin America* (Stanford, 1965).

Fernández was the leader of a group of young officers of middle-class extraction who refused to sanction the interference of senior officers in political matters. Most of the young officers of Fernández's type (unlike their superiors, who had been promoted for nothing more than their loyalty to Trujillo) were academy graduates trained in military centers at home and abroad. A number of them had been trained in the United States or in the Canal Zone by U.S. military experts. Some of them, ironically, were descendants of Trujillo's most hated generals.[9]

The activities of Colonel Fernández and his group were soon suspected by the generals serving the Triumvirate, which decided to get rid of Fernández by sending him to a diplomatic post in Spain. Other members of his group were less fortunate and were discharged from service. Among those summarily dismissed were Major Núñez Nogueras, Captain Lachapelle, and Captain Quirós Pérez. In the absence of Colonel Fernández another young officer, Colonel Hernando Ramírez, assumed the task of organizing the uprising within the armed forces. By the fall of 1964 a large number of young officers had been recruited from within the navy, army, air force, and the National Police. Colonel Fernández continued to play a leading role in preparing for the revolt, first from his diplomatic post in Spain, and later, from a new post in Chile. The date for the uprising was set for January 9, 1965; Colonel Fernández was to arrive the night before in a cargo ship from Puerto Rico, and the next day a bloodless coup would be staged. Juan Bosch would return immediately from Puerto Rico, and the 1963 Constitution would be reestablished. However, a series of mysterious circumstances aborted the coup before Colonel Fernández sailed from Puerto Rico, and the rebels called off the entire operation.

In the winter of 1964 the political atmosphere in Santo Domingo provided an adequate setting for a coup or a revolution.[10] The newspapers carried unconfirmed accounts and rumors of coups and countercoups planned by various political factions. Troop movements from one area of the country to another were frequently reported, and antagonism among different groups within the armed forces was indicated. Corrup-

9. Two such men were Colonel Fernández Domínguez and Colonel Caamaño, whose fathers were among the worst of Trujillo's henchmen. See J. de Galíndez, *La era de Trujillo* (Buenos Aires, 1962), pp. 85, 91, 167.

10. Chalmers Johnson, *Revolutionary Change* (Boston, 1966), p. 119.

tion and graft were at an all-time high, despite the sincere efforts of President Donald Reid to curb them.[11] Also, there were signs that Donald Reid intended to be a candidate in the forthcoming general elections, which helped raise against him accusations of *continuismo*.[12] Finally, since the leaders of the two majority parties, Juan Bosch of the PRD and Joaquín Balaguer of the Reformista Party, were in exile, and their followers could not obtain reassurance that they would be allowed to participate in the elections, the whole idea of elections appeared to be little more than political farce.

By the end of 1964 at least four different groups were engaged in plotting to overthrow the government. The first group, described above, wanted to restore the 1963 Constitution with Bosch as president. The second group was organized as a grassroots movement among the rank and file within the army. The leader of this group, Captain Peña Taveras, was later to play an important role in the April revolution. This group merged with the first group of young officers in terms of aims, but maintained an independent organization. The third group was organized by Colonel Neit Nivar Seijas of the powerful San Cristobal sector. The goal of this group was to bring Joaquín Balaguer—who in 1960–61 had served as a puppet president for Trujillo—back to power. This group counted among its followers a number of high-ranking officers, including some generals antagonistic to the generals of the San Isidro sector because the latter were favored by Reid. Around the middle of February 1965, Colonel Seijas' opposition to the government became so evident that he was sent into exile. The fourth group plotting against the government was organized by a former PRD leader, Nicolás Silfa, who had cooperated with Molina Ureña in the general organization of the coup, but later cut his ties with Molina and proceeded to organize a group of his own.

The existence of these four groups (and possibly others) provides considerable evidence that discontentment with the government was

---

11. A sign of this effort was the discharge from active service of the notorious Chief of Police, General Belisario Peguero, and of General Elby Viñas Román, Secretary of the Armed Forces, for their participation in wholesale black-market operations.

12. A term referring to a political leader's machinations to perpetuate himself in power indefinitely.

widespread and that it pervaded not only civilian organizations but also the military structure which the Reid government depended upon for its existence. Not unsurprisingly, when the pro-Bosch group staged the coup on April 24 and the government appealed to different sectors of the armed forces, none of them came to its defense. On the other hand, it cannot be said that this lack of solidarity with the government was the result of the armed forces' hatred of Reid. As a matter of fact, after surrendering the palace to the rebels, Reid was merely kept under house arrest for a brief time and later allowed to go free. Discontent centered not around any one person, but around the system itself. Even the strongly "loyalist" San Isidro group was ready to compromise with the "rebels" and cast aside the Triumvirate which it had set up some eighteen months earlier. It was only when the "rebels" insisted upon the immediate return to constitutional government with Bosch as president that opposition to the "rebel" cause materialized and a genuine "loyalist" group emerged.[13]

Fighting for the Constitution

The civilian and military leaders of the revolt had agreed that the uprising would take place on April 26, 1965. On April 24, however, General Rivera Cuesta, the Chief of Staff, jailed six would-be rebel military leaders. The news of the crackdown quickly spread, and Captain Peña Taveras, leader of the rank-and-file movement, decided to act on his own to liberate the young officers. He and a group of noncommissioned officers succeeded in taking General Cuesta prisoner and freeing the six men. The uprising had begun. The swift reaction of the rebels took by surprise not only the government, but also the men who had so carefully organized the revolt.[14]

13. Although the military organization was hardly "loyal" to the government of Donald Reid, still it may be called "loyalist" in the sense used by Chalmers Johnson in *Revolutionary Change,* p. 140. The "loyalists" (in this sense) did not defend Reid, but did fight to maintain the oligarchic system they had set up in 1963. Henceforth, the words "rebel" and "loyalist" will be used without quotatation marks, and will identify groups without necessarily implying an ideological connotation.

14. Coups and revolutions usually benefit greatly from the surprise element involved in the rebel uprising. Here, however, surprise was common to both factions.

Government officials, including Donald Reid, and rebel organizers, including Molina Ureña, first heard of the revolt when Peña Gómez, a radio commentator and PRD leader, broke the news to the public in his radio program at 1:45 P.M. What followed can best be described as a highly confused situation. While most rebel leaders reacted positively, rallying together to help the young officers who had unexpectedly started the revolt, most government officials and loyalist military officers waited passively for new developments. Reid tried desperately but without success to rally the support of the generals. Only General Wessin in San Isidro showed clear signs of opposition to the claims of the rebels. But he too failed to give the government any actual support.[15]

Under instructions from Juan Bosch in Puerto Rico, Molina Ureña was sworn in as provisional president after Reid resigned early on the morning of April 25. Conversations for a settlement between the young officers and representatives of the generals reached an impasse when Colonel Hernando Ramírez made clear that the rebels would not accept the new military junta suggested by the generals. For the rebels the issue of return to the 1963 Constitution with Bosch as president was not negotiable. This impasse was followed by the generals' order to the air force to strafe the Presidential Palace—where negotiations were still in progress.[16] Civil war followed, with the air force from San Isidro taking the initiative in attacking rebel strongholds in the capital city.

What had started as a conspiratorial coup[17] soon turned into a mass uprising. The populace particularly from the *barrios altos,* the poorest slums in the north of the city, threw itself into the streets, at first to celebrate the downfall of the government, later to help the rebels build barricades and organize the defense of the city. Student and labor leaders used radio and television broadcasts to rally support "for the honest military fighting for the Constitution." The attacks of the air force on the Presidential Palace and the Duarte Bridge greatly exasperated the crowds of onlookers. By April 26 the military rebels were handing out weapons to civilians ready to fight by their sides. The rebel military command

15. From private interview with Donald Reid.

16. From private interview with Colonel Benoit, head of loyalist negotiators and later president of the military junta.

17. Coup is understood here not as a "palace coup," or a personal struggle for power, but in the sense used by Chalmers Johnson, *Revolution and the Social System* (Stanford, 1964), pp. 49–56, "an attempt at revolutionary change made by elitist groups."

understood that their strength lay in numerical superiority, not in military hardware, since San Isidro was in command of the air force and the tanks.[18]

Information obtained in private interviews with rebel and loyalist leaders seems to confirm what had been suggested by other writers,[19] that from early on April 25 the military attachés and other officials of the U.S. Embassy in Santo Domingo set about to build a loyalist front in opposition to the demands of the rebels.[20] Evidently the presence of U.S. officials among them—air attaché Colonel Thomas Fishburn at San Isidro, naval attaché Colonel Ralph Heywood at Haina, and Lee Echols, U.S. police adviser at police headquarters—boosted the morale of the loyalists and helped iron out differences among them. On April 27 the loyalists staged a major operation by land, sea, and air to take the city from rebel control. The navy and the police force reversed their decisions to side with the rebels and joined forces with the generals to crush the uprising of the young officers.[21] The three day battle that followed was the fiercest of the war. Casualties were heavy on both sides, mainly among the civilian population exposed to the raids of the air force. It was estimated that nearly two thousand persons were killed during those three days.

Around 3:00 P.M. the tanks from San Isidro crossed the Duarte Bridge into the city. Rebel leaders decided to halt the fight by requesting the mediation of the U.S. Embassy in an attempt to negotiate with the generals. U.S. Ambassador W. T. Bennett, who had just arrived in the country, declined to mediate and suggested that total surrender to the loyalist forces was in order.[22]

The reaction of the rebels to this suggestion was mixed. Some civilians

18. On April 26, the rebels counted on the support of practically all important military garrisons in the country with the exception of the air bases at San Isidro and Santiago. General Wessin had tanks in San Isidro, but only around six hundred men under his command. Commodore Rivera Caminero went to see Molina Ureña on April 26 to promise him the support of the navy. General Despradel, Chief of Police, had also pledged loyalty to the new regime.

19. Tad Szulc, *Dominican Diary* (New York, 1965), p. 32.

20. From a private interview with an official of U.S. Embassy who on April 26 emphasized that the United States could not accept the return of Juan Bosch.

21. J. B. Martin wrote that: "on April 27 at 12:30 P.M. loyalist Air Force officers left a meeting with the U.S. naval attaché to begin bombing." See J. B. Martin, *Overtaken by Events* (New York, 1966), p. 652.

22. Ibid., p. 653.

and a few military men sought refuge in foreign embassies. Most of the leaders—headed by Colonels Caamaño and Montes Arache—went back to the battlefield.[23] All of them were outraged by the attitude of the U.S. ambassador. With no choices open to them but dishonor or death, the rebels made a desperate counterattack. The air raids continued all day, but the tanks from San Isidro, once inside the city, were trapped by the rebels.[24] Some of the tanks were destroyed, some were captured, and others fled back to San Isidro. By seven o'clock, the rebels once more controlled the city.[25]

On the night of April 27 the leadership cadres of the rebels had to be reorganized. Provisional President Molina Ureña, Minister of Defense Colonel Hernando Ramírez, and some others had requested political asylum. Colonel Caamaño, who had been appointed by Molina Ureña as Chief of Operations and had played an important role in the negotiations with the U.S. ambassador, was now the highest-ranking rebel officer. He assumed total responsibility for the rebel movement.

A number of civilian leaders who had joined the revolution in the past two days began to emerge in important leadership roles. These men generally had a high degree of organizational ability; some of them had had military or guerrilla experience. Such men as Héctor Aristy, André de la Rivière, Manolo González, Pichirilo, Juan M. Román, and Fafa Taveras proved to be extremely valuable to the rebel organization. Their participation in leadership roles gave the rebel movement not only new military expertise, but also tinged its political goals with radicalism, since most of these men could be considered to the left of the original rebel leaders. It was clear, however, that, because the exigencies of the situation were military rather than political, the regular army officers maintained

23. For a list of the rebel officers who stayed in the battlefield, see Appendix 3.

24. According to General Wessin's own testimony he only had around six hundred infantrymen in San Isidro. See U.S., Congress, Senate, Committee on the Judiciary, *Testimony of Brigadier General Elías Wessin y Wessin*, 89th Cong., 1st sess., Oct. 1, 1965.

25. About 9:00 P.M. Colonel Caamaño went to see Rafael Herrera, editor of *El Listín Diario*, and told him that the whole city was again under his control. By 11:00 P.M. that same night J. C. Estrella, editor of *El Caribe*, received a call from Caamaño, who protested strongly against the cover story in the paper for the next day. Editor Estrella then hurried to insert a bulletin reporting that the rebels had regained the city from the loyalists. (See *El Caribe*, April 28, 1965). Information from private interviews with editors of both papers.

control of their leadership positions and of the rebel movement throughout this first stage of the revolution.[26] The usefulness of the civilian leaders became apparent for two reasons: first, a large number of casualties and some desertions had decimated the ranks of the regular troops siding with the rebels, forcing the rebel command to depend more on civilian fighters; second, because the civilians distrusted the armed forces in general, civilian leaders could obtain allegiance from the irregular troops more easily than could the army officers.

By April 28 the rebels had strengthened their position in the city. Coordinated attacks were launched against the Ozama Fortress, the headquarters of the National Police, and the transportation barracks—the only points in the capital still held by the loyalists.[27] The rebel command prepared for a massive attack on San Isidro. By this time the generals in San Isidro were demoralized by their failure to take the city the day before. Colonel Morillo López was sent to survey the situation at the Duarte Bridge, where he found only a few loyalist troops; they were tired and frightened, and their morale was alarmingly low. Upon Morillo's return to San Isidro, the generals made an attempt to recruit more troops from neighboring garrisons; they could get a reinforcement of only twenty-five men.[28]

The following episode is indicative of the political atmosphere and the forces at work in the crisis. Antonio Martínez Francisco, a rich businessman, was the Secretary General of Bosch's PRD when the revolution broke out. As a moderate, he sought mediation from the U.S. Embassy when the fighting started to get out of hand. His plea went unheard by U.S. officials. On April 28, Martínez sought political asylum in the Mexican Embassy, where he received a phone call from Arthur Breisky, Second Secretary at the U.S. Embassy, who asked him to come to the embassy to discuss important problems with W. T. Bennett. Martínez agreed, and a car arrived to take him from the Mexican Embassy. Inside

26. From private interviews with rebel civilian and military leaders. At a later stage some civilian leaders would take up more relevant leadership positions to solve the political impasse caused by four months of negotiations.

27. The Presidential Palace was abandoned by the rebels after the air raids of September 27. That same night it was taken over by loyalist troops under the command of General Atila Luna.

28. From personal interview with Colonel Morillo López who later became Chief of Police during the Provisional Government.

the car he found a loyalist colonel and a CIA agent who took him at gunpoint to San Isidro. There he found the U.S. official who had led him into the trap, as well as U.S. air attaché Fishburn, surrounded by Dominican generals. He was forced to read over the radio an appeal asking the rebels to surrender their weapons.[29]

Earlier the same day the generals had agreed to set up a military junta to counteract the government established by the rebels on April 25. Three unknown colonels from the army, navy, and air force were chosen to rule the country. Colonel Pedro Bartolomé Benoit of the air force was appointed head of the junta.[30] In the afternoon of April 28 he held a staff meeting with his officers in San Isidro and after presenting them with the facts, he suggested that help from the United States should be officially requested to deal with the rebels. A few hours later the first 400 U.S. Marines landed in Santo Domingo.[31] President Lyndon Johnson said the landing of the troops was necessary in order "to give protection to hundreds of Americans . . . and to escort them safely" back to the United States.[32] As events developed, other excuses were given and an additional 30,000 U.S. troops were disembarked in Santo Domingo.

The U.S. Intervention

There is no doubt that the outbreak of the revolt took the U.S. Embassy entirely by surprise. Ambassador Bennett was on a routine trip to Washington, and a number of the members of the military mission were at a weekend conference in Panama. Naval attaché Heywood was on a dove-shooting trip with General Imbert (who was later to become head of the U.S.-sponsored loyalist government), and air attaché Fish-

29. From private interview with both Martínez Francisco and the loyalist colonel who took him to San Isidro on April 28.

30. It has been suggested that the military junta of San Isidro was created by the direct suggestion of U.S. Embassy officials in order to legitimize the relations between the U.S. government and the loyalists. See Theodore Draper, "The Dominican Crisis: A Case Study in American Policy," *Commentary*, 40 (Dec. 1965), p. 48.

31. Theodore Draper had also discussed at some length the exchange of cables between Colonel Benoit, Ambassador Bennett, and Thomas C. Mann.

32. U.S., Department of State, *Bulletin*, 52, no. 1351 (May 17, 1965), pp. 738–39.

burn was playing golf with General Santos (head of the air force) when the revolution was announced over the radio. From that moment until April 27 when Ambassador Bennett came back to Santo Domingo, the U.S. Embassy was run by Chargé d'Affaires William Connett, who had been in the country only six months. Quite active too in those four days were Second Secretary Arthur Breisky, the military attachés, and the four-man CIA station.

The degree and direction of the U.S. military attachés' involvement with the loyalist forces[33] and the various attitudes of U.S. officials toward loyalists and rebels would suggest that President Johnson's order to land the Marines was perfectly in agreement with the ideological position taken by the United States from the beginning of the revolution. The scope of this chapter prohibits a detailed description of the number of occasions on which, according to eyewitnesses and newsmen's accounts, officials of the U.S. Embassy were reported interacting closely with high officers of the loyalists. It seems that as a result of this interaction the loyalists were encouraged before April 27 to set up a common front to attack the rebels; after the fiasco of April 27, they were persuaded to request officially U.S. intervention. Also, evidence furnished by top rebel leaders in private interviews indicates that at least five attempts were made by the rebels from April 25 through 27 to obtain U.S. Embassy mediation in the crisis, and that these attempts were turned down by U.S. Embassy officials who rebuked the rebels for being "irresponsible and Communist."[34] Some of the men who sought mediation from the U.S. Embassy were upper-middle-class businessmen, such as Martínez Francisco, Enriquillo del Rosario, and Antonio Guzmán;[35] others were young military officers trained in the United States—Colonels Francisco

33. Juan Bosch has claimed that the U.S. naval and air attachés "ordered" the loyalist General Santos Céspedes to bomb the rebel garrisons and the Presidential Palace, and that the air attaché was responsible for the printing of leaflets charging communist infiltration of the rebel movement. See Draper, "The Dominican Crisis," p. 40.

34. J. C. Estrella, *La revolución dominicana y la crisis de la OEA* (Santo Domingo, 1965), p. 10.

35. The first was Secretary General of Bosch's party and later became Secretary of Finances of the Balaguer government. The second had been Dominican Ambassador to Washington, and is presently Ambassador to the OAS. The third was to become the candidate for the presidency in accordance with McGeorge Bundy's peace formula a few weeks later.

Caamaño and Ramón Montes Arache, for example. From information obtained from rebel leaders, it seems that all other contacts made by U.S. Embassy officials with the rebel government in the first days of the revolt were aimed at persuading the rebels to give up the fight or to get safeguards for U.S. citizens.[36]

With the landing of U.S. troops in Santo Domingo on the evening of April 28, the situation changed drastically. The loyalist generals and their troops received a boost in morale and soon started to broadcast threats and appeals to the rebels to surrender or to face total extermination.[37] The rebels, on the other hand, realized from the moment the U.S. Marines landed that new strategies had to be put into effect, since the focus of action was no longer military but political. Unquestionably, the rebel leadership did not at any time contemplate actually fighting the U.S. troops. However, they thought they would have to enroll whatever military power they had—together with any support they might receive from the masses—and their claims for legitimacy and constitutionality, to bargain at the conference table for those goals the United States had prevented them from achieving in the battlefield.

Despite the claim by President Johnson and other U.S. officials in Washington and in Santo Domingo that the U.S. intervention had only humanitarian purposes or that U.S. troops were neutral to both factions, it became clear to people in Santo Domingo that such claims were far from the truth. From the start the U.S. troops sided and fraternized with the loyalists and actually helped them dislodge the rebels from their positions. The first landing was conducted in the port of Haina, where the loyalist Rivera Caminero was boss. The second landing was made at San Isidro, where Wessin was in command. On April 30 troops of the 82nd Airborne replaced the loyalist troops at the Duarte Bridge and took over

36. Chargé d'Affaires Connett reported to Washington that he "did not believe representations to the rebels would, at that time, serve a useful purpose; in fact, any representations by the Embassy might associate the U.S. prematurely with some combination of persons who might fail, or might prove not to serve the national interest." Center for Strategic Studies, *Dominican Action, 1965: Intervention or Cooperation?* Special Report Series, no. 2 (Washington, D.C., 1966), p. 17.

37. According to Ambassador Martin, some loyalist elements became so belligerent after the landing of U.S. troops that they did not want to sign the cease-fire agreement worked out by the Papal Nuncio. *Overtaken by Events,* p. 663.

the strategic position of Molinos Dominicanos and the camp of Sans Souci, from which they could dominate the rebel city across the Ozama River. The Marines from Haina moved into the city and created the International Security Zone around the U.S. Embassy and the other embassies. This territory was seized by force from the rebels and was later enlarged.[38]

In a surprise attack on the rebel zone U.S. troops advanced from the west and east late at night on May 2 to create a "line of communication" between the International Security Zone (the U.S. Embassy) and the International Airport near San Isidro. Caamaño protested that the action was an open violation of the cease-fire agreement signed by him, the loyalists, and the U.S. Ambassador only three days earlier. The creation of the U.S. Corridor or "line of communication" obviously had as its purpose the division of rebel forces in the city. Ten days later when General Imbert started Operación Limpieza (Operation Clean-up) against the rebel forces in the north of the city, Caamaño's forces in the downtown area could not go across the U.S. corridor to help them. When all irregulars were wiped out in the north, Ciudad Nueva in downtown Santo Domingo became the last rebel stronghold. While Operation Clean-up was in progress, the U.S. occupation forces offered Imbert logistic and strategic support.[39] The borderlines of the International Security Zone were enlarged on several occasions without the consent of the rebels: every time the lines moved further into the rebel zone; the territory taken from the rebels was never given back to them.[40]

38. The ISZ was established in the morning of April 30 before the OAS in Washington approved Ellsworth Bunker's motion to create such a zone around some foreign embassies. Actually the OAS once more was rubber-stamping and legitimizing what the U.S. had already done. Finally on May 5, Caamaño agreed to sign the Act of Santo Domingo in which the existence of the ISZ was officially recognized. Despite the fact that the Act of Santo Domingo set the limits for the security zone, this was enlarged on several occasions after May 5 against the will of the rebels.

39. I personally observed Imbert troops moving freely from the ISZ to attack the rebels in the north. My observation has been corroborated by other eyewitnesses.

40. On June 15 when heavy fighting broke out between U.S. and rebel troops, the latter took some forty city blocks from the rebels along the line of communications.

The Government of National Reconstruction

On the evening of April 30, when the cease-fire agreement worked out by the Papal Nuncio was about to be signed, John B. Martin, a former U.S. ambassador to the Dominican Republic, arrived in San Isidro as a special envoy from President Johnson. The mission entrusted to Martin was "to assist W. T. Bennett to open up contact with the rebels and to keep the President closely informed of the situation."[41]

Ambassador Martin spent approximately seventeen days in Santo Domingo seeking to negotiate a settlement. He went to see Caamaño twice in the rebel zone, and he flew to Puerto Rico once to see Bosch. The rest of the time Martin spent in negotiations with the loyalists, particularly in the task of setting up the so-called Government of National Reconstruction. Although the military junta created on April 28 by the loyalists to request the landing of U.S. troops was still operating in San Isidro, Martin began a series of discussions with civilian and military leaders, the purpose of which was to set up a new junta that would command the support of the sectors opposed to the rebels.

Only a few hours after his arrival in Santo Domingo, Martin was visiting his former friend Antonio Imbert Barrera, one of the two surviving assassins of Trujillo. Martin admitted that he did not know who Caamaño was, and had to see Imbert to get some information about the rebel leader.[42] Forty-eight hours after his arrival in Santo Domingo, Martin had made up his mind about the complex crisis: the revolution was dominated by the communists and Caamaño was purely a front for them.[43] It seems that only twenty-four hours after his arrival he had also made up his mind about the formation of a new "coalition government." Imbert Barrera was chosen by Martin to head that government on the assumption that Imbert's title of "national hero" meant massive popularity.[44]

The test of Imbert's popularity came when Martin tried to recruit

41. J. B. Martin, "Struggle to Bring Together Two Sides Torn by Killing," *Life,* 58 (May 28, 1965), pp. 28–30, 70a–73.

42. Martin, *Overtaken by Events,* p. 666.

43. On May 2, Martin held a press conference in which he told newsmen the revolution was being controlled by the communists. See also *Overtaken by Events,* p. 698.

44. See José Figueres, "Revolution and Counter-Revolution in Santo Domingo," *Dominican Republic: A Study in the New Imperialism,* ed. Norman Thomas (New York, 1966), p. 49.

some respectable civilian leaders to participate in the new government. Scores of politicians, professionals, and businessmen—among them, Dr. Felix Goico, Dr. Nicolás Pichardo, Dr. Luis Julián Pérez, Antonio Guzmán, and Dr. Jordi Brossa—were invited to take part in the new junta. All, however, declined to participate in a government headed by General Imbert.[45] Eventually three civilians, practically unknown in Dominican public life, agreed to join Imbert as members of the new junta. The fifth member in the junta was Colonel Pedro Bartolomé Benoit, President of the San Isidro Junta. On May 7 the five-man junta was sworn in—after the military junta in San Isidro resigned in its favor. Seven days later General Imbert sent his troops to start Operation Clean-up in the north of the city, despite the cease-fire agreement signed by all parties concerned in the crisis. The 30,000 U.S. troops in the capital maintained themselves officially neutral in the fight, although unofficially it was obvious that Imbert's troops were receiving logistical and strategic support from them.

General Imbert had not yet completed Operation Clean-up when Washington sent another team of negotiators to Santo Domingo. The head of the team was McGeorge Bundy, Special Assistant to the President in national security affairs. With him came Undersecretary of State Thomas C. Mann and Deputy Secretary of Defense Cyrus R. Vance. The purpose of the new negotiations was to set up a government of national unity with broad popular support, which would exclude extremists from both sides. General Imbert, who was now successfully completing a large-scale military operation, flatly refused Bundy's proposals for a new government headed by Bosch's Minister of Agriculture, Antonio Guzmán.

The so-called Guzmán formula raised high expectations in Santo Domingo as well as in Washington. The rebels had accepted it and the Catholic bishops published a pastoral letter giving their support to the new solution.[46] It seems, however, that Imbert's supporters in Santo

45. Martin, in *Overtaken by Events,* p. 683, wrote that "these men refused to accept responsibility." From private conversations with some of these men I concluded that they did not refuse to accept responsibilities, but they did decline to take part in a junta that obviously would not enjoy popular support.

46. D. Brugal Alfau, *Tragedia en Santo Domingo* (Santo Domingo, 1966), p. 254. See also pp. 256–61—the letter addressed by General Imbert to the Catholic bishops in response to their appeal for unity: Imbert refused to be treated as "one of the contending factions" because he had control over the whole country.

Domingo and in Washington managed to rally enough support to make Bundy's proposals fail.[47] Bundy returned to Washington on May 26; by the end of May, General Imbert wrote a letter to President Johnson in which he complained of U.S. interference in the internal affairs of the Dominican Republic:

> To set up rules and political norms, to pass judgment on which government is good and which is not, to establish their norms and to choose arbitrarily those who would rule the destiny of a nation . . . is a very dangerous hazard in history, and a very deplorable transgression of international juridical principles, which the United States is obliged to honor.[48]

Shortly after Bundy's return to Washington, the U.S. representative to the OAS, Ellsworth Bunker, requested that a three-man Ad Hoc Committee be sent to the Dominican Republic to work out a settlement. The OAS voted approval of the U.S.-sponsored resolution on May 31 and on June 3. Bunker arrived in Santo Domingo with his two committeemen, Ambassadors Ilmar Penna Marinho of Brazil and Ramón de Clairmont Dueñas of El Salvador. For three months they engaged in discussions with rebels and loyalists, until finally, on September 3, Héctor García-Godoy was inaugurated as Provisional President. The solution presented by the Ad Hoc Committee was again unacceptable to General Imbert, who this time chose to resign in open protest against the new interference of the United States in Dominican internal affairs.[49] The Institutional and Reconciliation Acts, however, were signed by the rebels on the one side,

47. According to Tad Szulc, correspondent to the *New York Times* who was covering the crisis, on the same day that Mr. Bundy was expecting the final approval from Washington to set up the new provisional government, a new set of instructions entirely unacceptable to the rebels was sent to him. *Dominican Diary,* pp. 270–71.

48. From photostatic copy of original in my files. My translation. The person who furnished the copy could not guarantee that the letter was actually sent to President Johnson. There is some certainty, however, that the letter was signed by Imbert's junta.

49. The resignation of the five-man junta and its cabinet (with the exclusion of Rivera Caminero, Secretary of the Armed Forces) took place on the night of August 30, and was publicly broadcast over television. That same night the junta forces fired some sixty mortar rounds into the rebel zone. See Brugal, *Tragedia,* p. 218.

and on the other by the military establishment, which had evidently been the operative power behind Imbert's government for the past four months.[50]

The Constitutionalist Government

Early in the morning of April 27, Provisional President Molina Ureña appointed Colonel Hernando Ramírez as Minister of Defense and Colonel Caamaño as Minister of the Interior. Later in the day, when Molina Ureña realized that Colonel Ramírez was suffering from a severe attack of recurrent hepatitis, Colonel Caamaño was entrusted with all military operations undertaken by the rebels. That afternoon in the U.S. Embassy, Colonel Caamaño seemed to play an important leadership role in the discussion with Ambassador Bennett. When Molina Ureña and Colonel Ramírez sought asylum in foreign embassies after the meeting, Caamaño and Montes Arache went to the Duarte Bridge to lead the fight against the loyalist troops. As was mentioned earlier, later that evening Caamaño and Montes Arache were in full control of the city. The next day they led their troops in several successful attacks against the last loyalist stronghold in the city, the Ozama Fortress. On the night of April 28 Monsignor Clarizio, the Papal Nuncio, made arrangements with Caamaño for a cease-fire. On the next day Monsignor Clarizio went to Ciudad Nueva to see Caamaño, and from Puerto Rico Bosch communicated over the phone with both Caamaño and the Papal Nuncio.

From this evidence it is fairly clear that Caamaño had become the military leader of the revolution. The rebels, however, had emphasized from the start that they were fighting to reverse the status quo and to restore a legitimate constitutional government. Their original goal was to reestablish the 1963 Constitution and to bring Bosch back to the presidential office. Molina Ureña's claim to the provisional presidency until Bosch could return was also regarded by the rebels as legitimate, since Molina had been Speaker of the House under Bosch. The rebels had also reestablished the 1963 National Assembly ousted by the coup against Bosch. On April 27, however, Molina requested asylum, and after the landing of the U.S. Marines on April 28, it became clear that Bosch

50. See the communiqué of the armed forces published the next day in ibid., p. 220.

could not come back to the country. The rebels were about to lose their claims of legitimacy.

On May 3 the Dominican National Assembly gathered in Ciudad Nueva and in an emergency session elected Colonel Caamaño Constitutional President according to Article 105 of the 1963 Constitution.[51] Of fifty-eight votes, Caamaño obtained forty-nine, and was immediately sworn in as President.[52] The next day Caamaño gave a public speech at Independencia Park and appointed some members of his cabinet. Colonel Montes Arache was appointed Minister of Defense and Héctor Aristy Minister of the Presidency. Other appointments included Dr. Fernando Silié Gatón, former Dean of Economics at the university, as Minister of Education, Dr. Jottín Cury, former UCN deputy, as Minister of Foreign Affairs, Dr. Salvador Jorge Blanco as Attorney General, and Dr. Antonio del Rosario, President of the Social Christians, as Delegate to the OAS.[53]

Caamaño realized that to be able to deal adequately with the situation his "constitutionalist government" had to maintain a semblance of government as opposed to a "band of rebels," as they were called by the U.S. and the loyalists. To accomplish this task, he had to consolidate his position politically and militarily. He chose two of the most able men in the rebel leadership to be instrumental in this double task: Héctor Aristy and Colonel Montes Arache. The former was in charge of setting up the bureaucratic machinery needed in any political structure. The latter undertook the task of restructuring the rebel forces, civilian and military, for the defense of the city.

It cannot be said, however, that one man, no matter how able, organized the government or its military setup. It was only with the help and dedication of such men as Jottín Cury, Bonaparte Gautreau, Peña Gómez, Aníbal Campagna, Salvador Jorge Blanco, and others that Héctor Aristy succeeded in organizing effectively the different depart-

51. It became clear to the rebels from Martin's conversations with Bosch in Puerto Rico that the U.S. would not allow either Bosch or Molina Ureña to rule the country. See Juan Bosch, "A Tale of Two Nations," *The New Leader*, 48 (June 21, 1965), pp. 3–7. Also see Martin, *Overtaken by Events*, pp. 676–80.

52. See the proceedings in the official publication of the Constitutionalist Government, *Gaceta oficial de la República Dominicana*, May 4, 1965.

53. *La Nación*, May 6, 1965. The names of all senators and congressmen who attended the meeting that elected Caamaño are published in this issue.

ments of the Caamaño government. Likewise it was only with the help of dedicated and expert leaders such as Lachapelle, Alvarez Holguín, Núñez Nogueras, la Rivière, Pichirilo, and Manolo González that Colonel Montes Arache managed to set up an elaborate network of units to defend the city twenty-four hours a day against the attacks of a far superior enemy.

Caamaño and Aristy became an efficient working team. The former, with a military background but no political experience, represented the moderate right. The latter, with some political and business experience, represented the moderate left. Together they discussed and set policies acceptable to both left and right within the rebel movement. They sat together at the conference table to discuss policies with rebel leaders or with international representatives.

The new government headed by Caamaño lacked the ideological homogeneity of the group which had originally planned the revolution under Molina Ureña. Together with members of the PRD, there were in Caamaño's government dissident members of the conservative UCN and the Social Christians. The military group, whose leadership was so important to the revolution, was also bound to represent its political opinion. Héctor Aristy, Jottín Cury, Virgilio M. Reyna, and others were dissenters from still other parties. Finally, the members of the Marxist parties were also entitled to have a voice in the process of decision making.

It was not an easy task to give leadership to and secure support from such heterogeneous groups. Tensions and differences of opinions were frequent between the "moderates" and the "extremists." Clear disagreements on policies and revolutionary strategies existed among the more radical groups. Caamaño, however, always managed to secure the support necessary to maintain his leadership position not only in military but also in political matters.[54]

To consolidate his government Caamaño had to reorganize his military structure to face the new situation. The man chosen for the job was

54. On July 8, 1965, the supreme rebel leadership held a secret meeting to decide whether Héctor García-Godoy could be accepted as Provisional President. After a lengthy discussion in which the different sectors within the rebel leadership argued in favor of or against the motion, a vote was called. The vote was four

Montes Arache, who had shown both personal courage and leadership ability in the battle at the Duarte Bridge. There were in the rebel zone about thirteen hundred regular troops, including officers and enlisted men. To these, four thousand civilian fighters were added at different stages of the war. There were among them many veterans, but there were also many young men who had never received any military training. These supplementary troops were necessary if the rebels were to maintain a state of alert twenty-four hours a day along the borderlines of the rebel zone. The task before Montes Arache was to give these men some kind of military training to enable them to fight a far superior enemy, and to keep up their morale during the months of negotiations that lay ahead.

To provide the civilians with some military training, Montes Arache used as many military officers as he had available, as well as civilians who had some military experience—such as Pichirilo, Manolo González, André la Rivière, and Fafa Taveras. A training school was set up in which navy frogmen trained the civilians in urban guerrilla tactics. To maintain the morale of the rebel organization, Montes Arache and other military officers agreed to let the civilians organize themselves into commando units. Montes Arache realized that his job was to coordinate these units scattered all over the city and to give them leadership together with logistic and strategic support. Thus, the commandos, which had originally started as a means of self-protection and an expression of solidarity among members of informal groups, became the most powerful instrument of defense in the hands of the rebels. By the end of May there were in the city 117 commando posts in which five thousand men lived, ate, and slept together. These men, most of them civilians, were closely supervised and controlled by the Caamaño government, from which they received leadership and to which they gave military support.[55]

---

yes, two no, one abstention. Before dismissing the meeting, Caamaño asked if he could count on the support of those who had voted against the motion. Of the two votes against the motion, one declared that his party would support the decision. The other showed "reservations." However, despite these reservations, García-Godoy was accepted as Provisional President by the Government of Caamaño.

55. See the list of commandos in Appendix 5. The organization of the commandos is given in more detail in the next chapter.

Negotiations for a Settlement

Negotiations toward a settlement of the crisis started as early as April 25 when rebels and loyalists sat at the conference table in the Presidential Palace. When the rebels rejected the generals' proposals for the creation of a mixed military junta made up of rebels and loyalists, and emphasized that their constitutionalist claims were not negotiable, the negotiations became deadlocked. From the moment the loyalists strafed the rebels and opened the civil war, no direct negotiations between the contending factions were possible, and recourse was made to different mediators.[56]

The rebel leadership made several appeals to different groups to mediate in the crisis, first to the U.S. Embassy and diplomatic corps, later to the Papal Nuncio, the OAS, and the Latin American leaders consulted by President Johnson: Romulo Betancourt, José Figueres, and Muñoz Marín.[57] Finally, the rebels appealed directly to the United Nations Security Council. The rebels never rejected the mediating offices of any group that was thought capable of helping solve the crisis, and participated actively in the mediations of J. B. Martin, McGeorge Bundy, and and the OAS Ad Hoc Committee.

The negotiations lasted four months, during which time the top rebel leaders were dedicated to almost constant study and discussions of the proposals. Because of the heterogeneity of the personalities and groups within the rebel camp, they probably spent as much time in reaching agreement and ironing out differences among themselves as they spent in their negotiations with the loyalists. Rebel leaders, however, were able to present at the negotiating table a series of proposals that were rather consistent with the ideological position their faction had taken from the beginning.

Concessions, naturally, had to be made by both sides if the deadlock

---

56. I have been able to identify twelve different groups of negotiators who tried successively—some of them at the same time—to find a solution to the crisis. These twelve teams were made up of diplomats and politicians of national and international reputation. Of these teams, only those of the Papal Nuncio, the UN Representative J. A. Mayobre, and the Ad Hoc Committee of the OAS were able to make any positive contribution to the solution of the crisis.

57. On May 10, 1965, the rebel government addressed a letter to the OAS requesting the mediation of these three leaders in the Dominican crisis. See Estrella, *La revolución dominicana,* p. 40.

was to be solved. First it was Imbert who agreed to Martin's suggestion that he send some of the loyalist generals out of the country.[58] It was then the turn of the rebels to make a concession; in the negotiations with McGeorge Bundy the issue of Bosch returning to occupy the presidency was dropped entirely and the rebels agreed that Antonio Guzmán should fill the vacancy until 1967, when Bosch's term was due to expire. Later, in their negotiations with the OAS Ad Hoc Committee, the rebels abandoned two more substantial issues, the immediate return to the 1963 Constitution and the expulsion from the country of Wessin, Santos, and Rivera Caminero.[59]

Another issue on which the rebels had to compromise was the imposition by Ellsworth Bunker of Héctor García-Godoy as Provisional President. The rebels accepted him after delivering a note of protest to the OAS on July 9, 1965. In it they emphasized that by imposing García-Godoy as President, Ambassador Bunker was stepping out of the role of mediator and becoming the arbiter of the fate of the Dominican people. In this issue, again, a certain amount of conflict developed among the rebels' different ideological sectors. The moderates including the PRD were willing to accept García-Godoy, while the more radical groups rejected him as a member of the oligarchy. Caamaño, however, was able to implement a majority decision arrived at by a democratic vote of the top rebel leaders.

A few days before the inauguration of García-Godoy, Caamaño resigned as Constitutional President before the National Assembly and a crowd of people who gathered for the event at the Ozama Fortress. In his final speech, Caamaño emphasized:

> We could not win, but they could not overcome us either. . . .
> It is true that we had to yield, but the invaders who came to
> destroy our revolution had also to bend before the courage of
> our people. . . . The accomplishments of our revolution are
> embodied in the Institutional and Reconciliation Acts: elec-

58. The rebels never considered this gesture an essential step in the settlement because Wessin, Santos, and Rivera Caminero, the three top loyalist military officers, remained in their jobs.

59. From a communiqué of the PRD published in *La Nación* on June 30, 1965, it was clear that the rebels understood that they had to reach a compromise: "They [the United States] came to crush our revolution and they have been forced to negotiate with us: this constitutes an extraordinary success for our movement."

Civilians showing support for the rebel cause at a public rally, July 12, 1965. Sign reads "Again—Yankees out."

tions will be held shortly. Freedom of the individual and human rights will be granted to all Dominicans, who will also enjoy the right to live in their own country without fear of deportation. But most important of all: there has been a democratic awakening in our national consciousness—an awakening against coups d'etat and against administrative corruption, nepotism, and interventionism.[60]

On August 31 the Constitutional Government signed the Institutional and Reconciliation Acts, ending the civil war and giving way to the Provisional Government. On September 3 Héctor García-Godoy was sworn in as Provisional President. Colonel Francisco Caamaño was present at the inauguration ceremony. The war was over.

60. *Ahora*, no. 108 (Sept. 18, 1965), pp. 39–42. My translation.

Chapter 4

The Paramilitary Organization

⚜ After the landing of U.S. troops in Santo Domingo, the focus of the revolution shifted from military to political activities. Obviously for political negotiation to be effective, the rebels had to maintain their military strength. When the rebel command took the initiative in the first days of the uprising, it relied almost exclusively on the regular army officers and enlisted men who had initiated the revolt. After the rebel forces had been surrounded in Ciudad Nueva by U.S. troops, the rebel commanders realized that they could do little more than maintain their position and defend the city from a surprise attack by U.S. or loyalist troops. Since the rebel army had suffered many casualties and desertions during the darkest hours of April 27–28, the rebel command then had to rely heavily on civilian fighters who had been involved in the revolution from the beginning. From the organization of these small defense units made up of civilian fighters, a new structure emerged, which became known as the commando.

The first commando post was organized on April 26 by Manolo González with some members of the Communist Party (PSP).[1] After the battles of April 27–28, the civilian fighters taking part in the operations began to organize into other small groups operating alongside the

1. This group was disbanded by the Central Committee of the PSP when on April 27 it realized that if the San Isidro forces took the city, all members of the party would be exterminated if found together.

46

better-equipped and better-disciplined units of the rebel army. By this time, however, civilian fighters in the rebel military organization outnumbered the regulars four to one.

As mentioned earlier, Caamaño entrusted the defense of the city to Colonel Ramón Montes Arache, former director of the elite Navy Frogmen Academy. Montes Arache soon realized that to defend the city around the clock against the attacks of a militarily superior enemy would necessitate the use of as many civilians as possible. He encouraged the formation of new units and offered strategic and logistic support to those already in existence. By mid-May about 120 of these units, made up of four thousand civilians, were operating in the rebel zone.[2]

While some basic military training and discipline were necessary, these units maintained a distinctly civilian character. Because of the mixture of civilian and military traits in these organizations, I have called them paramilitary. This chapter describes two units that I feel were representative of many others in the rebel zone, although they were radically different from each other in several organizational dimensions. They were not the only types of commando that existed in the rebel zone,[3] but they represent the two basic types of commando organizations. The first unit, San Miguel, was set up within the structure of an informal organization (the barrio), while the second, San Lázaro, was founded upon the structure of a formal organization (the PSP).

My observations of these two commandos will illustrate many similarities between the two units. Not only were these posts set up in neighboring communities, but these areas were similar in size and socioeconomic background; they also faced the same military threat and the same problems in providing food, clothing, and security. Yet significant differences were apparent in the organization, morale, discipline, and effectiveness of these commandos. One basic reason for these differences was the leadership and organization within each of these posts.

An additional and most important reason for describing these two

2. See Appendix 5. There were 5332 men enrolled in the 130 commando posts listed. Approximately 1300 of them were members of the armed forces.

3. Because the commandos were organized informally and even spontaneously to cope with a sudden emergency, they were not formed according to any centralized plan. Indeed, each one generally took its character from its leader and membership.

commando posts is that I became closely associated with these two units, since the headquarters of San Miguel was next door to my apartment and San Lázaro was only two hundred yards away. Physical proximity helped to create several relationships, as well as some interdependence between these two commando units and the organizations I was running. Although I was in close contact with several other commandos—Poasi, Pedro Mena, El Lido, Barahona, Pedro Cadena, and Luperón, four months of daily interaction made me most familiar with San Miguel and San Lázaro.

San Miguel

The people of this barrio, known throughout Santo Domingo for their toughness, form a community in the heart of the city, independent in some ways of the rest of the city. They are proud of their name—*Migueletes*—and any resident of less than three years is considered a stranger. San Miguel harbors in its alleys and narrow streets many *tigres*.[4] To control them, the police had set up a small station next to the church. "But the cops did not dare to go into El Jobo [a slum area] during the night," Chiro, a local tigre, told me.

When the revolution broke out, the tigres of San Miguel were eager to take over the police station, but dared not attack until April 28, when two navy frogmen with machine guns challenged the small police force. Then some tigres joined the frogmen to chase away the police. When the rebels captured the Ozama Fortress on April 30, many tigres obtained firearms. Some returned to San Miguel to sleep that night in the police station next to the church. The next morning Francisco, a former army sergeant, joined them with his machine gun and showed them how to use their firearms. Francisco was older than most of the boys and had military training as well as personal traits which made him the natural leader of the group. They elected him comandante, and Chiro was appointed subcomandante.

Francisco had about sixty boys under his command and four girls to help as cooks. Only thirty percent of the boys were from the barrio, so Francisco had to provide food and sleeping accommodations for the

---

4. The term *tigres* (tigers) is a Dominican slang term for gangs of neighborhood boys whose organization and behavior roughly parallels that of urban street gangs in the United States.

others in the police station which had three rooms and a single toilet. When Francisco asked Montes Arache and Lachapelle for supplies, he received some, but not enough. Some of the boys suggested breaking into a grocery store "to borrow" some food. However, Francisco, an idealist who had joined the revolution to restore law and order under the Constitution, would not hear of it. One day he said to me: "I did not join this movement so that I could eat. I have enough myself. I am a master carpenter and I have plenty of work. But there are many people who have no work and are starving: for them I joined this."

Francisco was not an authoritarian comandante; he gave orders in a soft voice, calling his followers *compañeros* (which roughly translates to "buddy")—a term with considerable effect. He had to spend much time away from San Miguel looking for food and ammunition for his men. Originally he had twenty-five weapons for his sixty men, but some of the tigres sold their weapons to get money for food or drink. The boys started to blame Francisco for the poor food at the commando post. When I arrived in San Miguel to distribute food, I visited Francisco and gave him five hundred pounds of rice and some cooking oil. I told him he could feed the boys with these supplies, and if any remained, he could let them give it to their relatives. Francisco asked me to explain this to the boys myself so they would not suspect he had kept anything for himself.

Francisco had brought with him a few boys from his own barrio, and this group, together with other commando members not from San Miguel, supported his leadership. But the boys from San Miguel, particularly the tigres—perhaps hostile to what they regarded as usurpation from the outside—grew increasingly aggressive toward Francisco and his followers. One day when Francisco was away looking for food, a bitter argument developed with everyone taking sides against everyone else. The argument almost ended in a gunfight before those opposed to Francisco succeeded in their coup to oust him as the comandante. After Francisco returned and was refused admission to the commando, he went to general headquarters to inform the high command of the situation. He was advised to remain at general headquarters while Lachapelle, a young army major, went to San Miguel. I observed the meeting between the boys of the commando and Lachapelle from behind the venetian blinds of my apartment. Lachapelle was angry with the boys for "making an issue of such small matters." He told them a new comandante and subcomandante would be appointed by the General Staff, and he promised to find them sleeping facilities and to improve their lot in general. He reminded them that the revolution was being fought to improve their lives, but that its goals were not yet accomplished.

Two days later Deschamps, a former police corporal, arrived as the new comandante. Deschamps was the opposite of Francisco: authoritarian, proud, selfish, and even cowardly. He never lost an opportunity to ask me for food and supplies for himself or for his friends. One day I gave him four hundred pounds of rice and twenty gallons of cooking oil for the commando post. Deschamps asked me to come to his post and tell the boys that one hundred pounds of the rice would be exclusively for the comandante and the other three hundred for the rank and file. Although I was outraged, I did not show my anger since I wanted to continue my relationship with him and the commando. I merely said, "I am sorry. I can't do that. It is not good for you. The most you could get for yourself is twenty-five pounds."

About a month after Francisco left San Miguel, the girls cooking for the commando post quit their jobs. When one of them came to see me, I asked her why they had changed their minds about aiding the commando. She told me that Deschamps had taken some liberties with them, and they could no longer stay. She also told me that four dozen bottles of German malt I had given Deschamps for the boys in the battle of June 15 had never reached them, but had been distributed to some of Deschamps' friends in the barrio.

During this period many commando posts from the northern sector of the rebel zone had been displaced from their barrios by the attacks of the U.S. Marines. Some of these commandos (Poasi, Pedro Mena, and Pedro Cadena) moved southward and settled near San Miguel. This settling was a clear indication of the weakness of Commando San Miguel. Jaime, a young student who was comandante of Commando B-3, told me that the men of Pedro Cadena had started to settle in his territory. Jaime told them that they would have to merge with Commando B-3 and obey his orders. The men of Pedro Cadena then decided to move further south and settled without difficulty in San Miguel territory.

On June 15, the boys had fought throughout the day without eating, so when firing from the U.S. lines slackened by nightfall, the boys started to search for food and accommodations for the night. The old colonial church was sheltering two hundred women and children who slept on benches and the floor. Outside the church I distributed cocoa, crackers, and sardines to the boys from the commando posts. I also gave powdered milk to some women in the barrio, who prepared it for the hungry fighters.

The streets around the church were covered with debris and electric and telephone wires. All day long the area had been under heavy fire from the unrelenting rifles and bazookas of U.S. Marines, and many windows and doors had been blasted open. There were no lights in the city and, by then, only sporadic gunfire broke the silence. During the night the hungry boys took advantage of the darkness and started to loot the grocery store across the street from the church. I looked for Comandante Deschamps everywhere without success; as usual he had vanished at a critical moment. I finally found him and complained that some boys were looting the store. He replied, "That is terrible. They shouldn't be doing that. But, you know, none of those tigres is from San Miguel; they are all from the north. And they are tough. You can't tell them not to do it, because they might shoot you." At that moment, a local tigre named Hugo passed by carrying several cans of Quik chocolate from the looted store. Deschamps ordered him to return the cans to the store, and although Hugo did not like the idea, he obeyed.

Later that night, Francisco, who had returned to the area to help in the emergency, asked me to accompany him to another store that had not yet been looted. Inside, goods lay scattered everywhere. Even though Francisco had not eaten all day, he did not touch any of the food lying around. He had a hammer and some nails, and with them he secured the doors of the store. After he had finished the job with great dexterity, we left through the back door, which we also nailed shut. Back at my apartment I gave him some cocoa and crackers for supper, and when he was about to leave I suggested he sleep in the church. After propping a bench against the door, he went to sleep on the bench with his gun beneath it.

Two hours later, Tungo, the new subcomandante of San Miguel, came to me protesting the looting that the tigres had done. He brought with him a television set and a radio belonging to the owner of the store and asked me to keep them in my apartment to save them from the tigres.

He then went back and brought two of the store's delivery bicycles. (Two months later Macaré, the owner of the store, came and reclaimed these items.)

Subcomandante Tungo was a young PRD leader who had worked in the low-cost housing department in Bosch's administration. He was sincerely committed to the revolution and led the boys to the front when fighting broke out. When I knew him, he was the leader of a group of eight or ten men who were not only his loyal followers during the revolution, but his friends.

Tungo sometimes invited me to eat with him. By this time there were no cooks in the commando post; the food received from Caamaño or me was distributed to the smaller groups formed after the breakup of the general group. Tungo's girl friend, Esperanza, was an excellent cook who cooked for Tungo's whole group. Tungo sometimes boasted that those boys were now eating better than ever before in their lives. After dinner, we usually sat on the terrace and discussed politics. One day in mid-June Tungo invited Professor Goldsen from Cornell and me to dinner. We started to argue about the power structure of the rebel forces and about the negotiations taking place between Caamaño and the Ad Hoc Committee. I argued that Caamaño should have negotiated in May when he was still in command of the northern part of the city and had a much more powerful bargaining position. Tungo, however, objected strongly, saying that at that time the United States wanted Caamaño to negotiate with Imbert, but that the rebels would negotiate only with the United States or the OAS, not with Imbert. Later in the evening we tried to explain to Tungo the fears the United States had about the revolution, pointing out that the Marxists in the rebel zone had a very powerful organization and that we noticed that the June 14th Movement and the MPD (Chinese branch of local Communist Party) had some of the most modern weapons available in the rebel zone.[5] Tungo disagreed with my arguments about the Marxists, and argued that the June 14th Movement and the MPD had better equipment only because they were in places

5. We had heard on May 2 the statement of President Johnson to the American people in which he announced that "a popular democratic revolution had been taken over and really seized and placed into the hands of a band of Communist conspirators." (U.S., Department of State, *Bulletin,* 52, no. 1351 (May 17, 1965), p. 744.) Tungo, as well as most other rebel leaders, strongly disagreed with such opinion.

more vulnerable to attack—Ciudad Nueva and the northeastern sector of the city—and therefore needed better weapons. I was unconvinced and replied, "I don't think that Ciudad Nueva is any more vulnerable than San Carlos, Santa Bárbara, or San Antón. Why should the boys of the June 14th Movement be manning so many .50 caliber machine guns and bazookas?" He could not give a reasonable answer, and finally said simply, "Well, some of them were the first to the arsenals and arms depots."

Two months later, when relations between Caamaño and the June 14th Movement had become somewhat strained, I again had dinner with Tungo. We discussed a speech Caamaño had made the day before which the boys of the June 14th Movement had frequently interrupted with their slogans against the negotiations Caamaño was conducting with the Ad Hoc Committee. Quite disturbed by the boys' attitude, Tungo said to me, "One day we are going to show them who is boss here."

As subcomandante of San Miguel, Tungo was on duty almost every other night. Sometimes after dark he would come over and invite me to join him on a tour of the area. First we stopped at the sentry posts of San Miguel in Mella Avenue where he checked the boys' weapons and ammunition. If a car approached while we were there, one took positions behind the sandbags and walls or in a doorway. From a distance the car would signal by switching its lights off and on three times and would then proceed without lights. As it approached, the sentry would halt the car with a shout of "alto!" From the stopped car the passengers would shout their identification. This procedure was repeated at almost every other block. Except for emergencies, no one was allowed to drive at night, and under the circumstances few dared to.

During this tour I noticed that most of the boys were either dressed in dark clothes or had removed their shirts. I later discovered why: one night while wearing a light shirt I was warned to be careful crossing intersections, "because the U.S. Marines will see you and shoot you on the spot."

Sometimes after our inspection of the sentries, Tungo invited me to visit neighboring commandos. As we left our zone, extra caution was necessary. At the first sentry post, we shouted the name of its group. When the sentries shouted back, we identified ourselves and only then could we proceed, knowing that we would be in the sights of their guns until we reached them. When we drew near, the boys became very friendly and chatted, exchanging bits of gossip and political information. Tungo was proud to introduce me to them, but most of the boys already knew me. They always asked me whether a solution was near, as though I knew more than they. Often I did not, because I was so busy with the health clinic and food problems that I did not even have time to read the newspapers.

Tungo was not a born leader like Pichirilo and Barahona, who had won their commando posts by their physical prowess and a certain amount of charisma. Tungo had no charisma, but he was proud that, despite a congenital limp, he had beaten all his school classmates in swimming, boxing, and other sports. One day during a false alarm in the barrio I saw Tungo rushing to the front calling the boys and giving them orders. One of the boys ran away screaming in fear, "The CEFA troops are coming with tanks!" An angry Tungo ordered two other boys to take away his rifle and put him in jail. He rebuked the boy saying, "If you can't stand like a man in an emergency, you had better go somewhere else."

Very few San Miguel boys took part in the June 15 battle against the U.S. troops. To be sure, one of their most dedicated leaders, Chez Javier, was killed at the front line and one other boy from the commando was wounded. Later the commando post was officially named after Chez Javier to honor him. During the battle, though, over thirty percent of the boys vanished from the area, some never to return. The vacancies were soon filled by boys from other parts of the city or from the provinces. San Miguel, like most other commando posts, had a continuous flow of personnel, with no more than twenty percent of the founders of the commando staying in it until the end of the revolution. Some boys moved to other commando posts they liked better; some quit altogether. Many who had dropped out of the commando, returned from time to time to sit in the park with their friends, discussing the situation in and out of the rebel zone. Francisco, for example, decided around the end of July to return to his carpenter's shop in a barrio north of the city. However, about once a week he came back to do some work for me either in the church or in the clinic. One day, after hearing that U.S. Marines occupying his barrio had put him in jail, I drove there to look for him and found him sitting with some friends by his shop. He told me that the

Marines had freed him after questioning him. He was very pleased that I had taken such interest in his case.

In most commando posts the boys were subject to military instruction, drills, and even political indoctrination. Not so in San Miguel. Some of the boys went to the "commando school" set up by Montes Arache and his frogmen to train civilian fighters in guerrilla tactics, but when they came back to San Miguel, they would sit chatting in the park while Deschamps spent his time drinking beer and playing cards with Traboux, "Miguel el loco," and other friends in the San Miguel slum of El Jobo. As the weeks passed, drinking around San Miguel became quite a problem, despite a rebel government order controlling the sale of liquor. Liquor was apparently a compensation for low morale, but it caused several unpleasant incidents, one of which affected the organization of San Miguel as a commando post.

Traboux was a "cowboy," a man with a machine gun operating in the rebel zone without allegiance to any commando post. Cowboys took advantage of the confused situation to go from place to place using their guns for personal interests. They were disliked by the commando boys because they were out for fun and would not accept the responsibilities or duties of the commando post. At the beginning of the revolution, many cowboys roamed the city, but their number had been greatly reduced through the efforts of the military police and the comandantes of different areas.

Several times I noticed that even the tigres of San Miguel were critical of Traboux and his friends. Traboux, however, was a good friend of Deschamps, so he stayed around San Miguel.

Early one night Traboux and two local tigres were caught stealing chickens in the market of Mella Avenue. While trying to jail them, Oscar Santana—a student engineer, comandante of El Lido, and an important leader of the June 14th Movement—was killed, allegedly with a .45 pistol that Traboux was carrying. After the shooting, I saw Traboux and Deschamps nervously arguing on their way to San Miguel. I never saw Traboux again.

The boys of El Lido and members of the June 14th Movement were so angry they wanted to wipe out all the tigres of San Miguel. By 9:00 P.M. I had managed to stop a fight between the two factions, but only after one of the tigres who had been caught stealing was fatally shot in the melee, and another one jailed. Traboux, however, was still at large, and the boys from El Lido were after him. Later, while I was at the general headquarters of the June 14th Movement attempting to save the jailed boy's life, Traboux appeared at the church and surrendered himself to Father Tomás Marrero, a young Canadian-trained Cuban priest working among San Miguel's tigres. The priest took him to general headquarters and handed him over to Héctor Aristy, thinking the fugitive would be safer in his custody.

Back in San Miguel the word had spread that Oscar Santana had been killed with Comandante Deschamps' .45 pistol. (This rumor was subsequently contested; although Traboux had been carrying Deschamps' pistol, it was not the murder weapon.) The boys of El Lido were in a violent mood, so Deschamps surrendered himself to general headquarters and remained under arrest there until the end of the revolution. That night Traboux was transferred from one prison to another until the temporizing Aristy finally placed him in the hands of the June 14th Movement leaders. After they assured me that the life of Traboux was not in danger and that he would be given a fair trial, I returned home to bed around 3:00 A.M. Two hours later Traboux was shot. The next day I went to see the June 14th Movement leaders to tell them that I considered Traboux's death murder and that I held them responsible. I then saw Colonel Montes Arache and President Caamaño to protest this miscarriage of justice. Caamaño ordered an inquiry, assigning the case to Colonel Lora Fernández, the Chief of Staff. Three days later Father Tomás and I went to see Colonel Lora to learn the results of the investigation. We sat in the center of the office with several officers standing around us. After some explanation, Lora said with a glance at Father Tomás' clerical collar, "Of course, I see that you look at the whole incident from a humanitarian point of view." I interrupted him: "Colonel, we are not here to protest from a humanitarian point of view. We are here as members of a society that wants to be democratic, protesting this violation of elementary human rights. To send a man to his death after a fair trial we consider justice. To kill a man the way they did is murder."*

After Deschamps' departure from San Miguel, a young man named

* Further inquiry into the case seems to indicate that Traboux was accidentally shot while imprisoned by the members of the June 14th Movement.

Peralta was elected comandante. Whether this election was free or imposed by the leadership of the June 14th Movement was never made clear, but Peralta belonged to the Movement; from this point members of the June 14th Movement gave regular conferences and lectures to the boys of San Miguel. The commando boys started to drill in the streets of San Miguel and officially participated in some general rallies. By this time, Tungo and the other boys who had been in San Miguel since its foundation withdrew from the commando post. Despite Peralta's efforts at indoctrinating and disciplining the commando, I had the impression that the commando had practically disintegrated. "It is not so much that we don't like discipline and order," a local tigre said to me. "What we don't like is that *they* (the June 14th Movement) want everyone to be like *them*."

San Lázaro

Only two hundred yards west of San Miguel is another barrio known as San Lázaro. People there are also from the lower middle class, but their houses, stores, and general way of life suggest a higher socioeconomic level than that of San Miguel. The two barrios are divided by the well-paved Santomé Street, but the social life and characteristics of the two neighborhoods have much in common. San Lázaro is built around an old church and convent much larger than San Miguel's rectory. In peacetime a group of sisters ran a grade school in the convent, and the adjoining building was used by the Cursillos, an upper-middle-class Catholic organization with radical right-wing tendencies. When the revolution broke out, the sisters of the convent, the priests, and the laity of the Cursillos left for the loyalist zone.

When Manolo González arrived in the barrio leading a group of rebels, he recognized the old colonial structure of San Lázaro, with its thick walls and small windows, as an ideal site for a commando post. He took over the abandoned church building for sleeping quarters, giving the boys precise orders: "No one is to remove anything from this place. We are using the Cursillos building and its facilities; the convent is not to be used."

The commando had nearly sixty men from different social strata and political affiliations. The largest and most influential group was from the PSP, the Dominican Communist Party which followed the Moscow line, but there were also men from the MPD and the PRSC (Social Christian Party). Many, including a few tigres, had no political affiliation. Cachorro, a former MPD member who had received guerrilla training in Cuba, was appointed comandante, and Manolo González the sub-commandante, although Manolo González was obviously the main figure. Fifteen percent of the boys were university students and were led by Tony Isa Conde, a university student of middle-class background. Twenty percent were men with technical skills and were led by Cachorro. The rest were unskilled and unemployed workers. Three or four women took care of the kitchen under the direction of Manolo González's wife, an attractive young middle-class girl.

The commando was organized into platoons of ten men, each under the direction of a group leader, and each had duties for the day or the week posted on a bulletin board in front of the comandante's office. Platoon leaders met with the comandante daily to discuss the orders of the day. Political indoctrination was an important part of the schedule and the boys were carefully trained in urban guerilla warfare. Once Manolo González said to me, "The boys of the June 14th Movement and some of our own boys were trained in Cuba for guerrilla warfare in the mountains. They now think they are in Cuba. They are wrong, and their training is worthless. Ours is an urban war. We had to learn it ourselves as we made it. Our war is in the *patios*[6] and in the alleys. We came to know each alley and each patio inch by inch. We learned how to hit the enemy and how to escape from him."

When Manolo González requested that I open a food distribution center in San Lázaro on May 22, I inspected the facilities of the convent and found everything as the sisters had left it, including a large framed picture of Generalissimo Franco in the living room of the Spanish sisters. Manolo asked me to use that section of the building and to take responsibility for the convent. I declined, because I could not stay there permanently. However, I did start using the convent for food distribution and opened the church to the public.

If I needed any help distributing food, my friend Tomás Marrero

---

6. A *patio* in Santo Domingo is a backyard common to as many as ten or fifteen houses in a very poor neighborhood. These people live a communal life and their children play together. The women do their washing and sometimes their cooking in the yard while the men play cards together after work.

would ask Cachorro for some cooperation and Cachorro would promptly send two or three boys to do whatever they were asked. Some of the middle-class girls who helped me distribute food were quite pretty, and they attracted the interest of the commando boys. The girls told me they did not like the boys loitering about while they were working, and I noticed too that the girls were less efficient when the boys were around. So I told Cachorro about the problem. He forbade the boys to loiter near the food distribution center, but he asked me to have the girls enter and leave through a side door. This minimized unnecessary communication between the two groups.

Occasionally, some food was left over after allotments were passed out; this was stored until the next distribution in a small convent storage room with no lock. I noticed once that some food had been stolen from the storage room, and when I reported the theft to the comandante, he told me he would take care of the problem. A week later he had caught the thief and put him in jail.

On several occasions I needed things we did not have in San Miguel, such as a rubber stamp we used to stamp the food cards we had given to the families of our barrio and desks for a classroom where we had begun teaching English to the tigres of San Miguel. On such occasions I went to San Lázaro and asked Cachorro or Manolo for help. They gave me what I needed, always requesting a receipt for their files.

Discipline in San Lázaro was strict; drinking was not allowed, and stealing was severely punished. Several times the boys from San Lázaro came in conflict with small bands of tigres attempting to break into the many small shops of Mella Avenue. One incident involved the boys of the commando and the "Americano Feo" (the "Ugly American"). He was called the Ugly American because he was tall, blond, and ugly. After taking part in the war in the first days, he had become a "cowboy" and drove about in a jeep captured from the U.S. Marines. He belonged to no organized group, but had friends in the barrio with whom he drank, played cards, and stole during the night. One night he was very drunk and was caught stealing by the boys from San Lázaro. He was sent to the Ozama Fortress for a couple of weeks and when he was freed, he fled the rebel zone and asked political asylum in a foreign embassy. He never returned to the barrio.

San Lázaro was not one of the most powerful commando posts; in terms of manpower or military equipment, such commandos as San Carlos, Poasi, Argentina, B-3, Pichirilo, and others were much stronger. Because of the political background of its PSP leadership, however, San Lázaro outranked most of them in political prestige with the rebel government. Manolo González was often consulted by the General Staff in military matters and by the government in political affairs. The boys thought highly of Manolo González's importance to the government and called him a "big shot." The San Lázaro leaders often participated in the solution of problems outside their own geographical demarcation. If San Miguel came under mortar fire during the night, Manolo González studied the damage, established the possible direction of the attack, and reported his intelligence to general headquarters. Comandantes from less important commandos, such as San Miguel and Pedro Mena, would merely join the crowds of onlookers, without taking any technical responsibilities.

One day while a businessman from San Lázaro was loading merchandise to take to his store in the U.S. zone, the boys of El Lido argued with him, trying to persuade him not to remove those items from the rebel zone. The businessman showed them a written permit Manolo González had given him from the office of the General Staff, but the boys tore the permit to pieces, criticizing Manolo for being an "old racketeer." After the businessman reported to San Lázaro, an outraged Cachorro informed the El Lido boys that he was the authority in that area and told them to withdraw to their own demarcation. He then went to general headquarters and returned with a copy of the permit and some of his boys with machine guns to insure the safe delivery of the load of merchandise.

Often I went to the commando posts to have dinner with the boys. San Lázaro had an excellent chef in charge of the kitchen and the food was much better than in San Miguel, although the variety was limited to beans and perhaps a piece of meat, with either rice or green plantain. One night after supper one of the boys started to show my associate how to operate a Mauser rifle. Conversing with the boys, I watched uneasily from the corner of my eye. Suddenly there was a blast, scaring us all; the bullet, fortunately, hit the ceiling of the room. Cachorro rushed in immediately and shook his head. "Compañero," he said, "you know we cannot play with or demonstrate firearms. I am sorry, but you must go to jail for twenty-four hours. Please take him away." Two other boys, obeying the order, led him off.

Relations between Cachorro and Manolo González were not always good; indeed, after the revolution was over, Cachorro told me they were no longer friends. He also told me that Manolo had brought too many members of the PSP into the commando, destroying the balance of power. Apparently most PSP members coming in from the provinces to join the revolution were incorporated into San Lázaro. One day Cachorro told me, "It had been understood that the newcomers should not outnumber the old members, to prevent the commando post from losing its own personality." Manolo González, on the other hand, blamed Cachorro for lacking the courage to go to the front line when the U.S. Marines attacked the rebel zone on June 15.

An incident described in similar terms by both men may help explain the enmity between the two. Shortly before the end of the revolution, Cachorro visited Niurca, a girl who helped distribute food in San Lázaro. (Niurca was the sister of subcomandante Tungo, and is now married to Cachorro.) Niurca was sick, and Cachorro stayed long enough to drink too much. She begged him to leave his gun with her when he started back toward San Lázaro, but he refused. When he passed the commando post of the Haitian refugees and they ordered him to stop, he opened fire on them. The incident was immediately reported to Manolo González who went to San Lázaro, took Cachorro out of bed, and had him jailed. The following morning, after Manolo reported, the General Staff removed Cachorro from his position, although they let him stay in San Lázaro. Roca, a student from the University and a platoon leader, was chosen new comandante and stayed in command until the end of the war.

Summary

Both San Miguel and San Lázaro were in the same neighborhood; both organizations drew heavily from the same socioeconomic elements (the unskilled laborer and the unemployed); both faced the same threat from the enemy; both faced the same problems in providing food and clothing; and both had approximately the same number of members. Nevertheless they were quite different in organization, morale, discipline, and efficiency. Why? Was it because the leaders of San Lázaro were of middle-class extraction? Perhaps, but such a condition may be considered a disadvantage when the rank and file of the group is of low socioeconomic status. Was it because San Lázaro operated with leaders and structures borrowed from a previously existing formal organization, the PSP, which gave support and stability to its leaders? Manolo González once said to me, "Those who received guerrilla training in Cuba are not the most useful to the revolution, but those are who have organizational abilities, even if they can't hold a gun. In two hours you can learn to hit the target and prepare Molotov cocktails. But it takes a long time to learn how to organize men into groups that can operate effectively in a given set of circumstances."

The same idea was voiced by Jaime, the young economics student and member of the June 14th Movement, who became comandante of Commando B-3, one of the largest commandos. Around the end of May this commando post encountered some serious difficulties when several factions brought it to a point of imminent disintegration. The commando had been organized by Fidelio Despradel, a leader of the June 14th Movement, and although Jaime was not a member of the organization, he rushed to the commando to confer with leaders of the different factions. He brought them together, and by the end of the day they asked him to stay and become their comandante. To do so, Jaime gave up an important job in his party, but he felt that the only way to keep the unit together was to take command. He immediately set out to give the organization an entirely new structure, dividing the men into smaller units, appointing a leader in each group, and entrusting the men with various responsibilities. Jaime enjoyed great prestige among the rank and file. This he explained to me by saying, "When there is work, I am the first to do it. When we have to fight, I am the first in the front line."

Jaime had considerable organizational ability, which was apparent in his work in the leadership of the June 14th Movement and later in a patriotic organization set up by Héctor Aristy after the war. Jaime is a cosmopolitan, white, middle-class boy who had been at the university for two years and then traveled in Europe and Cuba. There were other leaders, however, such as Barahona, Pichirilo, and El Indio, who were less cosmopolitan than Jaime or Manolo González, but who successfully organized efficient commando posts. These men had little training or experience in organizing, but they nonetheless manifested great organizational ability. In my opinion, these men combined native organizational ability with a high degree of *machismo* (which translates roughly into courage, toughness, and physical prowess). The commando groups organized by these men were ruled in a personal way by one man's will, whereas those organized by Manolo, Jaime, and Santana seemed ruled by patterns of behavior established by other organizations, of which the commando post was only an offshoot. For example, if Pichirilo or Barahona had been involved in an incident similar to Cachorro's drunken firing on the Haitian post, I am sure no one, at least in their own commandos, would have dared to jail either of them.

The comparison of San Miguel and San Lázaro reveals the two main avenues along which commando organizations developed. On one hand, informal groups of people from the barrio, groups of friends and relatives from the same community, or gangs of tigres evolved into commandos such as San Miguel, Pedro Mena, Pichirilo, and Barahona. On the other hand, some formal organizations already operating in public life whose leaders decided to combine their memberships with other individuals formed such commandos as San Lázaro, Poasi, and Argentina. Both kinds of groups were numerous, and both were relevant to the revolution. The first kind relied heavily on the organizational abilities of the leader, particularly on his charisma and *machismo*. The second kind relied heavily on the organizational structure of the parent organization. The commandos of the first group were more effective in war situations (particularly if they had a truly charismatic leader). The second group of commandos grew in importance from a political standpoint, particularly during truce periods, because they seemed able to maintain high morale in times of inactivity and because the parent organizations seemed able to prevent their disintegration during periods of political negotiation.

One final observation is that all commando posts, regardless of their origins and the nature of the leaders, were autonomous and rather informally ruled. They resembled large families or communities more than army units and observed a minimum of formalities. In most commandos, the only officers were the comandante and the subcomandante who took the comandante's place in his absence. Commandos of more than sixty or seventy men, however, required more officers, since there were more duties than two men could handle. But the majority of the posts had only about thirty men who lived together, eating and sleeping in the same place without regard to rank or social distinction. When I asked a boy in a commando one day whether another fellow was an officer, he replied, "There are no other officers apart from the comandante and subcomandante. In this country we are tired of so many officers. Now we are all the same."

After September 3, 1965, when García-Godoy was inaugurated, the rebel command ordered the commandos to disband. Some of the boys surrendered their weapons; others wrapped them in plastic bags and buried them in their patios or hid them in old boxes. For some, the journey home was only around the block; for others it was to another sector of the city, perhaps next door to a police station or the barracks of CEFA troops; and for still others, it was far away to the provinces. Those from La Vega, Santiago, Macorís, Romana, and other important towns rented old buses and returned home in groups, perhaps for fear of being shot if they went one by one, or perhaps because they truly believed they had won the revolution.

Repressive moves against them would soon start. By 1966, some 250 men from the commandos had been assassinated without the law proving the identity of a single assassin.[7]

7. Among these casualties was Pichirilo, who was shot in the back in the summer of 1966. For an assessment of the situation up to 1967, see J. Bosch, "El Pentagonismo sustituto del imperialismo," *Ahora* (1967), p. 45.

Chapter 5

The Civic Organization

The major political and military events of the revolution made newspaper headlines, and some of them have been documented in committee reports compiled for the U.S. Senate hearings. However, another series of events, that of the civic organization, was hardly noted by the news media although these events were as important to the existence and understanding of the revolution as the activities already described.

The revolution was fought on two different levels: one a level of high leadership—general organization and major negotiations; and the other a level of medium and low leadership—local organization and face-to-face interaction between the four thousand irregulars who supported the uprising and the thousands of people in whose environment the revolution materialized.

Without the support of the Dominican civilians the revolution clearly could not have sustained itself through the long months of negotiations. The solidarity of the people and the civic organization was an essential base for the strength and morale of the political and military activities at the upper levels of the revolution. My experience of living for almost five months with these people on the lower level of the revolution enables me to describe many activities in which I was directly involved. To my knowledge my notes were the only documents made on this phase of the revolution.

65

Work in the Hospitals

I spent the first three days of the revolution in my house on Independencia Avenue, which is in an upper-middle-class sector of the city, collecting all available information on the revolution from the radio, television, and newspapers, and through telephone contacts with friends in different parts of the city; I also drove around the city daily to see what was happening. On Monday, April 26, I took several friends to donate blood and visit the wounded in two hospitals in the north of the city. When the main battle between the rebels and the loyalists started on Tuesday, April 27, my friend Father Tomás and I again started toward these hospitals to help the wounded.

After driving as fast as we dared through a deserted city under attack by navy and air force rockets, we arrived at Morgan's Hospital around 1:30 P.M. Confusion and hysteria reigned: crowds of women and children were pouring into the building from the neighborhoods around the Duarte Bridge, at that moment under heavy strafing. Dozens of wounded also continued to arrive although the hospital was already full. We knew no one in the hospital, but Father Tomás began to organize the second floor while I started on the ground floor. In the operating room on the second floor, doctors and nurses were performing delicate operations as bullets hit the windows and walls of the room. When the director of the hospital asked me to hold the refugees on the ground floor, away from the wards and the operating room, I begged the crowds to sit in the corridor, away from the windows and doors. Babies cried, and women held them against the walls with the few belongings they had been able to carry from their homes. Before nightfall, I gave them some cocoa for supper which I had found in the kitchen. The next day was still worse since food stored in the hospital was inadequate to feed so many.

By about 4:00 P.M., I thought the CEFA troops of General Wessin had taken over the whole city. The presence in the hospital of two rebel army regulars with their submachine guns troubled both the doctors and the Spanish sisters who operated the hospital. They feared a battle if loyalist troops tried to take over the hospital. Although the sisters and doctors agreed that no one in the hospital should carry arms, none dared ask the rebel soldiers to leave. Finally they asked me if I could persuade them to go. I called the soldiers to an empty room and told them that we did not need their protection since the hospital was for all wounded, loyalist and rebel alike. After a long discussion they agreed to leave. Immediately I felt guilty for sending them into the streets where they might be killed by CEFA troops, so I suggested that they change from their army uniforms into civilian clothes and leave their weapons in the hospital. One of them, however, put a hand grenade in his pocket. Ten minutes after he left, he ran back and asked me to keep the grenade, because loyalist troops were searching everyone in the streets. When I saw the same boy three weeks later in the downtown area held by the rebels, he embraced me claiming I had saved his life.

We were isolated in the hospital. By this time all communications in the city were interrupted, and electricity and water supplies were exhausted. Not knowing what was happening, I went to my car, which was parked outside the main lobby, to get news over my car radio. Soon a group of men who had been sitting in the lobby surrounded the car. As I switched stations, I could hear the men saying: "That's us!" or "That's them!" In confusion I turned to them and asked, "Who are 'we' and 'they'?" They all answered at once, " 'We' is the rebel station, and *pueblo* [people]. 'They' is Wessin and the military." At this moment I began to understand what the whole thing was about. The elitist coup of April 24 had turned in these days into a mass popular uprising of the populace against the armed forces and the oligarchy.

In spite of sporadic gunfire during the night, the Red Cross ambulance kept bringing more wounded to the hospital. With everything in darkness, the doctors were forced to operate by flashlight. I asked the driver of the Volkswagen ambulance if we could use its engine to supply power to the operating room. Throwing a cable from a window we connected it to the ambulance's generator; a spotlight then enabled the doctors to perform some urgent operations. The doctors and nurses who had worked until early morning were exhausted when fighting broke out again in the morning and more wounded started to arrive. Doctors and nurses from other parts of the city came to help, but after several hours they too were tired. At this point doctors and medical students from Santiago, the second largest city in the country, volunteered to come and aid with the wounded.

Two days later the Red Cross and Peace Corps volunteers came with corn meal, wheat, powdered milk, and drugs. The director of the hospital told me that some of the patients were becoming weak because they would not eat the food. "Many of these people," he said, "are accustomed to eating only plantain and beans. If they don't, they die."

"Why don't you buy some?" I asked.

He replied, "We have neither the money nor transportation to go buy them."

I drove to Villa Consuelo, a poor neighborhood in the heart of Santo Domingo. After crossing barricades and driving back and forth to get to the market, I stopped near Amado García Avenue where I could see barbed wire barricades and for the first time U.S. Marines with tanks and howitzers. Although I explained I was driving to the market to buy food for the hospital, they would not let me through. I turned back and started over again. When I finally got to the market, I spent all the money I had in my pocket—$13.00—to buy plantain. Then I returned to the hospital.

The director of the hospital asked me to drive him downtown to Catholic Charities headquarters for food. First we drove to the power plant and then to the telephone company, appealing to them to repair the hospital lines as soon as possible. Finally, we arrived at the Catholic Charities warehouse on George Washington Avenue. The rebel officer in charge gave us all the food we could take,—a relatively small load since I was driving a small Austin. When one of the men who helped to load the car asked for a ride home, I assented, despite the fact that he took the room of two bags of corn meal. A few blocks from the hospital he asked me to stop. After he got out of the car, he started to take several big bags he had helped load. When I asked him what he was doing, he replied, "This is my share." I angrily grabbed him by the arm. "This food is for the wounded in the hospital," I said to him. "We did you a favor giving you a ride and now you want to take our food? Take your own bags and get lost." By this time the director was at my side cursing the stranger. As people gathered around us, the stranger understood that we meant business and he left. We drove on to the hospital, and the wounded had food for another day.

By Wednesday, April 28, I had moved on to the Moscoso Puello Hospital further north. I had been there only once before, to give blood. Now I arrived with another Jesuit priest, Father Lemus, and we offered our help to the director, Dr. Vicini, who welcomed us and immediately set us to work. Father Lemus took care of the wounded in the operating room, and I served as a handyman to Dr. Vicini with two Peace Corps boys as my assistants. My first task was to learn to operate the gas lamps the Peace Corps boys had brought for the emergency. When I arrived at the director's office, I found several doctors on their knees trying to make the lamps work. Finally Dr. Vicini and I succeeded in lighting them, and we instantly became "experts." No one else was allowed to operate the lamps, and lighting became a routine operation for me every evening.

The doctors of Moscoso Puello were all exhausted, and they slept by turns only three or four hours a day, often several men in a single bed. The wards were filled to capacity and more wounded were still coming. The doctors had to stop working at night since there was no electricity, and gas lamps could not be taken into the operating room. There was, however, a small generator in Dr. Vicini's office, but no one knew how to operate it, since hospital electricians had not reported to work the last five days. A Peace Corps boy and I read the instructions and, after three hours of experimenting, managed to start it. We put it in the garden outside the operating room and connected a cable to the big lamps over the operating tables.

I stayed in this hospital for over ten days at the height of the crisis, helping the doctors and nurses in whatever way I could. Sometimes my job was nothing more than taking a cup of coffee to an exhausted surgeon; at other times I changed the linens or carried buckets of water up and down the stairs because we had no running water.

As time passed, the shortage of food and drugs became a serious problem; there was no food for the doctors who were working eighteen to twenty hours a day. I went to a nearby church to ask the priest for food. He invited me to eat with him and afterward, gave me all the food he had in storage from Catholic Charities. I took this food to the hospital in a Red Cross ambulance, so that the hungry people of the barrio would not think that the priest was giving the food to some friends.

When the doctors had a few minutes free, they would sit in the dining room or lobby, listening to newscasts or asking friends for information. Most of the young doctors favored the rebels; the older ones, however, did not seem to be sympathetic to them, although I saw none of them arguing politics.

In both hospitals the administrative staff was rather conservative, often accusing some young doctors of being communists, although I met only one medical student who I felt could be classified as such.

In both hospitals, many medical students came daily to help the doctors. They normally supervised the wards and first-aid cases and also took over most tasks handled in the United States by registered nurses. In Santo Domingo most nurses are "practical nurses" and have little or no formal training. Even when fighting was in progress, however, most of these nurses showed a dedication and courage by coming to work every day. I occasionally heard complaints from the administration that some of them had not reported to work, but this was understandable, since many lived far away and all means of transportation were interrupted.

In both hospitals the minor employees such as cooks, janitors, and floor sweepers continued to work, despite the general fear and confusion. The Spanish sisters of Morgan's Hospital also showed dedication and courage during the revolution. I was surprised, however, that no other sisters from their own community or from other religious communities in Santo Domingo came to help them or take their places for a few days. There was a clear ideological gap between the sisters and the medical staff of the hospital. The Catholic Church—as an organization—was loyalist in its sympathies—which explains the reluctance of many sisters to work in the rebel zone. The Peace Corps nurses also performed well during the revolution. In Moscoso Puello, a Peace Corps girl tearfully told me the U.S. Embassy had ordered the volunteers to leave the besieged barrio and come to the hospital. "If I cannot stay with these people now when they are in danger, I cannot go back to them later," she said. Later, apparently still concerned for their safety, the embassy ordered all Peace Corps nurses to leave even the hospitals and to be ready for evacuation. The nurses wrote the ambassador that they would stay in the hospitals at their own risk. One day one of the doctors told me, "If these girls had not been here, we would have been unable to do one-third of what we did."

Work in San Miguel

In the second week of May, when I thought that a political settlement was near and an end to the fighting imminent, I decided to return home to rest and think about the situation. The day the Imbert government was sworn in, I went to Santiago to see what the situation was in the provinces. After returning once more to Santo Domingo, I tried to organize a group of friends to study the political situation and take a stand regarding the events we were witnessing. By this time Imbert's troops were successfully carrying out the so-called Operación Limpieza (Operation Clean-up) in the north of the city. Rumors were spreading that after the war was over in the north, Imbert would go into the downtown stronghold of Ciudad Nueva to crush the rebels. A propaganda campaign was launched to show the world that all rebels in Ciudad Nueva were communists.

On a rainy Sunday afternoon, May 16, when Operación Limpieza was in full swing, I decided to go to the rebel zone with a friend. When we crossed Checkpoint Charlie at Avenida Bolívar, I began to fear that I might never return alive. After we left the American tanks, howitzers, and Marines behind, we walked along deserted streets. When we crossed Independencia Park in the heart of downtown Santo Domingo, we began to see rebels with machine guns hiding in doorways and on rooftops. In El Conde Street we could see small groups of rebels at every intersection. As a jeep passed by, my friend recognized the driver and waved to him. He stopped and came back to greet us. He was the French paratrooper, André de la Rivière, dressed in combat outfit with a machine gun slung from his shoulder. We stood together on a corner in the rain while André criticized the Papal Nuncio for asking him outright whether he was a communist. He was angry with Caamaño for letting Viriato Fiallo, the head of the loyalist UCN, go free from the rebel to the loyalist zone without a trial. After talking for half an hour, André drove us near the U.S. lines, because it was almost curfew.

On May 19 I went back for a second visit to the rebel zone. This time it was a sunny day, but the city still looked grim; I could hear gunfire from the north where Operación Limpieza was being completed. At noon on Friday, May 21, the twelve-hour humanitarian truce worked out by U.N. representative Mayobre went into effect. I decided to take advantage of the truce and move into the rebel zone that Friday afternoon, fearing that Saturday would be too late, because Imbert had promised repeatedly "to finish up with the Communists in Ciudad Nueva." With me went a young Cuban priest, Father Manuel Ortega, who had studied political science at the University of Berlin the year before. We took some food, a transistor radio, and a few books and papers, and left for the rebel zone. We had requested permission from the bishop to use as our base the old colonial church of San Miguel in the heart of downtown Santo Domingo. Although neither of us had ever been in that part of the city, we had been told that the rebels had turned the old stone church into a fortress armed with machine guns and surrounded by sandbags.

Like most other churches in downtown Santo Domingo, San Miguel had been abandoned by the local priests as soon as the revolution broke out. Of the fourteen Catholic churches which normally served the area, only five were still open by May 21, and two of these were administered by young priests who had moved in after the churches were abandoned in the first days of the revolt. On Sunday, May 23, we opened the churches San Miguel and San Lázaro to the public; a week later Father Tomás Marrero joined us and opened the church of El Carmen. By the end of May, eight Catholic churches in the rebel zone were once again serving the population, and at least five of these churches were administered by young liberal elements within the clergy.

When we arrived at San Miguel, the janitor was nailing a big lock on the front door of the church in preparation for leaving early the next day. He had been alone in the church for three weeks, and he was unwilling to sit there and wait for the CEFA troops. He showed us our quarters: a small apartment annex to the church with two small rooms, one downstairs and the other upstairs. He told us that the upstairs bedroom was not safe because the tin roof did not offer much protection during the air raids. He himself had slept on a cot downstairs. Father Ortega also decided to stay downstairs, but I did not like the odors there and chose the upstairs. Before I went to sleep that night Father Ortega came upstairs with his belongings; he had also decided to face the air raids rather than the downstairs odors.

We knew no one in San Miguel. When we stepped out of the car, some women in Juan Isidro Street looked at us with surprise and curiosity. When I waved, they waved back and looked at each other. After I deposited my belongings inside I said hello to several boys standing two houses from the church in Jose Reyes Street. The house had a flagpole in front and had been hit recently by gunfire. It turned out to be the San Miguel police station now occupied by the boys of Commando San Miguel. When I asked to see the comandante, the boys ushered me into the house. The comandante was conferring with some other men in a small windowless room. When I entered he stood up, smiled, and introduced himself in a soft voice: "Francisco, Comandante de San Miguel." We shook hands and I told him that I had taken over the old church and would be available to help in any way I could. He said my help would be greatly appreciated, especially during the fighting, because there were no medical doctors around. Embarrassed, I told him I was not a doctor. He replied, "In any case, you know more than we do, and I'm sure you'll be able to help."

Later in the evening I was talking with some boys from San Miguel when a thin man in combat outfit and carrying a machine gun approached and asked to talk to me in private. He had a clear Spanish accent. We walked toward San Lázaro where he asked if Father Ortega and I could also take care of that church. I agreed to open San Lázaro to the public and to use its facilities as a food distribution center. The man with the machine gun was comandante in San Lázaro; he was blunt and authoritarian, but friendly even when giving precise orders to the boys. He was better educated than those around him and had a gentleman's bearing. At that time his name, Manolo González, did not mean anything to me, but I tried to remember it. Soon I was to find out who he was and what role he played in the revolution.

The Food Problem

San Miguel is a lower-middle-class neighborhood in the heart of Santo Domingo surrounding an old colonial church dedicated to that patron saint. Behind the church is a poor slum called El Jobo, where 150 families had formed their own community, linked to the rest of the city only through two small unpaved alleys. Most houses in the barrio have electricity but no running water. Many families have small radios and a few have television sets. Children play naked in the narrow alleys and the women cook in their patios while the men play cards under a big seibo tree.

Across from the church, a public park is surrounded by houses belonging to middle-class families. At one corner of the park stand a bar and a grocery store and at the other end is the three-story private clinic of Doctor Dinzey. The police station commando post was across from the park near the church.

Main street of the San Miguel barrio. The church that was used as a food distribution center is to the left, out of the photograph.

After my first night in San Miguel, I realized that lack of food was the primary problem in the barrio. Markets and grocery stores had been closed for almost a month, and people in the rebel zone had no money since all work in the city had stopped with the outbreak of the revolt. Although many had stretched their food supplies and cash reserves, most families were now desperate. Also, limited refrigeration facilities among the lower-middle-class and poor families made extended food storage impossible.

I phoned the OAS, CARE, and Catholic Charities trying to get some food for the barrio.[1] Each agency noted my request, but all passed the petition on to Catholic Charities which had been assigned the task of distributing food to the people. The next time I called Catholic Charities, an aggravated director complained that I was trying to pressure him

1. See Figure 5, p. 168.

through other agencies. I was embarrassed and confused by his anger, because I was trying only to get food from whatever source I could. I was wholly unaware at the time that power politics were already at work in the mechanics of these organizations.

Two days later Catholic Charities informed me that I could have a truckload of rice. I drove to the international zone and then to the government zone where I was given twelve thousand pounds of rice in two-pound bags. By the time the bags were unloaded in San Miguel and San Lázaro, about seven hundred people were waiting in line in front of each church. The preceding day we had gone from house to house in the barrio, giving out tickets for food distribution. The procedure started in an orderly fashion with some barrio girls distributing three bags of rice to each person in line, and the boys of the commandos maintaining order with their machine guns. To prevent use of the same ticket more than once, I cut the upper right corner from each ticket we honored. The process had continued for over two hours when the people still in line became nervous and started to push one another. Sensing that a riot might break out at any moment, I decided to stop the distribution for a while. Protected by the boys from the commando, I stood in the middle of the crowd and raised my hands for silence. At the top of my lungs, I shouted that there was rice for everyone, but we needed order for the distribution and that we would honor first those tickets given out the day before. Despite what I had said, hundreds without tickets continued to stand in line. When all with tickets had received their three bags, we allowed those without tickets to get their share. But the line never seemed to get shorter. We then noticed that some were coming two and three times to get more food. At that point we gave the remaining rice to the commando boys for themselves, in payment for their help unloading the trucks and keeping the people in line.

Our next food distribution followed a similar pattern. But this time an orderly and equitable distribution was even more difficult because we had received different amounts of rice, beans, and cooking oil. At one point a riot was so close that the commando boys had to fire over the heads of the crowd. Elsewhere in the city where food was being distributed, fights and disturbances had developed, and on those occasions everyone grabbed what he could. One day I saw a woman carrying on her head six gallons of cooking oil, when in my barrio we could hardly give families a quart for the week. We were determined that inequitable portioning of food should not happen in our barrio.

The city was divided into different sectors: each person in charge of distributing food to a sector was responsible for issuing punch cards to the families in his area. Although food distribution was restricted to card holders, the mechanics of distribution could be organized as each sector head saw fit.

I was in charge of the central part of the city from Mella Avenue to Nouel Street, which I divided into four sectors. I took care of San Miguel and made Father Tomás responsible for San Lázaro, Reverend García, Minister of the Evangelical Church, for the Evangelical Center, and Doña Tina, a volunteer worker from the community, for Mercedes Center. Our area had fifteen thousand people according to a house-to-house census. Each family was issued a punch card with the name, age, and address of the head of the household printed on the card, together with the number of children and dependents. The census took Father Tomás two full weeks, but when he finished, we knew exactly how many rations to prepare when the truckloads arrived each week.

Before we issued the punch cards, we stamped them with our own seal to differentiate them from those of the other sectors. People from other sectors frequently tried to use their cards in our distribution, but our system frustrated this practice, and, at least temporarily, ended it. Two weeks later I noticed that many people were waiting in line with cards bearing the address of our sector but not our seal. I soon found that the office of a political party in the city was distributing the cards to people from all over the city and sending them to us for food. This action was not only highly irresponsible since we did not have food enough for the whole city, but it also had the appearance of a political maneuver. Politely but firmly, I sent the holders of the unvalidated cards back to the politicians. An hour later, the mayor of the city and other officials came to persuade me to honor the cards. I refused. They insisted that I should honor the cards, if only for one day, to help them save face. I knew that if I agreed once, I would have to do so again and again. When I told them that if I had to do it their way, I would rather let them take care of food distribution, they begged me to continue the distribution in my own way and apologized for the interference.

Another major problem in organizing the food distribution was the selection of trustworthy men and women who would cooperate without expecting too great a share of the items in return. The problem first arose when the trucks arrived with the food and twenty or thirty men volunteered to help unload. When the task was completed, they all expected some recompense, even though they knew their wives would soon collect the family share. Every time a truck of food was unloaded, we went through the same argument with "volunteers." I finally decided that only commando boys would be asked to help and I made it clear that their work was a service to the community for which no reward should be expected. At the end of each distribution, however, I gave the comandante two or three hundred pounds of the food that was left for the boys.

Once the food was in our compound a team of twelve to fifteen persons in each sector had to be organized to distribute it as efficiently as possible. Once again, those who helped us wanted more than their share as a reward. When I refused their requests, they would then get angry with me and I with them, and our work was hampered. Slowly, I ended the system of extra rations for my helpers and eliminated from the teams those whom I could not trust, those who favored their friends in preference to others, or who stole food when I was away. I also eliminated those who were not hard workers. I found in the end that my teams were made up of white middle-class boys and girls, mostly of Lebanese extraction. (There is a large Lebanese group in Santo Domingo, most of whom are middle-class.) This situation posed a new problem: a group of white middle-class people distributing food to a crowd of dark poor Dominicans. I took pains to bring into my teams some colored boys and girls of the barrio. They were carefully chosen and I found that they performed as well as the others. Once Father Tomás had organized his club in San Lázaro, he succeeded in entirely replacing the middle-class group with his tigres.

After this, the food distribution presented no major problems. We spent one day a week at it and everything was done routinely. Women lined up on one side and men on another. At the entrance a girl punched cards to avoid repeats. Pregnant women entered first, and the rest entered in groups of four to be given the food allotted each family for that week. They left through a different door, so those still in line would

Women from the San Miguel barrio waiting for the weekly food distribution

not get excited and try to steal their food. Every week twenty to thirty thousand pounds of food were distributed in this way—without major difficulties or unpleasant incidents—to a population on the verge of starvation.

The Danger of Epidemics

When we had arrived in San Miguel, the streets were littered with garbage, and it was difficult to drive a car without getting a flat tire from the debris of barricades and half-burned rubbish. There was no garbage collection and sewers were broken in many places. Only one hospital in the rebel zone was operating and we were afraid an epidemic might break out at any moment in this city where more than three thousand had been killed in the streets. In the middle-class sector of the city the Red Cross had set up a center for vaccination against typhoid,[2] and I decided to set up a center in San Miguel also. The Red Cross office gave me the shots, alcohol, and the instruments to apply the vaccine, and we put up a Red Cross sign in front of the compound and announced over a small public address system that all children should

2. This center was set up in the zone controlled by U.S. forces.

be vaccinated. Slowly their mothers brought them in. After our team of two boys and two girls from the barrio had vaccinated them, we recorded their names on Red Cross papers, which were taken to the main office daily. Some two thousand children and adults received the three shots at regular intervals.

To set up the vaccination center I had needed the signature of a physician who lived in the area. Once our vaccination campaign was over, I thought the physician might come once a week to our barrio health center to care for a few sick women and children. A medical student volunteered to help the physician, but I had to get the drugs for the patients. With a few bottles of cough syrup, aspirin, and anti-biotics some friends had given me, we opened a health clinic. At first the doctor and medical student used my apartment twice a week to care for the patients. Although the drugs were soon gone, more and more patients came to our makeshift clinic. One day Tungo, the subcomandante from San Miguel, urged me to use Dr. Dinzey's clinic which had been closed since the battle of June 15. He told me that the rebel forces had taken over private clinics in other parts of the city—Abel González, San Luís, and Cruz Peña—and groups of young doctors and medical students had set up a medical post (*comando médico*). Tungo said he could get an order from the rebel Ministry of Health to open the clinic for our use. I compromised and telephoned Doctor Dinzey's assistant, who had taken refuge in the international zone, for permission to use one room in the ground floor as an outpatient clinic. He proved eager to let me use the facilities, probably for two reasons: to discharge his own feeling of responsibility, and to prevent a rebel take-over of the premises. He sent me the keys the following day. After an inventory of furniture, medical supplies, and drugs, I sealed off some of the clinic offices and set up my health center in two small rooms on the ground floor.

Since the number of patients grew daily, I requested medical help through the headquarters of the PRD and PRSC, and through personal contacts. By the end of the second week, we had to take over the whole building; thirteen doctors (one cardiologist, one gynecologist, three pediatricians, and eight general practitioners), plus seven medical students, five nurses, three laboratory technicians, and two receptionists were taking care of more than a hundred patients daily. Contacts were made for referrals to other specialists throughout the city for difficult cases. Our patients were treated without charge. Soon the main city hospital started to refer problem cases, particularly in pediatrics and obstetrics, to our clinic.

The organization of the health clinic presented some major problems. We had the difficult task of scheduling the work of our voluntary doctors and medical students, some of whom had obligations in other hospitals and in private offices, so that every day we would have from three to five doctors for consultation. The doctors, students, and nurses were dedicated and efficient; some were in their offices by 8:00 A.M., and worked until 1:30 P.M. The nurses came every day with amazing regularity, even though some had to come from as far as fifteen miles away.

Our main problem, however, was getting drugs and medical supplies. We organized a group of university students to request medical samples from pharmaceutical manufacturers and distributors, the Red Cross, and the Ministry of Health. The group collected many kinds of samples from both domestic and foreign manufacturers. Jose Licha, a medical student of Lebanese extraction, and Danilo Caro, an architecture student from Cornell, collected most of the supplies. Although the supplies helped temporarily, the number of patients continued to grow. One day, Dr. Sigarán, a physician who lived in the rebel zone and came to the clinic every day, said to me, "If we don't have drugs, I won't come back to the clinic. Our prescriptions are useless to our patients if we can't give them the drugs because they haven't the money to go elsewhere." At that point I joined the team of students collecting medical samples. I visited not only offices in the rebel zone, but in the international and loyalist zones as well. I also went to the OAS, CARE, the Ministry of Health, and the head of the Evangelical Church. Monsignor Clarizio, the Papal Nuncio, was particularly interested in helping the health clinic, and he brought thousands of pounds of medical samples from Puerto Rico. Unfortunately, some of these were new products, which only a few Dominican doctors were familiar with. Although most distributors were quite generous in supplying medical samples, very few would give regular stock. Although no pressure of any kind was ever used to obtain drugs from distributors, firms with offices in the rebel zone, such as Gassó y Gassó, Eli Lilly, and Frank Rodríquez, were far more generous than those with offices only in the other zones. Only one distributor for an American firm flatly refused to donate any drugs. He said he could not give drugs to a clinic in the rebel zone. Even after I pointed out to him that nearly 86 percent of the patients were coming from the loyalist zone, he refused to cooperate. When the employees of another American firm which had declined to cooperate with our clinic learned that their firm would not help us, they collected twenty-three dollars among themselves for the clinic.

At the suggestion of the OAS, I went to the loyalist Secretary of Health to ask for medical supplies. I was ushered into the office of Dr. Pichardo, the Under-Secretary of Health in the Imbert Government, who lectured me about medical services in the city and said there was no need for me to run a public health clinic. I interrupted him, saying "Whether my services are necessary or not, I don't know. But at 6 o'clock every morning there are over one hundred women and children waiting outside the clinic to receive medical attention. Over 86 percent of these people come from your zone, and it is for them that I request medical supplies." After the interview, he gave me a written order for their warehouse, where I was given a bottle of aspirin, one hundred vitamin tablets, two packages of cotton, and two bottles of alcohol. That was the total contribution of the Dominican Department of Health to a clinic caring for over 125 patients a day!

Every morning before going on my search for medical supplies, I had to organize the appointments for the day. Josephine Salas, a medical student, helped distribute appointment cards to the patients. Priority was given on the basis of arrival time at the clinic and the seriousness of each case. During the morning the doctors could see only about one hundred of the daily crowd of nearly one hundred seventy patients. Consequently, Josephine and I screened the cases; when we thought that the patient's ailment was only malnutrition or a bad cold, we gave him vitamins or cold tablets and sent him home, scheduling for the doctor only those cases we thought needed further medical attention.

Some of the doctors who were sent by the PRD created minor problems with the appointment policy. They would disrupt our appointment schedule by bringing in their friends or members of the party to give them preferential treatment. Sometimes, after caring for these private patients, they would leave, and the other doctors would have to see the regular patients. At first, since the doctors were not being paid for their services, I did not object, but when the practice started to generalize, I called it to the attention of these doctors and told them that although their private patients were welcome in the clinic, they should follow the regular sequence of appointments. In spite of this, the practice continued and the staff of the clinic started to feel uneasy about it. I then called the doctors together and said that preferential treatment based on personal or political friendships could not be tolerated in the clinic. After this, two doctors stopped coming to the clinic and put pressure on a third doctor to discontinue his services there. When I noticed this, I informed Peña Gómez, leader of the PRD, of the situation. The dissident doctors did not cause any more trouble although my complaints apparently created some irritation among party members. Later a member of the PRD told me, "Señor, you must take it easy. You are trying to solve the problems of this country in a month; our problems are very old and much time and patience are needed to solve them."

When I left San Miguel in September 1965, the clinic had been operating for less than three months, yet it had served at least 2,200 outpatients, providing free medical care, laboratory tests, and drugs. We had records for each patient and we had in storage $1,500 worth of drugs and medical supplies, and had distributed over $6,000 worth of drugs. Before the end of the revolution, Doctor Segura, head of the *comando médico* in the rebel zone, asked for the names of all those who had worked in the clinic, so the rebel government could give them credit for their services to the Dominican people. Since Doctor Dinzey was planning to open his clinic again, we moved our medical supplies back to our apartment in San Miguel. On a visit to Santo Domingo after the revolution was over, I met Doctor Dinzey for the first time; he greeted me warmly and said, "Thank you very much for everything you did. Everything in the clinic was in perfect order when I came back."

The Human Rights Center

Shortly after our arrival in San Miguel, we were confronted with a series of cases of violation of human rights. Women tearfully told us of husbands or sons who had gone to work or to visit friends across the international zone and never returned. They had already gone to the police or to the local jails, but no one would tell them whether their husbands or sons were there. Others complained that the CEFA troops or the U.S. Marines had arrested some relative without a warrant and without filing charges. We started taking these complaints to the OAS Commission on Human Rights and to the Human Rights Center opened by the Papal Nuncio. As soon as word about our new activity spread, many people came from the northern part of the city to file their complaints. At that time, we put up a sign, "Human Rights," in front of our building. Catalina Navarro, a very efficient secretary, recorded all the pertinent information on the missing persons. This was then telephoned or delivered personally by José Licha to the Papal Nuncio's center. In a few days we would receive information from the organization the Nuncio had set up to trace missing persons. In turn, we conveyed this information to those who had placed the complaint with us. This procedure furnished information on some 230 cases, although fifty other cases remained unsolved.

The Tigres Club

Mention must be made of Father Tomás Marrero's organization of the Tigres Club. Since his arrival in San Miguel at the end of May, he had been working with a small group of tigres from San Miguel and from El Jobo. While he had been in Montreal, Father Tomás had developed an interest in studying and helping delinquent boys, and in San Miguel he found an excellent opportunity to work with some of these delinquents. During the evenings, Father Tomás spent hours sitting in the park across from the church talking with the tigres. After a few days, the boys followed him wherever he went; even while he ate his supper, they sat on the sidewalk outside the house waiting for him.

One day in July they decided to organize themselves into a club—the Tigres Club. They stole a tiger advertising sign from an Esso gas station and put it in front of the police station that the commando had recently abandoned. Led by Father Tomás, they cleaned, painted, and repaired the house. They organized themselves into "commando units," each with its own leader. By allowing the boys of the Tigres Club to organize into "commando units," Father Tomás was using what, at that time, was most appealing to the imagination of the young boys, the motivation to set up their own organization in imitation of what the men of the barrio were doing to defend the city. Each unit was given certain tasks for the week: to clean the club, to help with the distribution of food, or to sweep the streets and the park. Father Tomás suggested they also take odd jobs and pool their money to buy sporting equipment. In the evenings from 6:00 to 7:30, all club members had to attend an English course given by Father Tomás. The boys organized their own band and every other week presented a stage show in the church. On my last visit to Santo Domingo, Father Tomás was finishing a school he and the tigres had constructed. From time to time, however, the boys lapsed back into their old ways, breaking a few windows or getting into fights with other gangs.

One night the boys held a dance in the Club to celebrate their victory in a basketball tournament. I had invited Father Tomás over for dinner that evening but I worried whether he should leave the tigres unchaperoned at a party with girls. He reassured me smilingly, "They know how to take care of themselves. They don't need me anymore." When we returned after the dance, everything was in order. Things had really changed for the tigres of San Miguel.

Chapter 6

Characteristics of the Rebels

From the very beginning of the revolution, I had one question in mind: "Are the so-called rebels any different from the rest of their fellow citizens?" I drove back and forth through the city during the worst of the fight and I lived in the barrios altos for the first two weeks of the war before moving into downtown Santo Domingo where the United States troops had surrounded the rebels. I spent many hours interviewing the top leaders of the revolution, visiting the slums, and talking with the women who came to the clinic every day from the barrios altos and with the commando boys in the park or at night in their machine gun nests. I noted what was said at political rallies and conferences held in the rebel zone and observed carefully the behavior of both speakers and listeners.

Roughly speaking, the hundreds, perhaps thousands, of people with whom I came in contact during the five months of the revolution comprised a cross section of the Dominican population at large, since all social classes, strata, groups, occupations, educational levels, religious denominations, and political ideologies were represented among the revolutionaries. If it were true that the rebels were not basically different from the "loyalists," how was it possible that, at a given moment, the whole of Dominican society was torn into two warring factions unable to come to terms with each other for over five months? If a survey had been made two weeks before April 24, would it have been possible to determine at that time who would become rebels and who would remain loyalists? Would it have been possible to estimate how many would side with one faction and how many with the other? Were there any social traits that would distinguish in advance the rebels from the loyalists?

I set out to discover if there was a set of characteristics common to the rebels which would differentiate them from the loyalists and provide a better understanding of the rebels and the revolution. Although the rebel group was, roughly speaking, a cross section of Dominican society, it is quite probable that certain traits of the Dominican middle and upper classes were under-represented in the rebels and over-represented in the loyalists—traits such as Caucasian racial background, higher education, steady employment, and wealth.

An Ideological Frame

Two characteristics constantly present in the rebel group but rarely found among the loyalists were: a certain ideological frame and a deep feeling of alienation. Generally, ideological frame may be understood here to mean a set of ideas, values, and beliefs which defines society in general, what goals it seeks, and which means to implement these goals should be used in preference to others. Often a given ideology may be expressed through a set of theoretical propositions logically interconnected, as I have shown below in terms of the rebels. I do not suggest that the loyalists were without an ideological frame, and some probably subscribed to certain of the propositions subscribed to by the rebels, particularly those concerned with long-range goals. No loyalist could agree to all the propositions of the ideological frame without, of course, ceasing to be a loyalist and automatically becoming a rebel or a rebel sympathizer.

The following propositions attempt to present the basic ideas, values, and beliefs in the rebel ideology:

1. A need exists in the Dominican Republic for greater participation of all classes of people in the national life.
2. This greater participation in the life of the country implies development and redistribution of the nation's economic and cultural wealth.
3. To develop and redistribute the wealth of the nation, the "old

Trujillista oligarchy" must be removed from the sources of political, military, and economic power.

4. To remove the old Trujillista oligarchy from the sources of power, graft and corruption in the government, and particularly in the armed forces, must be eliminated.

5. To eliminate graft and corruption in the government, it is imperative to return to constitutional democracy with Bosch as president.

The ideas of greater participation of all people in the country's life and the redistribution and development of the nation's wealth are long-range goals, probably shared by many Dominicans on both sides of the revolution. Moreover, they represent the expectations of most of the world's underdeveloped countries. On the other hand, propositions 3 and 4 refer to ways of achieving those goals which, although specific to the Dominican people, are not necessarily shared by all Dominicans.[1]

The logical connection between propositions 4 and 5 is not theoretically very clear since as much corruption may occur in a democracy as in a dictatorial system; still, in the experience of the Dominican people the fact is that the only honest government they have known resulted from the democratic election of 1962.[2]

My interviews with rebel leaders and members of the rank and file during and after the revolution showed that an ideological framework containing these five propositions was essentially present in the minds of all rebels, although different levels of education would determine to what extent. An evaluation of which issues had contributed most to their decision to join the revolution showed that: (1) propositions 3 and 4 had been decisive for most military men and young politicians; (2) propositions 1 and 2 had been instrumental in the case of students and professionals; and (3) proposition 5 had been particularly decisive for the working people. At the height of the crisis, however, when decisions to support or oppose the revolution had to be made in a matter of hours,

1. In June 1966, Joaquín Balaguer, a former Trujillista who had the support of the oligarchy, won the presidential election in a landslide against rebel leader Juan Bosch. It is superfluous to say that Balaguer won for reasons other than that he was a Trujillista.

2. After an extremely harsh assessment of Bosch's administration, U.S. Ambassador J. B. Martin states: "Nor can one ignore the indisputable fact that his brief administration may well have been the most honest in Dominican history, if not in Latin America." J. B. Martin, *Overtaken by Events* (New York, 1966), p. 716.

A public rally in the rebel zone. Signs read "The 1963 Constitution is the only solution"; "Yankees—murderers"; "Show yourself worthy of your country (fatherland)."

the issues became centered around the most concrete means of achieving the goals of the ideological frame. Thus, the slogan—"Return now to the Constitution with Bosch as president"—became the rebel battle cry. Scores of boys and girls from the June 14th Movement wrote the slogan on the walls of public buildings and private houses. The crowds from the PRD blew the horns of their cars and trucks to the rhythm of their chant—"Juan-Bo-Presidente." However, it was not only the shouts of the crowds in the streets or the slogans broadcast by the radio stations which directed attention so sharply to the issue of constitutionality with Bosch as president. From April 24 on, when Donald Reid, Wessin, Imbert, and the generals made attempts to negotiate with the rebels, the rebel leaders' demand for a return to constitutionality with Bosch as president was made clearly and definitely. As soon as Donald Reid handed over the government to the rebel officers on Sunday, April 25, Molina Ureña was sworn in as "provisional president under the constitution" until arrangements could be made for the return of Bosch.[3] Later in the day, when

3. Actually, Molina Ureña was not sworn in until 5:45 P.M. By then, the negotiations had broken off and the air force had started to strafe the Presidential Palace. See *El Listín Diario,* Apr. 26, 1965, p. 4.

rebels and loyalists sat at the conference table to discuss a settlement, Colonel Hernando Ramírez, speaking for the rebel leadership, made it quite clear to Colonel Benoit, the main negotiator for the loyalists, that the rebels did not regard the issue of constitutionality with Bosch as president as negotiable. Wessin and the loyalists, who had ousted Bosch eighteen months earlier, could not agree to his return. Deadlock resulted and civil war broke out.[4]

The ideological frame that guided the behavior of the rebels was more distinct in the minds of the leaders at all levels than in the minds of the rank and file or the masses. The rank and file consisted generally of the three thousand regulars who started the revolt and the four thousand irregulars who joined the commandos. The masses included most of the people in the barrios altos (numbering perhaps two hundred thousand) who were favorable to the ideals of the revolution, but who did not take an active role in the paramilitary activities.

It was not an easy task to detect an ideological framework in the minds of these people, since most of them were illiterate. While visiting them in their shacks, eating with them, and helping them with food, clothes, and medical attention, I tried to find out why they favored the revolution. In simple words, these people clearly stated that they supported the revolution because they had suffered too much under the Trujillo regime with its corrupt police and military and because the rich had always had too much while the poor had had too little. By ending the abuses of the past, the revolution meant a change for the better. It promised to return Bosch to power, whom they liked because "he spoke our language and did not steal." It was for these very reasons that the military had sought an end to his regime.

At the height of the crisis, when a decision had to be made or the causes of the revolution had to be expressed briefly and precisely, the issues tended to focus on the return to constitutionality with Bosch as president. This was often true for the leaders of the revolution, but it was

4. In theory, rebels and loyalists at that moment would have agreed on the first four issues of the ideological frame. Both agreed to the ousting of Donald Reid, and only two weeks later the loyalists agreed to send the corrupt generals into exile. Both General Wessin and General Santos told me in private interviews that a social revolution was badly needed in the country. But they added, "We cannot allow this revolution to be made by the communists." In the eyes of Wessin and Santos, Bosch was a communist, despite the distinction made by U.S. officials that "Bosch is not a communist, but is weak on communism."

true for the masses at all times. Bosch represented education, employment, and human rights. For the illiterate masses of Santo Domingo, such concepts as the constitution, freedom, human rights, education, and employment seem to mean nothing unless they are embodied in a person or leader who has actually implemented them.

Alienation

The second characteristic found more often among the rebels than among the loyalists was a deep feeling of alienation. The individual felt he was not a part of the political process. Such alienation took the form of a feeling of powerlessness to influence or change the political institutions by which the individual is tied to the social system, a feeling of the meaninglessness of his existence within the frame of his society, or a feeling of estrangement from the role which links the individual to the community.[5]

In interviews with rebel leaders, I always asked "Why did you join the revolution?" The answer invariably started with a basic outline of the ideology describing long-range goals and the means for achieving them. If I tried to show them that it was quite possible to pursue such goals peacefully, they usually interrupted, saying, "No, you are wrong. Here it is impossible to achieve such goals through peaceful means." After making this remark, they freely expressed their feelings of powerlessness, meaninglessness, and estrangement.

Alienation within the context of Dominican life was expressed by five significant groups of rebel leaders: (1) the military, (2) the politicians, (3) the professionals, (4) the students, and (5) the leaders of organized labor. All these groups scored high in expressing feelings of meaninglessness. Although they expressed their feelings differently, their statements could be reduced to the following, respectively: (1) "There is no use in being a good military leader when the bosses use you for their personal interests." (2) "What is the use of preparing for the September elections? We know they will not be fair!" (3) "The only way a professional may serve this country is in private practice; as soon as one gets into politics, one becomes corrupt like all other politicians." (4)

5. Murray Levin, "Political Alienation," in *Man Alone: Alienation in Modern Society*, ed. E. and M. Josephson (New York, 1962), pp. 227–39.

"Why should I study when an illiterate colonel makes more money than a doctor, and a general has more influence than a cabinet minister?" ('5) "Have you ever seen a labor dispute in this country won by labor? We are never right! If we protest the abuses of management, we are branded as communists and the police or the army arrest our leaders."

In all groups except the military, feelings of powerlessness were high. The politicians protested that there was no sense in having elections if the candidates of the two majority parties (the PRD and Reformista) were in exile. Nor could they do anything about this state of affairs because the military would not let either Bosch or Balaguer return. Professionals and students alike felt greatly disappointed because fair competition was not the regular channel for social mobility. For political success what you knew was not so important as whom you knew. Labor leaders felt so utterly helpless in their relationship with the government and the armed forces that they had to seek support in international organizations such as the ORIT, CIO, CLASC, or in political parties such as the PRD, the PRSC, the MPD, or the PSP. On several occasions prior to the April revolution, strikes were called by different union leaders, but they always failed because of swift action by the police against the leaders.[6]

Alienation was also expressed by feelings of estrangement, a manifestation of the citizens' discontent at not fulfilling their roles in society. Strangely enough, labor leaders did not score high in feelings of estrangement, probably because they drew considerable satisfaction from what they actually were doing for their fellow workers. Professionals also scored low in feelings of estrangement since, understandably, they drew satisfaction from their private practices. It was the military officer and the politician who scored highest of all groups, followed by the students. One naval officer said to me, "I had always wanted to dedicate my entire life to the service of my country, but I found that the only thing I was doing was perpetuating the oligarchy." A young politician said, "By maintaining political opposition to the government the only thing we achieve is to give the Triumvirate a semblance of democracy."

6. In May 1964, organized labor (FOUPSA and CASC) called a strike against the government of Donald Reid. The workers held the barrios altos under their control for three days before the government succeeded in breaking the strike.

Table 1 shows the scores of the different rebel groups with regard to the dimensions of political alienation.

TABLE 1
ALIENATION OF REBEL GROUPS *

	Powerlessness	Meaninglessness	Estrangement	Scores
Politicians	+	+	+	3
Military	—	+	+	2
Professionals	+	+	—	2
Labor leaders	+	+	—	2
Students	+	+	+	3

* Based on interpretations made by author after interviews with approximately eighty rebel leaders.

My findings concerning alienation among rebel leaders apply also to the rebel rank and file and to the Dominican urban masses at large. No survey has been made to measure the alienation of the population in the northern sectors of the city of Santo Domingo, from Mella Avenue along and across the Ozama River to the east and up the Isabela River to the north. Approximately three quarters of the total population of the capital city live in this area, which is partly lower middle class and working class. It is near the river and is clearly a slum. The slum has no electricity, water supply, or sewage system. There are no schools, churches, hospitals, or any other community public services.[7] Studies of other Latin American cities have suggested that the masses of slum dwellers are alienated from the rest of their societies. On the basis of my own observations, I concluded that the masses in the barrios altos were so alienated from the middle- and upper-class sectors of the city that the two cities exist, physically juxtaposed, with practically no social interaction. Although considerable exchange of goods and services occurs between the two groups, this activity resembles the relationship that exists between a mother country and its colonies more than the normal flow of communications existing among different parts of a modern city. The masses from the barrios altos come to the city only for the services they cannot obtain in the north, such as education, medical attention, and political patron-

7. I was surprised, however, to find that the local branches of some political parties, such as the PRD, were either in the slum or very close to it.

age, or to offer their services to the upper and middle classes. Every morning, civil servants, working people, and domestic servants walk along Duarte Avenue or ride in the *públicos* (local inexpensive cabs), to the downtown sector; every evening they return to their homes in the north. The streets of the downtown sector are crowded with people trying to get jobs.

The masses from the barrios altos do not come to the downtown business section to shop. They have their own business section along Duarte and Mella Avenues where a string of stores owned mainly by merchants of Lebanese extraction offers them all kinds of cheap merchandise. During the day, in front of these stores on both sides of Duarte Avenue, Dominican peddlers display all kinds of black-market items on makeshift stands.

Entertainment is also different in the two sectors of the city. Movie theaters and taverns are the main diversions, but most of the city's movie theaters, including the two drive-ins, are located in the downtown middle-class sectors and their prices—from $.90 to $1.50 per person—are unreasonably high by Dominican standards. Several expensive night clubs and casinos are also located in the middle-class sector. In the poor sector north of Mella Avenue, movie theaters are of the lowest quality and prices are low—about twenty-five cents per person. Innumerable drinking places and brothels are also in the barrios altos. Whereas activity in the middle class sectors seems to cease at night, it begins then in the north; bars are open all night, and people drink and dance to the music of loud juke boxes.

Well over 60 percent of this urban proletariat living in the barrios altos are peasants who have come to the city within the last ten years from all over the country, from small towns in the provinces and from the *campo* (country). Over 80 percent are illiterate, and over 50 percent are permanently unemployed (*chiriperos*).[8] When they arrive in the city, they live for some months with relatives or friends from their own villages.

8. The term *chiriperos* is a Dominican term roughly equivalent to the U.S. "hard-core unemployed." In an interview with me, Professor Bosch estimated that of the 500,000 people presently unemployed in the country 400,000 were *chiriperos*. He pointed out that these men make less than $100 a year per family, and consequently have to live by borrowing or begging money from relatives or friends. See Juan Bosch, *Partido Revolucionario Dominicano: tesis sindical* (Santo Domingo, 1966), pp. 19–20.

After that, they build their own *ranchos* (replicas of their campo huts) with tin and wood from old boxes.

Their physical proximity to the city exposes them to many contacts and influences that probably would not have affected them had they stayed in the campo. Most listen to radio programs for music and information; even where there is no electricity some transistor radios are available. Those who go to the city in the morning return to the slums in the evening bringing back rumors, stories, and political gossip currently being discussed in the city, or one of the few men who can read may bring a copy of a newspaper, and his friends gather around him to discuss the news. Although discussion is mainly confined to crime or the sports section, a glance is given to the headlines on national issues. Often the stories and gossip transmitted orally by those who have been downtown are corroborated by the newspaper stories.

When the revolution broke out on April 24, radio commentator Peña Gómez appealed to the masses to support the revolution. The masses trusted him, because, although well-educated and a leader in Bosch's party, he was a Negro from a poor family. By 6:00 P.M. a curfew had been imposed on the city's population, but the people in the barrios altos rushed into the streets and celebrated the downfall of the Triumvirate until 3:00 A.M. Police patrols assigned to these barrios did not dare drive through that night. By Sunday, April 25, the masses were in the streets and thousands of people had gathered at the Duarte Bridge and at the Presidential Palace following the appeal of popular radio commentators who had taken over the main radio stations. By Monday, April 26, all the streets of the barrios altos were blocked with barricades to defend against the tanks from San Isidro. During the first two weeks of the revolution I estimated that from 80 to 90 percent of the people in the barrios altos actively supported the rebels by helping build barricades, giving them food, or helping the wounded.

After the U.S. Marines landed in Santo Domingo on April 28, the barrios altos were cut off from the main rebel stronghold of Ciudad Nueva. Two weeks later when Imbert started Operation Clean-up, his forces pounded the barrios altos with tank and bazooka fire. Caamaño's irregulars, with the help of the local populace, resisted this attack for a full week, fighting from house to house and from block to block.

My interviews with the rank and file of the commandos revealed that nearly 80 percent of the commando members were from the barrios altos. About 40 percent had been with the rebel leaders in the downtown stronghold since the beginning of the revolt, but nearly 60 percent of them had come across the U.S. corridor when Imbert's clean-up operation was completed. They had left their weapons behind and joined the crowds that daily crossed the U.S. corridor after being carefully searched for weapons by the Marines. Once in Ciudad Nueva, they reported to the rebel leaders and were incorporated into commando posts.

After dark I often sat in the park of San Miguel with the boys from the neighboring commando posts discussing different topics related to the revolution. From talks about their lives before the revolution, I compiled Table 2, presented in rough statistical form.

From these crude indicators, I concluded that these boys were highly

TABLE 2

CHARACTERISTICS OF REBEL RANK AND FILE

Characteristics			*Percentages**
1. Place of birth	(a)	Capital city	30
	(b)	The province	70
2. Location of home	(a)	In downtown sector	15
	(b)	In barrios north of Mella Avenue	85
3. Housing	(a)	Have a rancho of their own	45
	(b)	Live with relatives or friends	55
4. Education	(a)	Literate	60
	(b)	Illiterate	40
5. Occupation	(a)	Skilled in some trade	35
	(b)	Unskilled	65
6. Employment	(a)	Employed immediately prior to the revolution	40
	(b)	Unemployed immediately prior to the revolution	60
7. Political participation	(a)	Active in party politics	10
	(b)	Not active in politics	90
8. Religious practice	(a)	Go to church regularly	5
	(b)	Go to church occasionally	50
	(c)	Never go to church	45

* Approximations for a total N of about 95 rebels.

alienated from the life of Dominican society in more than one respect. The percentages of variables in 1, 2, and 3 indicate that these boys were not true citizens of Santo Domingo. Rather, they were members of that other urban conglomeration that lived physically close to the city, but which was not integrated into its social, economic, and political processes. Before the revolution they had felt like foreigners in their own capital city; they thought they could never enter department stores, banks, government buildings, and expensive movie theaters. The revolution gave them reason to believe that this would change and that they were at last really citizens of their own community.[9]

Variables 4, 5, and 6 indicate that the lives of these boys were hard, and that within the framework of the Dominican status quo, their lot stood little chance of improvement. They were members of the illiterate strata,[10] having little or no skills and chronically unemployed. They had lost faith in their leaders. They were tired of paternalistic promises, such as Trujillo, and later Balaguer, had made to the populace. Trujillo had granted himself the titles of Father of the Land and Benefactor of the Country. The rights to work, to education, and to public services were not really considered as rights but as benefits granted by Trujillo. The governments that had succeeded Trujillo's, except Bosch's, had maintained intact the socioeconomic structure of the nation. Whatever improvements due to result from the alteration of the political structure—mostly personnel changes—had not yet taken place or, at any rate, had not reached the populace.[11]

9. For nearly five months the rebels controlled the downtown sector of Santo Domingo, where, as mentioned earlier, most businesses, department stores, public facilities, and movie theaters are located.

10. The figure of 60 percent literacy is considerably higher than the 43 percent given for the whole country by the United Nations. See United Nations, *Economic Bulletin for Latin America* VI, no. 2, (1961), p. 43. It might be relevant to point out that the bulletin is using the 1950 census figures. On the other hand, if compared with the total population figures, the relatively high degree of literacy noted in this sample might indicate that even within the masses there was a process of natural selection in following the rebel cause, and that perhaps the better educated were, in their own strata, more motivated than others to follow the revolution.

11. In 1961 the total expenditures for the armed forces represented one-fourth of the total national budget, while public health received only 7.7 percent and agriculture 6 percent. See Interamerican Development Bank, *Institutional Reforms and Social Development Trends in Latin America* (Washington, D.C., 1963), pp. 144–45.

The government of Bosch had been an exception to the rule of paternalism. He had not promised the populace free benefits. In 1963 he had given them a constitution which promised every man the right to work, every child the right to education, and every farmer the right to a piece of land. For seven months Bosch had tried to implement the constitution to break the social structure established under Trujillo. The Trujillista oligarchy, however, supported by the military, ousted him less than seven months after he took office. Since then the status quo had been reinforced and the only way to modify it was by force. This the rebels were now trying to do.

Finally, from variable 7 and 8 it may be inferred how little these people had participated in the organized activities of the prerevolutionary society. The number who had participated in politics and in religious activities is well below the national average. Considering that the revolution was primarily a political issue, it seems remarkable that only 10 percent of this sample of the rank and file considered themselves political activists. The 5 percent attending religious services is also quite low, since national attendance figures show 10 to 15 percent for males and even higher percentages for females. Perhaps these low figures suggest substantiation of my hypothesis that deep feelings of alienation can be correlated with active participation in the revolution.

To conclude, two major characteristics commonly found in the rebel ranks distinguished the rebels from the loyalists. First, the rebels had an ideology seeking greater participation of all classes of people in the cultural and economic life of the nation, together with some specific ideas on means to achieve this goal. A second characteristic prevalent among the rebels was a high degree of alienation, manifested by feelings of a lack of political power and a meaningless existence.

Chapter 7

The Ideologies of the Revolution

The revolution had begun as a coup d'etat, an attempt to restore a political system that had been, the rebels declared, perverted temporarily by a bold exercise of power. In a flash, however, it had become a revolution, a conflict between two competing conceptions of society. This chapter examines the ideology that underlay this metamorphosis. Ideology here means simply what the revolution was *about*.

To tell this story, we draw eclectically upon what people *said* the revolution was about, but we reinterpret their statements by analyzing their beliefs. Their beliefs are closely related to official party doctrines and the analyses of economists and political scientists, but are by no means identical to them. Ideology here refers to the political, economic, and sociological concepts found in the rhetoric of the masses. This differs from the intellectual ideologists' reasoned, coherent, and cognitive written products which submit themselves to rules of evidence as they interpret the "objective events" of political, social and economic life.

All participants in any complex social event—especially a violent social revolution—are not reacting to the same set of objective events.

This chapter was co-authored by Professor Rose K. Goldsen from Cornell University, who visited me twice while I was living in the rebel zone in June and August 1965. I am deeply indebted to Professor Goldsen, not only for her work in this chapter, but for the generous help, encouragement, and insights she gave me during the course of my research and the production of the manuscript.

Not only do different events have different degrees of salience for each participant, but each also perceives and experiences "the same event" through his own set of ideas. These ideas act as a filter, a set of intervening variables, that modifies each person's definition of the event and helps him place it in the "right" perspective according to his particular point of view. The play *Rashomon* or the novels in *The Alexandria Quartet* have a certain objective core of occurrences in each version of their stories. But the common core is subjected to vastly different emphases, interpretations, and explanations of what *really* occurred. Moreover, the disparate interpretations are at least as much what the play and the novels are *about* as the commonality underlying each version of "the same" story.

Ideas of what society is, ought to be, and ought not to be; assumptions of what motivates people, the nature of causation and its agents; appropriate explanations of complex events; ideals, codes of behavior, values, cultural themes—all these constitute an ideology through which events are made meaningful to one who experiences them. But not all the ideas, assumptions, and beliefs a person or a group has are part of their ideology. There must be some principle of exclusion.

So we revert to another analogy to distinguish the "ideology" of the revolution from just any ideology[1] and to distinguish the ideology of the revolution for the masses of participants from the official doctrine of professional and intellectual ideologists.[2]

In this sense, an ideology is a sort of grammar. It is the job of a trained and analytic intellectual to occupy himself with grammar, specify its rules, point out its logic, and so on. The man on the street, who may know very little about formal grammar, nevertheless speaks the language and *makes* the grammar, since popular usage determines the rules of the language. Needless to say, this grammar may differ widely from the formal grammar, just as the ideology of the masses differs from the intel-

---

1. The same groups could have had other ideas, beliefs, and ideologies that were perhaps alien to the essence of the revolution. Only those cognitive elements that were relevant in the minds of the people in understanding and explaining what the revolution was about will be specified here.

2. In the next chapter, the positions of the political and other interest groups vis à vis the revolution are discussed. The term ideology is used there following the classical interpretation of Mannheim and others.

lectual doctrine of politics, economics, and sociology. The grammar of the masses resembles, but does not mirror, that of the language student.[3]

This analogy is apt in another sense. For the person trying to understand a new language, the dictionary meaning of words in a sentence provides only a minimal grasp of the meaning. But as soon as the grammar is clear—the relationship of the words to each other in the sentence —meaning is clarified. In the same way, knowing the formal grammar or the postulates of a given intellectual ideology enables one to understand the literates and intellectuals, but is not sufficient for an understanding of the language or ideology of the masses; the new grammar of popular usage must be grafted to the formal grammar before one can understand the meaning.

Taking the analogy no further, we will present as "ideology" the explanatory systems the people themselves used to account for the social rift the revolution dramatized, its causes and cures. From the rhetoric of the revolution—the people's explanation of the meaning of the revolution and why they were fighting—we will attempt to discern its "grammar," its ideology.

We reiterate the themes that recurred when people explained why they were fighting and why it was necessary to fight. In Chapter 6 we analyzed these themes in terms of their differential distribution among rebels and loyalists. Now, in contrast, we will try to discern what images of society these claims, refrains, and slogans implicitly referred to. They may be summarized as follows:

1. There is a need in the Dominican Republic for widespread participation of all classes of people in the life of the country.
2. The "old Trujillista oligarchy" must be removed from political, military, and economic power. They are a source of graft and corruption in the government, particularly in the armed forces.
3. We are fighting for a return to constitutionality—that is, the Bosch Constitution of 1963.
4. Both steps 2 and 3 are necessary for a more just distribution of the economic and cultural wealth of the nation.

3. To use the analogy rigorously, we could say that often both the philologist and the intellectual ideologist seek to present in a logical frame something that actually exists in the language and in the minds of people previous to and independent of the efforts of the scientist.

5. We are fighting to eliminate exploitation by the domestic oligarchy and foreign capital.

These themes have been phrased in the rhetoric of the rebels. But such a set of beliefs could scarcely differentiate a supporter of the revolution from an opponent. All these beliefs—although they might have been phrased slightly differently—were widely held on both sides of the demarcation line. Only the argument about which constitution should be binding really differentiated rebel from loyalist. If the activity in the Dominican Republic was a revolution, there must be something in these themes, some point of divergence, which implies sharply different images of society. In other words, although most rebels and loyalists in the Dominican Republic were agreed on the desirability of such goals, they must have disagreed on some aspect of these goals. It could have been the priorities for attaining the goals, the means of achieving them, or the weight and importance attributed to each. This is where the study of the ideological grammar of the masses can help us understand the revolution.

1. Greater Participation (Compromise vs. Correctness)

Virtually everyone agreed on point 1 that the people have the right and indeed the obligation to participate in their own government. The loyalists, however, were loyal to a de facto government, which supported military action against a popularly elected government. Why? What was the divergence in the two views of legitimacy?

One loyalist's answer was to deny the legitimacy of the PRD government in the first place, by accusing its members of being either communists in disguise, or communist dupes. Even if we take these claims at face value, where is the legitimacy of any opposing governing groups to which the loyalists were loyal, since neither the Reid Cabral government nor the Benoit nor the Imbert juntas came to power by popular mandate or permitted popular participation? One way to avoid this discrepancy puzzle is to say that those loyalists only *said* they believed in the legitimacy of popular participation without really believing it. And this is true for many of them. But it is equally true of many Constitutionalist supporters who paid lip service to popular self-rule. Thus, this argument cannot account for the contrasting ideologies.

The crux of the matter apparently concerns images of the role of pluralism, compromise, and checks on government authority. The principle behind popular participation in government is the notion that a society is composed of conflicting interest groups, each vying for power and privilege. It is in this tussle that a way to a tolerable compromise will be found. Indeed, the principle holds that such a compromise is the very goal to strive for; not the ideal solution as defined by any one of the conflicting interests, but a partial answer that all can live with. Nobody is completely satisfied with a compromise, but neither is anyone so desperately dissatisfied or disgruntled that the price of compromise is too high.

Stated negatively, this philosophy of a popular government is that every interest group is forced to live with some kind of *tolerable abuse*. The question of how much abuse is "tolerable" is, of course, a tricky one. Wessin and Imbert, who participated in the overthrow of the Bosch government, and the Reid Cabral government, who agreed to serve in its stead, must have felt that the abuse they suffered or would suffer from Bosch and his legislature was or would become intolerable.

The Jeffersonian position is that the "tolerable abuse" resulting from compromise is the goal of the democratic process and represents its very triumph. The absolutist position, common to both "leftists" or "rightists," is that this is a false goal. They maintain that popular participation can be effective only when the participants are educated to recognize the "correct" answers, policies, and procedures.

For many in the Dominican conflict, clearly this time had not yet come. On the right were many who felt that "the people" had voted blindly and incorrectly for the PRD and would be equally blind to support that same government again. This rationale supported the "correctness" of cancelling their vote and eliminating their participation in decision making—whether their vote had been by ballot as in 1963 or by armed conflict as in 1965. On the left, many saw popular participation in the PRD government as an interim device, perhaps tactically necessary for the moment.[4] But the occasion was an opportunity to "educate the masses" for a future situation where politics not of compromise but of "correctness" could prevail.

4. This was evidently the position not only of the PSP (see the Manifesto published on March 16, 1965 as quoted in J. I. Cuello and N. Isa Conde, "Revolutionary Struggle in the Dominican Republic and its Lessons," *World Marxist Review,* 8 [Dec. 1965], pp. 71–81.) and of the MPD, but also of the June 14th Movement and of the Social Christians.

To restate the positions:

Right: No popular self-government until "the people" are educated enough to make "correct" decisions and to avoid error.

Left: Popular self-government now as an interim measure to provide a chance to educate "the people" for a future time when they will then have learned to make "correct" decisions and avoid error.

Center: Popular self-government now because it represents the only chance for compromise and tolerable rather than intolerable abuse. While error is unavoidable, we hope that its results will not be insupportable.

Two of the stated positions, the right and the left, mention education of the masses as a prerequisite for unconditional participation in self-government. The center position does not deprecate education of the masses for political participation. To the contrary, Bosch stated specifically, that the *only* way to get this education is through participation itself—a kind of on-the-job training.[5]

So far this discussion has centered on participation in terms of efficiency—with proper education either as a prerequisite or as on-the-job training as the only way in which a popular government will arrive at "the correct" answer or the least costly compromise of differences. A further ideological divergence must be pointed out. For many, both on the left and right, democratic participation is viewed principally as a technique of government, but for the centrist position, it is an end-value in itself. "The kind of society we want" includes heavy emphasis on participation in self-government quite aside from its efficiency.

Strategic vs. Tactical Decisions

Another aspect of the issue of participation that helped distinguish between the ideological positions of rebels and loyalists was the distinction between strategic and tactical decision. On certain issues, to make the "correct" decision which we call tactical, some kind of "educa-

5. Juan Bosch, *Crisis de la democracia de América en la República Dominicana* (Mexico City, 1964), p. 108. "As the habit of walking is learned by the act of walking, one can only learn what democracy is by practicing it."

tion" or expertise is required, because "correctness" here is a measure of the "appropriate" (i.e., logical-technical-scientific) use of certain means to achieve certain ends. Other issues, however, require no special expertise to make the "right" decision, because "rightness" or "wrongness" is an ethical problem which is evaluated according to general cultural values and no one can claim the privilege or monopoly of defining what is good or bad for the collectivity. To clarify the matter, it is a tactical decision whether the U.S. should use atomic warheads, napalm bombs, or conventional hardware in attacking North Viet Nam: only the experts can advise the President what is "correct" in terms of technical criteria. However, the decision to attack North Viet Nam is an ethical issue, the "rightness" or "wrongness" of which is measured by a set of values of the American people. This is a strategic decision for which no one group is more qualified than another, because by sharing the same cultural values all have the right and responsibility to participate in the process of making that decision.

By overemphasizing the need for education and expertise for participation in decision making, and often grouping together decisions both tactical and strategic, the Dominican loyalists stripped the populace of any opportunity for deciding its own fate. The rhetoric of the revolution, on the other hand, strongly advocated that the right to make strategic decisions should not be the privilege of one group, be it the oligarchy, the military, or the educated, but that this privilege belonged to all Dominicans.

While the rebels did not claim that the masses should decide which sectors of the economy should be developed in preference to others, they did advocate citizen participation in deciding economic policies that seemed to favor one economic group over another. The rebels did not demand that the masses define the specifics of the constitution or the law, but they asked for citizen participation in deciding general policies concerning their own welfare or in selecting legislators and government executives.

2. Trujilloism and Corruption

The corruption of the Trujillistas and the necessity of their removal from the centers of power was a theme that recurred on both sides of the demarcation line, and as such cannot be said to split the society. This was true of corruption in general, whether or not it stemmed from Trujillistas. The ideological divergence is discernible only in the means of removing corruption.

One view is that a moral regeneration is necessary—either of individuals who are suffering from social and economic deprivation, or of power wielders who distort the social system because of their unregeneracy.[6]

These are familiar arguments. The unemployed are unemployed because *they* are unwilling to work. Thus, even though it is true that many are suffering, this problem is strictly social and economic, and political solutions will not get to the heart of the matter. If wages are raised, the workers will either drink more or work less. Until there is a change in the hearts of men, structural solutions are beside the point.[7]

A variation of this ideological position is that the moral regeneration needed is not that of the sufferer, but of those who hold power and make policy. Although politicians, police, and the military are generally regarded as corrupt en masse, the rebels differentiated in their day-to-day vocabulary between "the honest military" and "the military." If the dishonest could be made to see the light, or be replaced by honest and morally upright people, inequities would be corrected.[8]

A sociologist would call these kinds of explanation "non-structural." Toward the left the ideology becomes more structural. While many leftists would agree, at least privately, in whole or in part that the under-

6. For Dominicans in 1965, as for Cubans in 1952, it was a widely held belief that "all politicians are corrupt." It is significant that a play staged in Santo Domingo a few months before the revolution was the satiric comedy *Se busca un hombre honesto* (*In Search of an Honest Man*), in which the role of the main character was a clear personification of Juan Bosch.

7. The loyalist groups tended generally to demand changes at the individual level, either through moral-religious regeneration of the hearts of men—as some conservative sectors of the clergy and the oligarchy often suggested—or through the process of education—as advocated by some progressive conservatives.

8. It was not only the rebels who held this view. Some loyalist military, such as General Wessin y Wessin, Colonel Benoit, and Colonel Morillo, firmly believed that moral regeneration of the politicians and the military was absolutely necessary. On the basis of my personal contacts with these men and of information obtained from other sources I have no reason to question the sincerity of this belief.

privileged contribute to their own misery, and that replacing corrupt officials with honest ones would correct inequities to a large degree, these claims are not a satisfactory explanation. They may be true, but they do not strike at the heart of the problem. The revolutionist sees the need for a fundamental change in the political and economic institutions, not just in the honesty of one or a few men. For this, checks and balances are required to regulate the way power is granted and wielded. Changes are needed to base the civil service on efficiency and not on favoritism. Honesty is required in the private sectors of industry and commerce, so that appropriate taxes are paid, prices of consumer goods are not widely increased, and fair salaries are paid to the workers.

3. Social Justice and Constitutionalism

The revolution "was about" the Constitution.[9] Indeed, the rebels called themselves Constitutionalists and insisted they were fighting for a return to the Bosch Constitution of 1963.[10] The loyalists felt either that the

9. As early as April 25, hardly twenty-four hours after the revolution broke out, the slogan "Return now to the Constitution with Bosch as president" became the rebel battle cry. On that date I witnessed the contagious fervor of the crowds in the streets of Santo Domingo singing the slogan while boys and girls wrote the words on the walls of public and private buildings.

10. The Dominican Constitution of 1963 was the result of the Constituent Assembly elected in December 1962 under the supervision of the OAS. The Assembly worked from January to April 1963 when the document was published as the law of the land. Juan Bosch had begun his presidential term on February 27, 1963. This constitution, the first of its kind in modern Dominican history, replaced the provisional one adopted by the Council of State in 1962 to rule the country until elections were held. The 1963 Constitution, which resembles considerably the Cuban Constitution of 1940, advocates a liberal type of welfare state relatively advanced by Latin American standards. From April 29, 1963—when the Constitution was proclaimed—to September 26 of the same year—when Juan Bosch was ousted by an army coup, the Constitution faced mounting opposition in some ultraconservative sectors of the oligarchy, the church, and the military. In his book *Overtaken by Events* (New York, 1966), John B. Martin dramatizes how he tried to salvage the Constitution on the night of September 25 when Bosch was ousted. The U.S. Ambassador tried to convince the generals that perhaps Dr. Rafael Molina Ureña, the Speaker of the House, could take over the presidency as established in the Constitution, but the generals would not agree to follow a constitutional solution.

Constitution was not worth fighting for, or that it had to be opposed.[11] And yet, from my conversations with many of the commandos who declared that they would defend the 1963 Constitution with their lives, it was clear that they and even some of their leaders had a very sketchy and inadequate idea of what was written in the 1963 Constitution. Certainly many, perhaps most, of the poor, illiterate, unskilled, and unemployed were unable to articulate the difference between the 1963 Constitution and the 1962 Constitution they refused to accept. Even the more literate, educated, and intellectual participants were, after all, not constitutional lawyers and could not very well have sustained a pro-constitutional position in an argument with a trained antagonist. What, then, was the symbolic appeal of the Constitution?

Rights vs. Privileges

Apparently, a very simple "grammar" was at the bottom of this conflict. The rebels and their supporters believed that the document they were fighting for made certain guarantees: a job,[12] a minimal level of welfare,[13] and an education.[14] Equally widespread was the belief that the 1963 Constitution would protect a citizen from police brutality, from arbitrary imprisonment, and guaranteed certain human rights—particularly the right of all citizens to live in the country and not to be deported to a foreign land.[15]

For thirty years, Trujillo had implemented an elaborate system of

11. Shortly before the elections of 1966 I had an interview with a high-ranking officer of the loyalists, in the course of which I asked him: "In a few weeks elections will be held in which Bosch is a major candidate. What will you and the armed forces do if he is elected president?" He looked me in the eye and said: "You don't understand! He cannot be elected because we [the armed forces] cannot accept him or the 1963 Constitution."

12. See *Constitución de la República Dominicana* (1963), art. 2, pp. 13–21. It is important to notice that while the 1962 Constitution only mentioned "freedom to work" (art. 8, no. 3) suggesting that "the law" would provide for other specifications, the 1963 Constitution dedicated ten articles to regulate different aspects of work emphasizing that "the existence of the nation is based on work" and declared work a fundamental obligation for all Dominicans.

13. Ibid., art. 14.

14. Ibid., art. 35–40.

15. Ibid., art. 55–84, especially art. 66. Deportation was a favorite method of Trujillo and of subsequent governments for getting rid of political foes.

political and economic paternalism. He owned the land, industry and commerce, utilities, and communications media. Dominicans had no rights or opportunities but those that Trujillo granted them. After Trujillo's death, the Council of State succeeded in holding together his political and economic empire under semblance of institutional order. The Constitution of 1962, by which the Council of State was to rule the country until a Constituent Assembly could be elected, reflected the same paternalism that Trujillo had exercised.

The Constitution of 1963, on the other hand, emphasized the right of the individual to work, to an education, and to some kind of social security, while stressing the obligation of the state to guarantee conditions appropriate for the exercise of these rights.[16] The grammar of the revolution was heavy with terms such as "rights of the individual," "equality under the law," "opportunity for all." The grammar of the loyalists was built on such concepts as "free enterprise," "the right to own property," "free education," "freedom of speech and association." The spirit of these concepts was elicited from conversations with rebels and loyalists, although they were unable to formulate them with so many abstractions and of course, could not quote the relevant articles of the constitutions.

Who Were the Trujillistas

Equally widespread was the belief that the 1963 Constitution validated the state's claim to the lands and resources expropriated from the Trujillo family and the Trujillistas. Although names were not mentioned in either the 1962 or 1963 Constitutions, it was clear that both documents provided the state with the right to expropriate the properties of those who had used official positions to enrich themselves or others, that is, the Trujillistas.[17] While it was relatively easy for the state to take over property owned by Trujillo, it was more difficult to determine where the state had the right to expropriate property of the Trujillistas because of the numerous Trujillistas that had appeared during the thirty years of dictatorship. The problem was not only to decide which Trujillistas

16. *Constitución* (1963), art. 2.
17. *Constitución* (1962), art. 9; *Constitución* (1963), art. 22.

should lose their rights but also to establish a just law to deal with so many different cases.

While the Council of State was in power in 1962 there was no difficulty in implementing the expropriation law since the matter was handled by provincial and local courts.[18] After Bosch came to power, however, the National Assembly decided that these expropriation cases could not be handled by local courts, but only by the National Assembly itself.[19] The new law was never fully implemented because Bosch and the National Assembly were ousted two months after the law was approved.

Despite the fact that all Dominicans—rebels and loyalists alike—agreed that the lands of Trujillo and his associates should be expropriated, they were deeply divided on the application of the principle. Again the issue of popular participation is relevant. The loyalists thought that the courts (often under control of the Trujillistas) should be given authority to expropriate, while the rebels thought that only the elected Assembly should decide cases in which the patrimony of the people was in jeopardy. The question was not whether the masses were capable of identifying the Trujillistas, or what methods of expropriation should be used, since these were tactical decisions for which expertise was required. What was at stake was whether, once the strategic decision of punishing the Trujillistas was made, the task should be entrusted to the courts or to the National Assembly. The loyalists said: "To the courts, because they have the legal expertise." The rebels said: "Not to the courts, because they are controlled by the Trujillistas. But to the National Assembly, because they represent the country and have expertise." Both sides seemed to attribute some Machiavellian intentions to each other. The loyalists did not trust the National Assembly because it represented and was controlled by the

18. Many of these courts were evidently controlled directly or indirectly by the Trujillistas since no major changes were introduced after the downfall of Trujillo.

19. See *El Caribe*, July 26, 1963, for the text of the new law. The same newspaper published on the same day an open letter of the Dominican Association of Landowners to President Bosch, in which the law of expropriations was strongly opposed and accused of "inciting the masses to vandalism" and of "destroying the concept of private property in Dominican law." Three days later several associations of businessmen, entrepreneurs, industrialists, and landowners published a communiqué in which the law of expropriations was blamed for "transforming the country into another Cuba in the Caribbean." *El Caribe*, July 29, 1963.

masses. The rebels did not trust the judiciary system because it represented and was controlled by the Trujillistas.

4. Human Rights and Welfare State

Because both the 1962 and the 1963 Constitutions were written in reaction to thirty years of Trujillo dictatorship, during which the most elementary human rights were constantly violated, both documents were specific in their guarantees of individual rights. Significantly, however, the 1963 Constitution declared that no Dominican citizen could be expelled from the country.[20] This article was intended to stop the practice, introduced by Trujillo and continued by the Council of State, of exiling political opponents. The Bosch Constitution appreciated the democratic right of minorities to disagree.[21]

Although some deplorable excesses were committed in the rebel zone,[22] it was clear that even in the midst of the highly disorganized and confusing situation, the rebels maintained their belief in human rights, and that, despite a few occasions in which violations occurred, the law was enforced.[23] This was not the case in the loyalist camp, as revealed in the Interamerican Human Rights Commission report on their investigation of violations of human rights.[24] Our Human Rights Center in the rebel zone also processed about 230 cases of violation of human rights, of which 90 percent were committed in the loyalist zone.

20. *Constitución* (1963), art. 66.

21. The practice of deporting political adversaries is still enforced in the Dominican Republic. Joaquín Balaguer, former president of the country under Trujillo, was deported by the Council of State. He went back to the country during the 1965 revolution and is now president of the country. Some members of the Council of State as well as some rebel and loyalist leaders are now in exile.

22. I am referring here not to the "tales of horror" described by misinformed U.S. journalists, and propagated by U.S. Ambassador W.T. Bennett. (On this see Theodore Draper, "The Dominican Crisis," *Commentary*, 40 [Dec., 1965], pp. 43–44.) I am referring to some abuses of power and even crimes that I personally witnessed and have related in other parts of this book.

23. The rebels were always willing to allow representatives of the Church or of international organizations to visit those they had in prison. They also set free U.S. soldiers they captured.

24. See full document in J. C. Estrella, *La revolución dominicana y la crisis de la OEA* (Santo Domingo, 1965), p. 53.

Concerning the welfare of the people, the 1962 Constitution contented itself with guaranteeing "freedom to work," "freedom of education," and advocated some kind of paternalistic subsidy for the poor. Without implying that the economic needs of the masses did not concern the loyalists at all, it seems that the state was concerned only with protecting certain individual freedoms and the collectivity in the economic and social sectors, and assumed that general progress and prosperity would automatically follow.

The rebel grammar describes the opposite point of view: "Let us guarantee the deprived uneducated masses not freedom to work and to educate themselves, but, rather, let us guarantee them work and education. Let us give them not bread and medicine, but social security and health. Economic development and prosperity will follow. Our country is so rich that if our leaders were honest men we could all live like kings!" The moral regeneration theme occurs on both sides.

Admittedly, both factions seem to agree that freedom, work, health, and education are worthy long-term goals, but they differ in their order of priority and in the means of achieving them. The role assigned by each faction to the government and to private sectors in attaining those goals seems to be particularly relevant here. The ideology of the loyalists placed special emphasis on the assumption that if the individual is industrious and capable, he will get an education and work. Those who don't succeed fail because they are neither industrious or able. The function of the state will be to punish or correct the bad and to subsidize the disabled. Any other attempt of the government to correct the situation was taken as an infringement of individual rights and freedom and as an obstacle to the "right" development of society. A Machiavellian character was often attributed to those who disagreed with this liberal position.

The ideology of the rebels, on the other hand, emphasized that the individual cannot really be free until he has education, work, and security. The individual alone cannot obtain these goals without the state's assistance. The function of the state is to protect the individual from powerful forces at work in society against which the individual is powerless. The primary function of the government is therefore not only to guarantee certain individual rights, but also to guarantee conditions under which those rights may be exercised by all. Any ideological disagreement with this grammar was also considered a Machiavellian position. For example, the rebels did not believe that the loyalists thought that their own system of free enterprise and private ownership was more conducive to economic development; they felt that the loyalists were only concerned with their own profits. Similarly, the rebels believed that the loyalists' liberal ideas were not sincerely based on the principle of freedom, but rather they were only concerned with their own freedom.

Together with the issue of a welfare state comes the problem of who will pay for it. To say that the masses should pay for it is to beg the question because by definition the masses are poor and uneducated. Even the rebels admitted that it was not feasible to ask the upper and middle classes alone to do it. A somewhat more realistic solution, that the state should pay for the costs of social reform with the cooperation of all economic and social sectors, was agreed to by all sides. The disagreement started when specific laws had to be formulated as to how the costs were to be divided among the various sectors.

5. Private vs. State Economic Development

In most countries where the government undertakes basic social reforms, it immediately has to embark on such major enterprises as agrarian reform, land distribution, nationalization of industrial concerns and utilities, and perhaps the expropriation of foreign holdings. These create serious problems for any government nationally and internationally. By a quirk of history, this issue was not a pressing one in the usual sense for the Dominican Republic, but it intruded itself in a very special way.

After the assassination of Trujillo in 1961, the dictator's vast land and industrial holdings, and those of his family, had reverted to the state. Without expropriating any foreign company and without further hurting private interests, the Dominican government found itself in possession not only of the best land, but also of the sugar mills, power plants, transport and utility systems, and other industrial or commercial enterprises operating in the country. The issue facing the government was the best way to operate these resources to develop the country economically. And here again Dominican society was ideologically divided, each faction deeply entrenched in its position with no desire to compromise. On the contrary, each often made Machiavellian interpretations of the other's point of view.

On the one hand, the loyalists claimed that the private sectors (national or foreign) were the only ones with sufficient technical expertise to develop the Trujillo holdings now under state control. The rebels, on the other hand, maintained that the question of development was not one of pure expertise, that is, not a purely tactical problem to be solved on the grounds of technical knowledge, maximum efficiency, and ratios of input-output. The rebels claimed that prior to that tactical decision was a strategic one on the use of the immediate profits from the Trujillo holdings.

This basically is the familiar argument of capitalism—or some combination of private and state capitalism—versus socialism. While this is certainly a fundamental issue, it is not the center of the controversy, since the nonintellectual revolutionaries and a good many of the intellectuals were simply not qualified to justify their support or antagonism to these economic decisions in the economic terms. The more fundamental and widely felt ideological issue concerned the goals of society. The rebels felt quite strongly that—whatever the economic arguments might be, and whatever economic decisions might be taken on this score—the highest priority should be given to satisfying the welfare needs of the population. The question of priorities in distributing output was foremost in their thinking.

Certainly, many naive rebels who held this view had a rather primitive notion of what this entailed. They visualized the dollar profits going into their own pockets, rather than into the pockets of the "foreign capitalists" or the home-grown "oligarchy." The slightly more sophisticated saw profits being plowed back into schools rather than factories. But the underlying policy issue of both these images leads back to their priorities: widely spread welfare gains for all on a modest scale rather than a short-term policy of capital investment in production enterprises.

Chapter 8

Interest Groups, Political Parties, and Formal Ideologies

It would be unrealistic to study the groups or organizations that participated actively in the revolution without giving some attention to their ideologies. Without making a political analysis of their different ideologies, I will attempt to describe these groups and their alignment in the revolution, to suggest that this alignment was an outgrowth of their formal ideologies. Formal ideology is here understood as a set of values, norms, and beliefs shared by all group members, which focuses on the goals of the group and the means of achieving them, and which directs the action and behavior of the group members. At the risk of over-simplifying the issues, I have attempted to place these groups on a simple continuum of ideologies, shown in Figure 1 on page 130.

On April 24, when the rebel group announced over the radio that their uprising was aimed against the unconstitutional system of government and that their main goal was return to the 1963 Constitution with Bosch as president, many Dominicans suddenly understood that this was not an ordinary palace coup, but something far more serious.[1]

It seemed apparent that the military rebels were not seizing power merely to become the rulers of the nation, as other military groups had previously done; on the contrary, they were seizing power to reestablish a constitution under which only civilians were entitled to govern. They were also planning to bring back to power a man who had been

1. Chalmers Johnson, *Revolutionary Change* (Boston, 1966), p. 140.

114

ousted eighteen months before for "being a leftist and letting the communists take over the government."[2]

For many Dominicans, the PRD represented an ideological commitment; a coup staged by its members would not be merely a palace coup, but would necessarily involve some major changes in the social structure of the country. Major changes in Dominican society would necessarily affect the structure of other groups whose ideologies might not be totally or even partially in agreement with those of the PRD, and the military coup of April 24 was a fact that no group in the country could disregard. Whether the coup would succeed in evolving a process of change guided by the ideology of the PRD remained a question largely dependent upon the positions taken by other ideological groups.

One by one, all ideological groups started to take sides. Forty-eight hours after the military revolt had begun, practically all the country's important ideological groups had aligned themselves with one faction or the other. The alignment of these groups in the revolution is described in the following pages. Evidence of their alignment is taken from various sources: written documents or incidents which show the group's political actions, the communication and interaction of the groups, or their geographic situations. All the groups described are guided by ideologies that may best be classified as Dominican versions of nineteenth- and twentieth-century Western ideologies, such as capitalism, communism, or Christian Democracy.

Ideological Groups Supporting the Revolution

The Partido Revolucionario Dominicano (PRD)

The political ideology of this party resembles closely the ideological frame described earlier.[3] Its leaders organized the revolution because they were convinced that no other path was open.[4] Despite the internal divisions, the bulk of the party supported the revolution since its inception. An approximate measure of the PRD membership can be gained from the official figures of the two elections in which the party partici-

2. CEFA, *Libro blanco de las fuerzas armadas y de la policía nacional de la República Dominicana* (Santo Domingo, 1964), pp. 39–95.

3. See Chapter 6.

4. Juan Bosch, *Crisis de la democracia de América en la República Dominicana* (Mexico City, 1964), p. 94.

pated. In the 1962 election, the PRD polled 628,044 votes of the total 1,054,944, or 59.5 percent. In 1966, a year after the revolution, the PRD polled only 487,650 votes of the total 1,321,695, or 36.9 percent,[5] although in the capital, where the revolution was fought, they had 144,631 votes out of a total of 256,142, or 56.4 percent.[6] These figures suggest that even after the revolution the PRD was a popular political organization, particularly in the cities and industrial areas.

After Bosch was ousted in 1963, the PRD made some inroads into the middle class, particularly among groups of professionals and military officers. Several of the most powerful labor organizations such as FOUPSA, POASI, and ASOCHOIN also had close ties with the PRD. From the start all these groups sided with the PRD, and they stayed in the rebel zone until the very end of the revolution. While the press has emphasized that some leaders of the PRD sought political asylum when Wessin's troops were entering the city on April 27, no one has pointed out that none of the leaders of the groups just mentioned asked for asylum.[7] The organizational structure of the PRD in the capital remained intact and functioned actively during the four-and-one-half months of the revolution.

The Partido Revolucionario Social Cristiano (PRSC)

The Social Christian Party, like nearly all other political parties in the country, was divided and highly disorganized at the start of the revolution. The liberal wing of the party was headed by Caonabo Javier and Antonio del Rosario who had succeeded in securing the support of most of the party membership. On January 30, 1965, the PRSC

5. It would be a gross misunderstanding of the Dominican situation to believe that the failure of Bosch to win the 1966 election was a total rejection of the revolution; the issues seem to be much more complex than that. It suffices to point out that the candidate of the "extreme right," Rafael Bonnelly, polled only 45,073 votes in 1966, or 3.4 percent of the total vote. The victory of Balaguer must be attributed to a set of factors that are beyond the scope of the present study.

6. Naciones Unidas, Consejo de Seguridad [United Nations, Security Council], *Informe del secretario general sobre la situación en la República Dominicana*, June 4, 1966.

7. Miguel Soto, Pedro J. Evangelista, Marcos Vargas, and Gilberto Peña were among the labor leaders of the PRD who were still fighting in the rebel zone when other PRD leaders went into hiding. The importance of these leaders to organized labor in Santo Domingo is well known to those familiar with Dominican affairs. See *El Listín Diario*, Apr. 27, 1965, p. 3.

signed the Pacto de Río Piedras with Professor Bosch and Secretary General Martínez Francisco, representatives of the PRD. According to this widely publicized pact, the two parties agreed to "build a common front to reestablish constitutional order in the Dominican Republic, and to act together if faced with any event that might bring a democratic solution to the misfortunes affecting the Dominican people."[8] The Santo Domingo Social Christian Party, like other such parties in Latin America, does not have a unique ideology of its own, but promotes the middle-of-the-road ideology of European Christian Democracy. This ideology refuses to accept either completely individualistic or collectivistic theories of society, but borrows from both. Dominican Social Christians, like most other Social Christians in Latin America, have placed special emphasis on criticizing the monopolistic and imperialistic polices of the United States and the Soviet Union.

The potential strength of the PRSC may be estimated from the fact that the PRD, which polled over a half million votes in the 1962 elections, decided to sign the Pacto de Río Piedras with the Social Christians alone. In 1962 the Social Christians polled around 50,000 votes, and in 1966, despite the fact that they only polled 30,134 votes, their party became the third largest in the country. Andrés Lockward, leader of the PRSC, explained to me in an interview before the elections, that because of the polarization of forces around Bosch and Balaguer, the PRSC would get fewer votes than in 1962. I attended the national convention of the PRSC in April 1966, when it was decided that they would join the PRD in supporting Bosch as presidential candidate.

Christian Democracy, as an ideology, receives its major support from the middle class, particularly young professionals and students. Many workers have also responded favorably. The Autonomous Confederation of Christian Trade Unions (CASC), although politically independent of the party, plays an important role in spreading the Christian Democrat ideology among peasants and workers; in the universities and high schools, the BRUC and JRC perform the same function among the students. Christian Democracy is also highly favored by the young liberal element within the Catholic clergy.

The members of the different Christian Democrat organizations sided with the rebels from the outset. In a communiqué published on April 26, the PRSC declared that it fully supported the revolution and

8. From photostatic copy of original document in my files.

encouraged its members to do likewise.[9] On April 27, the organization
of students, JRC, announced their support of the rebels,[10] and a similar announcement was made the same day by the top leadership of
CASC.[11]

The members of the different Christian Democratic organizations
participated actively in the war against the loyalist forces, both in the
organization of several commando posts and in top-level negotiations.[12]
Until the very end of the revolution, the Social Christians remained
in the rebel zone with the Constitutional Government of Colonel
Caamaño.

The Marxist Organizations

The Marxist organizations include three different political groups
active in Dominican politics since the death of Trujillo: the PSP, the
June 14th Movement, and the MPD.[13] The total membership of the
three groups is estimated by U.S. observers at less than 6,000,[14] and
its hard-core membership at approximately 100.[15] Their participation in
Dominican public life, however, has always been significant. Although
their role in the April revolution has often been overemphasized while
the role of other groups has been greatly underestimated, there can be
no doubt that these parties did have considerable influence in the revolution. Whether the importance of their role depends on the military
and political support they gave the rebels, or whether it depends on
the ideological opposition the rebels faced because of their acceptance
of this Marxist support, is a question as yet unanswered. There is no

9. *El Listín Diario,* Apr. 26, 1965, p. 14. On April 27, the same newspaper
carried a speech of Dr. Rosario, president of the party, in which he encouraged
the membership to fight together with the PRD for the Constitution. He also
announced that he would arrive from Puerto Rico with Juan Bosch.

10. *El Listín Diario,* Apr. 27, 1965, p. 3.

11. *El Caribe,* Apr. 27, 1965, p. 9.

12. In Chapter 3 it was pointed out that the Social Christians participated in
the deliberations about accepting García-Godoy as provisional president.

13. The PSP and the MPD were involved at some time in their history in dealings with Trujillo and his son Ramfis. See J. B. Martin, *Overtaken by Events* (New
York, 1966), p. 40, and *Libertad* (official newspaper of the MPD), Sept. 3, 1965,
p. 3.

14. Center for Strategic Studies, *Dominican Action—1965: Intervention or Cooperation?* Special Report Series, no. 2 (Washington, D.C., 1966), p. 61.

15. Martin, *Overtaken by Events,* p. 129.

reason to believe, however, that the events would have taken a different direction had the Marxist groups abstained from participating in the conflict.[16]

The Partido Socialista Popular (PSP)[17]

The PSP is the country's official communist party following the Moscow line, often through Cuban channels. Founded as an offshoot of the Cuban Communist Party in 1946, at the invitation of Generalissimo Trujillo,[18] it has always been a minority party with its greatest appeal among the intellectuals and the upper-middle-class students of the university. The party's total membership is estimated at between 500 and 700.[19] The PSP has often been bitterly attacked by other Marxist parties, particularly the MPD, for "being revisionists, doomed to be entirely destroyed in the same manner as the imperialists."[20]

Although the PSP had originally agreed to support the formula of "return to a legitimate government through the electoral process," the party published a document on March 16, advocating a new solution: "return to the Constitutional government of Juan Bosch without elections."[21] In interviews with several leaders of the PSP, I was told that they had not known that the revolution was being planned. They maintained that their hostile attitude toward any participation by the regular

16. In private interviews with a high-ranking loyalist officer and with one official of the U.S. Embassy, for example, it was emphasized that Bosch could never be allowed back in power, regardless of how much proof of his cooperation or non-cooperation with the Marxists was uncovered. It would seem obvious then that real Marxist participation in the revolution was not as important to the loyalists and interventionists as was the propaganda charge (and excuse for intervention) that Marxists had fomented and taken over the revolution. See statement of President Johnson, May 2, 1965, U.S., Department of State, *Bulletin*, 52, no. 1351 (May 17, 1965), p. 744.

17. This party is now the Partido Comunista Dominicano.

18. See J. de Galíndez, *La era de Trujillo* (Buenos Aires, 1962), pp. 216–20, where a fair assessment is given to the meaning of the double play between Trujillo and the PSP.

19. Center for Strategic Studies, *Dominican Action*, p. 61.

20. Communiqué of Official Pre-Congress of the MPD held in the rebel zone from August 16 to 24. See *Libertad*, Sept. 3, 1965, p. 1.

21. The Pacto de Río Piedras between the PRD and the PRSC, signed on January 30, 1965, had already advocated such a solution. I have found no evidence that the PSP knew that the revolution was being planned, although its leaders could have guessed that such action was imminent. See also *Manifesto of the PSP*, published on March 16, 1965.

Dominican armed forces in a revolution had alienated them from any possible contact with the military; the military had gone instead to the moderate parties, such as the PRD or the PR (Balagueristas). "We failed to see," a spokesman for the PSP said, "that an armed uprising was inevitable. Consequently, our party found itself unprepared for the uprising and was unable to head it, although as far as possible it took a firm and resolute part in it."[22]

Despite being unaware and unprepared, the leaders of the PSP threw their lot with the rebels. Some of their student leaders were present at the Presidential Palace on the morning of April 25 when the young army officers put Donald Reid under arrest. Others armed themselves at the places where weapons were being distributed to civilians. Still others organized civilian groups to help the rebel military units. The PSP contributed further to the rebel cause, providing expertise in guerrilla methods and political advice during the negotiations.

The June 14th Movement

Founded in 1959 to fight the dictatorship of Trujillo, this group was allied with the conservative UCN until their split in 1962. The June 14th Movement is similar to the July 26th Movement that helped Castro fight Batista from 1956 to 1959. Nationalism is perhaps its most important ideological characteristic; it leans heavily toward a socialist concept of society, and the fight against the imperialism of the United States has become the mainstay of its ideology.

The June 14th Movement appealed most strongly to the young professionals and the upper-middle-class youth, whose parents had perhaps collaborated with Trujillo. Their most famous leader, Doctor Manolo Tavárez Justo, together with several students and professionals, was killed in the mountains by army troops while fighting for the return to constitutionalism after Bosch was ousted. Although this incident attracted scores of young boys and girls to the party's ranks, the June 14th Movement polled only 4,427 votes in the entire country during the 1966 elections.[23]

Since early in 1962 the June 14th Movement has been considered

22. J. I. Cuello and N. Isa Conde, "Revolutionary Struggle in the Dominican Republic and its Lessons," *World Marxist Review,* 8 (Dec. 1965), pp. 71–81.

23. This figure does not represent the total membership of the party, since many of its members—being under twenty-one—were not allowed to vote, and still others voted for Bosch.

Leader of the June 14th Movement addressing a crowd on the day of the group's anniversary. Caamaño (profile) and Aristy are to the extreme left.

a potential political power in the country, and as such, allegedly has been a target for infiltration by such disparate forces as the Communist PSP and the American CIA.[24] When the revolution broke out, the leadership of this party gradually committed itself to fight with the rebels. Since most of its members are aged 18 to 25 and because many of its leaders had received guerrilla training in Cuba, the Movement soon became a military asset to the rebels. Similarly, many of its members were able to give leadership to civilian groups in the early stages of the revolution because of their party discipline and their middle-class education. Their leaders also participated in top-level negotiations within the rebel leadership. They organized and controlled a number of commandos and were influential in commando training. They lost a good number of men during the conflict, including such leaders as Juan Miguel Román, Euclides Morillo, and Oscar Santana.

The Movimiento Popular Dominicano (MPD)

The MPD, founded in Havana in 1956 as an exile splinter of the PSP with its greatest leader, Máximo López Molina, was often involved

24. See Bosch, *Crisis,* p. 32, and Tad Szulc, *Dominican Diary* (New York, 1965), p. 70.

in dealings with Trujillo and his son, Ramfis.[25] Although the MPD calls itself a Marxist-Leninist party, its ideology parallels the hard orthodox line of Mao Tse-tung, and it maintains close ties with Maoist ideological groups in Latin America. The party advocates violent revolutionary change as the only means to the dictatorship of the proletariat. It has launched bitter attacks against the PSP, accusing it of being revisionist, and in 1963 it accused Juan Bosch of being a "puppet of the imperialists."[26]

The MPD has made little progress in its ten years of existence. Only a small group of middle-class professionals and students have embraced the party, and these have become its leaders. A few workers have also supported the party's position, but its total membership is estimated at only around three hundred.[27] The MPD has never been officially or legally recognized as a political party.

The leadership of the party was taken entirely by surprise when the revolution broke out. Initially they thought that the revolution "was only a coup organized by the military with help of the CIA to prevent a real revolution of the masses."[28] It was not until April 27, forty-eight hours after the revolution's start, that the leaders of the MPD committed themselves to the revolution. Their major stronghold became a commando post near San Miguel known as Commando Argentina.

The MPD was not asked to participate in the negotiations and was quite critical of some decisions made by the rebel leadership, insisting that "the bourgeois wing of the rebels" had succeeded in imposing compromises upon the rebels.[29] After the inauguration of the provisional government, the MPD advocated a "common front against imperialism," but their plan was rejected by the PRD and PRSC.

The groups siding with the rebel forces during the revolution are presented in Table 3, along with the parties' ideologies, the groups or class from which their leadership emerged, their actual or estimated membership, and the groups to which their ideological appeal was directed.

25. After the April revolution López Molina was expelled from the party as a revisionist. On the relationship between him and Trujillo, see Bosch, *Crisis,* p. 39.
26. Ibid., p. 177.
27. Center for Strategic Studies, *Dominican Action,* p. 61.
28. From private conversation with MPD Secretary General Gustavo Ricart.
29. See *Patria,* Aug. 25 and 26, 1965. See also *Libertad,* Aug. 11, 1965, p. 5.

TABLE 3

IDEOLOGICAL GROUPS SIDING WITH THE REBELS

Group	Ideology	Leadership	Appeal To	Membership
PRD	Economic nationalism Democratic left Welfare state	Lower middle class Professionals Organized labor	Urban masses Lower middle class Young military officers	628,044 (1962) 487,650 (1966)*
PRSC	Christian Democracy Anti-imperialism Nationalism	Middle class Professionals University students Organized labor	Middle class Peasants Working class	50,000 (1962) 30,134 (1966)*
PSP	Communism Moscow line	Middle class Professionals University students and faculty	Middle class	Between 500 and 700†
June 14th Movement	Nationalism Marxist socialism Castro line	Middle-class youth University and high school students	Middle class	4,427 (1966)*
MPD	Marxists-Leninists Peking line	Lower middle class Workers	Working class	Estimated at 300†

* Figures from official returns of the elections of June 1, 1966, Naciones Unidas, Consejo de Seguridad, *Informe del secretaria general sobre la situación en la República Dominicana*, June 4, 1966.
† Estimates taken from Center for Strategic Studies, *Dominican Action—1965: Intervention or Cooperation?* (Washington, D.C., 1965), p. 61.

Ideological Groups Opposing the Revolution

The Military Structure

Although no military group in Latin America, much less in the Dominican Republic, has distinctly formulated a formal ideology of its own, it has been traditional since Spanish colonization for military men to think of themselves as guardians of the nation. They "protect" it not so much against outside attacks as against internal attempts to overthrow the established order. This is particularly true where the dictator has often favored the military, while they, in turn, have protected the dictator.

For thirty years the military in Santo Domingo helped maintain a government which endowed them with a privileged social position. Dominican military officers generally had obscure origins and they found in the army avenues of social mobility not otherwise open to them. After Trujillo's death, the military was regarded by some as the only force strong enough to keep the country from chaos. They maintained their powerful structure and enhanced it with two prerogatives never permitted by Trujillo: (1) the use of power for self-aggrandizement, and (2) the power to interfere with the civilian government.[30]

There is little doubt that the military, which had put Donald Reid in power after ousting Bosch, was dissatisfied with Reid, primarily because he had tried to curb these privileges. When the young officers proclaimed a coup against Reid on April 24, the older officers did not move to protect the established order. When the young officers announced a return to the 1963 Constitution with Bosch as president, however, the older military men felt their own positions were endangered. Even during negotiations between the rebels and the generals, the generals were ready to accept almost everything the rebels stood for, with the definite exception of the return of Bosch and the 1963 Constitution.[31] When the generals realized that the rebels would not relent on these

30. Acting on such premises, the military staged a coup against the Council of State on January 16, 1962, and against Juan Bosch on September 25, 1963.

31. Shortly before the elections of June 1966, in an interview with a high-ranking loyalist officer, I was told, "We cannot accept either Bosch or the 1963 Constitution." Ambassador Martin, back in 1963, had asked General Viñas whether the military would accept Molina as president after the ousting of Bosch: "It was useless," Viñas said. Molina Ureña was "a leader of the hated PRD." Martin, *Overtaken by Events*, p. 581.

issues, they ordered the strafing of the Presidential Palace and civil war followed.

Regardless of the actual role of the communists in the revolution, one fact cannot be overlooked: some elements in the military structure were convinced that the military was the Dominican nation's strongest bulwark against a communist threat and that they were duty-bound to oppose any social movement even slightly associated with communist or leftist parties. Since the military is often inclined to regard a change of the status quo as communistic, its opposition to the revolution was inevitable. This concept of the armed forces' role in the country is in line with the traditional idea of the military as the guardian of the established order. This strongly anti-communist stand has been encouraged by the United States' benevolent attitude toward the Dominican military since the death of Trujillo. Other forces within the country have also favored this stance of the military, since the proximity of Cuba has raised the possibility of "another Cuba" in the minds of many politicians and army officers, both in the Dominican Republic and in the United States.[32]

The Oligarchy and Upper Middle Class

The Dominican families which may be classified as oligarchs include such locally well-known names as Cabral, Vicini, Bermúdez, León, Cáceres, Pastoriza, and Espaillat. These people are well-educated, rich landowners who marry among themselves and educate their children in the United States. They owe their wealth not to Trujillo, who hated them, but to their ancestors. Trujillo tolerated them on the condition that they would not interfere with his regime, and they did not. Most of them are Catholic, paternalistic with their servants and laborers, and humanitarian towards the populace. Nonetheless, the farm laborers on their *fincas* (farms) are illiterate, live in unsanitary shacks, work under unhealthy conditions, and still earn almost the same wages their ancestors did at the beginning of the century.

Close to the oligarchy, although not on the same level, are the five thousand families of the upper middle class.[33] High-ranking government employees, entrepreneurs, professionals, and businessmen who

32. See CEFA, *Libro blanco,* pp. 162–68.
33. Juan Bosch, *Partido Revolucionario Dominicano: tesis sindical* (Santo Domingo, 1966), p. 62.

have worked their way up the social ladder comprise this class. With the exception of the seven months when Bosch was president, the upper middle class, together with the oligarchy, has run the country since the death of Trujillo. They control the country's industrial concerns and agricultural production, the Church, educational institutions, and the judiciary system. As a pressure group, they exercise considerable influence over the military and police.

The ideological position of both the oligarchy and the upper middle class is best described as semi-colonial capitalism. They consider the peasants and the urban proletariat unproductive and unable to govern. By using the masses' cheap, unskilled labor in a plantation economy and by supporting a right-wing dictatorship, the oligarchy believes that it has fulfilled its duties as a political landlord.

In 1963, the oligarchy and upper middle class opposed Bosch because he had given the populace a voice in governing the nation. In 1965, when they realized that the rebels intended to return Bosch to power, they again sided with those opposing Bosch and the populace. Although they did not mobilize themselves against the revolution, they did help others prepare for it. The Imbert government, created by U.S. intervention, was welcomed by the middle class. The oligarchy, using different pressure groups, even succeeded in having one of its members appointed to head the Provisional Government.[34]

The United States Embassy

One of the most powerful ideological groups in Dominican politics is the U.S. Embassy. Juan Bosch wrote, "If a captain of the U.S. military mission had suggested that the government should be overthrown, my government would have fallen in less than an hour because that captain had more power over the high command of the Dominican armed forces than the Dominican people, its President or the Constitution."[35]

The U.S. Embassy in Santo Domingo, staffed with career diplomats in close contact with Washington, unquestionably followed the State

34. See discussion of rebel leaders over accepting García-Godoy as provisional president in Chapter 3.

35. Bosch, *Crisis,* p. 202. Ambassador Martin's *Overtaken by Events* unintentionally shows the interference of the U.S. Embassy in Dominican internal affairs.

Department's ideological line, and this ideology influenced policies and decisions on Dominican affairs before and after April 24.[36] Political stability and the maintenance of the Dominican status quo were obvious and important elements in the U.S. Embassy's ideology; any internal or external attempt at subversion was to be discouraged, curbed, or eliminated. Such an ideology could not permit violent social changes directed toward altering the structure of Dominican society; a coup d'etat could be allowed, but not a revolution.

Several indications have been presented that clearly show how officials and military attachés of the U.S. Embassy committed it to oppose the rebels even at the early stages of the revolution. This commitment was reinforced on April 28, when the U.S. Marines landed in Santo Domingo. From that moment, the U.S. Embassy ceased acting merely as a powerful pressure group in Dominican politics and became instead the de facto government of the country.

The Catholic Church

The internal structure of the Dominican Catholic Church is backward, poor, and weak compared to that of the Church in Mexico or Colombia. With few exceptions, the intellectual standard of its clergy is low and the Church's wealth, in terms of money and land holdings, is very limited.[37] The ratio of priests and churches to the total population is one of the lowest in Latin America. The Sunday contributions from the whole country are likely to be less than the amount from a single middle-class parish of Boston or New York.[38]

Compared with other organizations within the country, however, the

36. See Theodore Draper, "The Dominican Crisis: A Case Study in American Policy," *Commentary*, 40 (Dec. 1965), pp. 33–68. In his analysis of the crisis, the author writes that the impression created by some journalists of an "innocent Washington and a frightened, incompetent embassy seems to be somewhat fanciful." Draper implies that despite all its "misinformation" and "blunders," the U.S. Embassy in Santo Domingo was following a line entirely consistent with the directions given by Washington.

37. Several times I visited the Archbishop of Santo Domingo in his old, lower-middle class home across from the cathedral. I also visited the "palace" of the bishop of Santiago, which by U.S. standards, would be considered a slum dwelling.

38. An average middle-class parish in New York collects from $2,000 to $4,000 a week. In San Miguel, the average Sunday collection was $4.50. The richest parish in Santo Domingo does not collect more than $400 on a Sunday.

Church's power and influence are relatively great. It is quite influential among the upper and middle classes, in the military establishment, and among the peasants. Its influence is almost minimal among the urban proletariat and the working class, the intelligentsia, and the university students.

The Church's social ideology is very much in line with that of the Spanish Church and those Latin American countries which still follow the Spanish traditions. As in Spain and Colombia, a concordat exists between the Vatican and the Dominican Republic. According to this, the Catholic faith is the official religion of the country, Catholic instruction is given in the public schools, Church laws regulate marriage and divorce, and parish priests are salaried by the state.[39]

In 1963, Bosch blamed the upper middle class, the military, and the Church for his downfall and for the disruption of democratic processes in the country. Essentially these same groups rallied support against him and the 1963 Constitution in 1965. The Church, however, took a less overt stand than the other groups: the official hierarchy did not attack either side, but appealed for peace,[40] later endorsing the U.S. formula for a "government of national unity with broad popular support.[41]

At this point, a distinction must be made between a cosmopolitan Church as represented officially in Santo Domingo by the Papal Nuncio and unofficially by several young priests, mostly Cubans and Spaniards trained in Europe or the United States, and the local church as represented by the bishops and the local clergy. The first group was active in helping to solve the crisis and showed considerable solidarity with the rebel faction.[42] The second group abstained from the conflict. Evacua-

39. In the 1963 Constitution no mention was made of the concordat, civil divorce was allowed, and nothing was said about religious teaching in schools. The Church was dissatisfied with both Bosch and the Constitution because of such changes.

40. See *El Listín Diario,* Apr. 27, 1965, p. 1.

41. In May, the Catholic bishops published a pastoral letter supporting efforts to create a government of national unity.

42. The work of the young liberal clergy was concerned mainly with social assistance to the people in the rebel area, which was under seige for over four months. The young priests' moving into the zone when the old conservative priests had left gave the rebels grounds for feeling that "the Church was not abandoning them but was actively sharing their own hardships." *Patria,* May 14, 1965.

tion of most of the clergy, including the bishop and the sisters from the rebel zone to the loyalist or U.S. zones was perceived by many as a sign of loyalist sympathies. There were other indications that the clergy in the latter group were critical of the rebels and that they openly favored the loyalists.

The Church's position may be described as officially and overtly uncommitted, but unofficially and covertly favoring the loyalist cause along with sectors of the population such as the middle class and the military, with whom the Church had been intimately tied in the past.

A Continuum of Ideologies

In Figure 1, these groups are shown on a continuum of ideologies. The dimension represented by the continuum is the ideological position of each group on structural change within Dominican society. The position of each group was determined by its reaction to the revolution, a phenomenon which affected all the groups simultaneously. The revolution materialized as a historical event which demanded drastic structural changes in the social system and the groups under study accepted or rejected the event to different degrees. For example, within the prorevolutionary faction, the moderates of the PRD were not advocating the same means of implementing change as the extremists of the MPD. Similarly, the U.S. Embassy was obviously less radical than the military or the oligarchy in sponsoring total destruction of the rebel forces.[43]

In the center of the continuum are the large urban and peasant masses who constitute nearly 90 percent of the population. The urban masses were placed to the left of the peasant population because they seemed more inclined to accept changes in the system. Both urban and peasant masses, however, lacked what we call a formal ideology, at least in the sense used in this chapter. They constitute an uncommitted proletariat which all other ideologies attempted to influence.

The second band represents the middle class on the right and the PRD on the left of the continuum. The two groups are really not far apart ideologically, particularly the lower midde class and the PRD.

43. This was particularly so after the middle of May when McGeorge Bundy came to Santo Domingo.

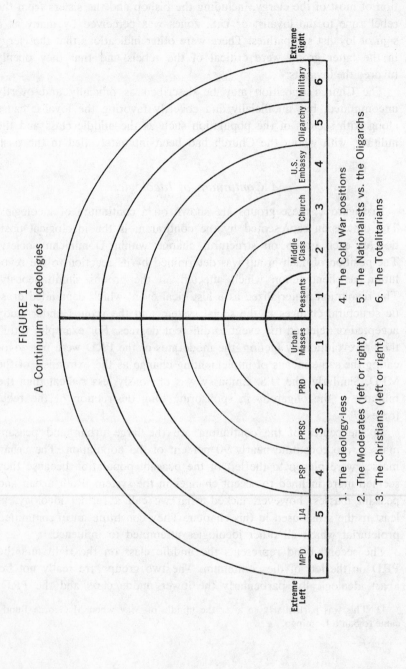

FIGURE 1
A Continuum of Ideologies

1. The Ideology-less
2. The Moderates (left or right)
3. The Christians (left or right)

4. The Cold War positions
5. The Nationalists vs. the Oligarchs
6. The Totalitarians

Extreme Left: MPD 6 | 1/4 5 | PSP 4 | PRSC 3 | PRD 2 | Urban Masses 1 | Peasants 1 | Middle Class 2 | Church 3 | U.S. Embassy 4 | Oligarchy 5 | Military 6 : Extreme Right

However, the middle class as a group did not favor the revolution. Both the PRD and the middle class advocate basic changes in the structure of the social system, but only by democratic means, such as agrarian reform without state expropriation of land or the protection of national industries without the nationalization of foreign ones.

The third segment of the continuum includes the Social Christians on the left and the Church on the right. These groups are more radical than the previous ones, not only in their attitudes toward change, but also in their attitudes toward implementation. The PRSC would probably advocate the expropriation of all foreign enterprises in the country and the immediate distribution of large land holdings to landless peasants. The only limitations of its ideological approach to change are those of a Christian framework, which they interpret in quite liberal terms. The Church also claims that her approach to change is contained in a Christian frame of reference, but it is a much more conservative one than that of the PRSC.

The fourth segment places the official Communist Party on the left and the U.S. Embassy on the right. Both groups appear to accept basic changes in the social structure, provided these changes are channeled through means acceptable to their respective ideological systems. Both groups contributed equally in turning the Dominican crisis into an international Cold War issue. There was a basic difference, however, between the actions of the two groups: the communists worked through the local PSP, so the men involved were Dominicans who had the right to decide which ideology they will follow; the capitalists, on the other hand, operated through the U.S. Embassy and with the landing of the Marines, a clear case of interference with the internal affairs of the host country.

To the left of the PSP on the continuum is the June 14th Movement, and to the right of the U.S. Embassy, the local oligarchy and upper middle class. Despite the fact that most leaders of the June 14th Movement are middle and upper middle class, the two groups are separated by a huge ideological gap. Regarding the dimension of change, the June 14th Movement, like the Cuban July 26th Movement, maintains that basic structural change is possible only if the internal structure (the oligarchy) and its external dependence (ties with imperialism) are entirely destroyed. The oligarchic groups, on the other hand, maintain that no structural changes are needed, and that only minor changes in the present situation would bring about modernization and progress.

The extremes on the continuum are represented on the left side by the MPD, and on the right by the old military structure. The ideologies of these two groups clearly suggest antithetical polarities. The MPD advocates total destruction of the present structure through violence by those at the bottom, and the military structure equates social change with communism, making social change unacceptable to them.

In summary, then, political parties and interest groups relevant in Dominican society have been described according to their ideological positions prior to the outbreak of the revolution. Their alignment and the degree of their commitment in favor of or against the revolution were found to be correlated with their particular formal ideologies. The continuum of ideologies seems to suggest that often groups and persons on opposite sides on the continuum might advocate the implementation of the same means to obtain contradictory goals.

Chapter 9

A Typology of Rebels

An ideological commitment and a deep feeling of alienation were suggested as characteristics that differentiated the rebels from the loyalists in the Dominican revolution. But what kind of people were the rebels, what motivated them to join the revolution, and what did they expect from it?

A typology of rebels is devised here, using as a point of departure the motivations and expectations of each type, listing those attributes which tended to distinguish between types, and offering as examples for each type some participant with whom the reader is familiar. Factors such as education, social class, and economic status have not been considered in making this typology, since people from every social stratum participated in the revolution and evidenced similar motivations and expectations.

An obvious difficulty in a typology is that some persons may fit into more than one category, since ideal types are not found in reality. It may well be that in considering the same person from different angles, I could have put him into more than one category, but I have tried to fit each individual into the category I found most appropriate.

Table 4 contains the five categories in the typology of rebels, showing the characteristic attributes of each and the names of some rebels who best typify the category. This is followed by a brief analysis of each type.

133

TABLE 4
TYPOLOGY OF DOMINICAN REBELS

Types	Attribute Set	Representatives		
		Politicians	Military	Others
I. Idealista (Idealist)	Nationalistic Visionary Altruistic Democratic	Bosch Molina Ureña J. Cury Peña Gómez A. Guzmán	H. Ramírez M. Arache A. Holguín P. Taveras N. Nogueras	M. González J. M. Román Tony Isa Conde O. Santana A. Lockward H. Molina
II. Acomplejado (Complex-ridden)	Break with the past Will to prove oneself Dedication	Aristy Casals	Caamaño F. Domínguez Capozi	Fafa Taveras Old members of PSP and MPD
III. Rebelde Profesional (Professional)	Personal abilities for leadership Machismo Authoritarian	Pichirilo Barahona Pujols	A. de la Rivière	Some members of MPD and the June 14th Movement
IV. Aprovechado (Opportunist)	Thrill-seekers Out for compensation Delinquent behavior		Deschamps	Tigres Traboux Johnny Adams Cowboys
V. Hijo de Machepa (Mass)	Adherence to group values and beliefs Identification with leader		Enlisted men in rebel camp	Commando rank and file

Type One: Idealista (Idealist Rebel)

The Spanish word *idealista* describes a person who wants to do things or attain goals beyond the reach of his peers, and also connotes unselfishness and altruism. For example, missionaries or Peace Corps volunteers are idealistas. A soldier who dies for his country, even when his action accomplishes nothing, or a man who enters politics not for financial gain but exclusively to serve his country is an idealista. The core of the concept gravitates around the pursuit of an ideal for the benefit of others, without regard for the cost to self.

In Table 4 are listed sixteen people I consider idealistas. This is merely a sample of the hundreds and perhaps thousands of revolutionaries who might be categorized here. They were fighting at the front, working as secretaries or cooks in government offices or commando posts, helping in hospitals, or teaching in the commando schools. Some were members of political parties or trade unions, and some were high school or university students.

Four attributes seem to describe and define this rebel group: (1) a highly nationalistic view of the revolution, (2) visionary solutions to the country's problems, (3) altruism in their aims, and (4) advocacy of democratic methods for ruling the country.[1]

The strong nationalistic feelings of practically every rebel should be evident from the preceding chapters. However, the idealista emphasized this aspect of the revolution so much that he would compromise on any other issue but this.[2] Illustrating this is an incident which occurred between Professor Bosch and American envoy J. B. Martin

1. It is clear that Dominican Marxist parties agreed to support Bosch and the return to democracy as a step toward the implementation of communism. See J. I. Cuello and N. Isa Conde, "Revolutionary Struggle in the Dominican Republic and its Lessons," *World Marxist Review,* 8 (Dec. 1965), pp. 71–81. For the typology, the fact that the Marxists advocated democratic methods (even though they considered them only a temporary phase) is sufficient to include them in the present category.

2. In signing the official document of reconciliation, the rebel group made a reservation regarding the stationing of the OAS Peace Force on Dominican soil. They insisted that it was "an exclusive and sovereign power of the Provisional Government to determine the date of the withdrawal of such force from Dominican territory. . . ." (See U.S., Congress, Senate, Committee on the Judiciary, *Testimony of Brigadier General Elías Wessin y Wessin,* 89th Cong., 1st sess., October 1. 1965, pp. 266–67.)

during the May 2 negotiations on a proposed agreement. According to Bosch, Martin "began to dictate conditions, . . . to declare that the revolution has fallen into Communist hands, and therefore the landing of U.S. forces was justified," to which Bosch replied, "I am not an American functionary, and Washington cannot dictate what I must do. I understand that you are defending your country's point of view, but I must defend my country's."[3]

Bosch has also been regarded by many as a visionary or a dreamer with grandiose plans which had little applicability to the actual Dominican situation.[4] Bosch and the others in this category envisioned the full advantages of a modern industrial urban society with a self-sustaining economy, without realizing that their country first had to emerge from the vicious circle of underdevelopment. Bosch's constitutional democracy attempted to set up political and social conditions which would permit a breakthrough from this elementary stage of development. His first attempt through the ballots had been halted by the military; the people were now trying a second time with a revolution. Clearly, Bosch and others in this category saw democracy as the only desirable climate for their political development.[5] This is particularly significant when we recall that Bosch's government represented the only democracy in the Dominican Republic in over a century.

These people also showed some altruistic motivation for planning and joining the revolution since practically all the persons cited under Type One are from upper-middle-class backgrounds. When asked why they joined the revolution when they could have lived a secure life with what they already had, they invariably replied, "Yes, I could have lived well, or better than the majority, but I could not stand by while hundreds of thousands of my fellow citizens were starving." Most were college graduates, and practically all the young officers in this category had studied abroad. Most had had the opportunity to progress in the established order through regular channels of social mobility. Peña Gómez told me that a U.S. Embassy official had offered him a bribe

3. Juan Bosch, "A Tale of Two Nations," *The New Leader*, 48 (June 21, 1965), p. 5.

4. J. B. Martin, *Overtaken by Events* (New York, 1966), p. 716.

5. From his self-imposed exile in Spain, Bosch has recently agreed that democracy cannot be the immediate goal of his party. He now advocates the doctrine of "dictatorship with popular support."

to stop his radio broadcasts against the Triumvirate.[6] Colonel Montes Arache told me privately of several young officers who had been ostracized because they were not willing to agree to certain deals suggested by the General Staff.[7]

In terms of motivations for joining the revolution and the expectations placed upon it, this first group is characterized by deeply sincere nationalistic feelings aroused by the internal corruption of the Dominican Republic political scene and the interference of outside powers in its affairs. Even though the structural changes they envisioned were perhaps not realistic in light of the country's situation, the urgent plight of their fellow citizens moved this group to start a revolution. It was the idealista's conviction that constitutional democracy should be a preliminary condition to the solution of the socioeconomic problems of the country.

Type Two: Acomplejado (Socially Complex-ridden Rebel)

The main characteristic setting apart the group of rebels from all other types is that all had something in their social backgrounds, their families, or simply their personal lives, from which they wanted to break free. (I refer here to a *social* criterion; it was not my concern to investigate psychological traits.) Each of the men in this group thought his background had handicapped him in his pursuit of ideological goals through the institutionalized channels of public life. In planning or joining the revolution, these men found a way in which to reestablish their personal positions on the basis of their own merits. In helping the country break abruptly with the structures of the past—corruption, oppression, abuse of power, and lack of freedom—they could simultaneously break with the structures of their own personal backgrounds. In creating a new nation, they also hoped to create new and entirely different images of themselves. In addition, these men wanted to prove themselves useful to society. For this reason they emulated the men in the idealista group. Some were as much idealistas as those in the first group; however, their emphasis was not so much pure altruism as it was rehabilitation of themselves through their usefulness to others.

6. From private interview on May 10, 1966.
7. From private interview on March 1, 1966.

Just as Bosch is typical of the idealista, so Colonel Caamaño is typical of the second rebel type. The Dominicans had not forgotten that his father was General Fausto Caamaño, one of Trujillo's most brutal henchmen.[8] Nor were his enemies slow in remembering that Caamaño had participated in the infamous Palma Sola massacre of 1962.[9] Caamaño's decision to join the rebels was obviously motivated by his desire to put his past behind him. When an American journalist asked him about his unpleasant past he answered, "What difference does it make now? The important thing is what we are doing for our country now. Let's forget the past."[10]

As a young army officer trained in the United States, Colonel Caamaño had been disgusted with the widespread corruption among senior officers of the armed forces. Early in 1965 he led a rebellious movement of protest within the police force, which succeeded in ousting General Peguero, the corrupt police chief. During the organization of the revolution, Caamaño became one of its top leaders, although at first his reputation was not as great as the leaders from the idealista group. On April 27, when the revolutionary leaders from the idealista group failed in their roles,[11] Caamaño emerged as the dominant leader, driven by a tremendous desire to prove his worth to his country.

Colonel Rafael Fernández Domínguez is also representative of this second type. The son of General Ludovino Fernández Domínguez, one of Trujillo's most hated butchers,[12] Colonel Domínguez had participated in the protection of the legitimate government against the dictatorial ambitions of General Rodríguez Echevarría early in 1962. Although he had been one of the original masterminds of the April revolution, Colonel Domínguez was in Chile when the revolution broke out on April 24 and was unable to rejoin the rebels immediately. From Chile he flew to Puerto Rico, but could not reach Santo Domingo until May 16. Four days later he was killed by the U.S. Marines while leading an

8. Tad Szulc, *Dominican Diary* (New York, 1965), p. 135. See also J. de Galíndez, *La era de Trujillo* (Buenos Aires, 1962), pp. 164–66.

9. This incident, which took place under the U.S.-supported Council of State, is related in Martin, *Overtaken by Events,* pp. 302–05.

10. Szulc, *Dominican Diary,* p. 135.

11. When I say "failed," I am not making a judgment on their conduct; I am merely stating a fact.

12. D. Kurzman, *Santo Domingo: The Revolt of the Damned* (New York, 1965), p. 125.

unsuccessful attack on the Presidential Palace.[13] With him also died Ilio Capozi, an instructor of Dominican navy frogmen and a former officer in Germany's SS. Capozi had joined the rebels on April 24, and his courage and technical knowledge became invaluable assets to the revolution. Both Domínguez and Capozi may have been motivated by the desire to make amends for their backgrounds, Domínguez by removing the shame his father had cast on his name, and Capozi by perhaps wiping out his past as an officer of the notorious SS in Nazi Germany.

Together with the attributes discussed above—the desire to break with the nation's past and their own—an extreme dedication to the revolution was common to all the rebels of this group. They stood fast not only on April 27 when many other rebel leaders were taking refuge in foreign embassies, but also on June 15 when the rebel zone was under heavy U.S. fire and extermination of the rebels seemed likely. Although the men in this category could also have taken asylum in foreign embassies, they stayed with the rebels, knowing that their chances of survival were minimal if they were to fall into the hands of the loyalists.

These men were dedicated, not only during the fighting, but also during negotiations. Perhaps the best example of this total dedication was Héctor Aristy. A civilian with a controversial background,[14] Aristy fought by the Duarte Bridge in the revolution's darkest hours, helping to reorganize the rebels after they had apparently been defeated by the loyalists. He was instrumental in setting up the rebel government and from that moment played a dominant role in all rebel negotiations.[15] The target for attacks from the loyalists and U.S. officials in the Dominican Republic,[16] he became Caamaño's closest political advisor.

13. The information I received from some rebel leaders who participated in the battle in which Colonel Fernández was killed is entirely at variance with the story presented by Martin in *Overtaken by Events,* pp. 697–98.

14. To his friends Aristy was a born rebel; he had opposed Trujillo in his teens and fought against Ramfis after his return from exile. To his enemies he was a playboy in politics, a double-agent of Ramfis, or even a communist fellow-traveler. Whatever his motives, he proved himself a very courageous fighter and showed one of the sharpest minds in the rebel side.

15. Martin, *Overtaken by Events,* pp. 669–71.

16. Szulc, *Dominican Diary,* p. 273. According to Szulc, one of the conditions imposed by Washington in exchange for accepting Guzmán as provisional president was the expulsion from Santo Domingo of Héctor Aristy and some other known communists.

After negotiations had been suspended for the night, he often appeared at the front lines to check the troops and encourage them by his presence. One night I reported to a commando post that a group of cowboys were trying to break into La Americana, a big hardware store on Mella Avenue. About an hour later the post comandante and Aristy himself came to thank me for cooperating with them in implementing law and order.

In summary, the complex-ridden rebels were men who sought in the revolution a means to break not only with the nation's past, but also with their own. They had high expectations that they could prove themselves useful to their country by helping to build a new society, and they showed themselves to be particularly steadfast in their support of the revolution.

Type Three: Rebelde Profesional (The Professional Rebel)

The professional rebels were endowed with natural leadership abilities, had considerable degree of machismo (courage, toughness, and physical prowess), and were highly authoritarian. They did not have a clear-cut formal ideology on politics or economics, but deeply resented the abuses of power and the corruption of the estabished order. They were supported by the masses with whom they lived and for whom they harbored deep feelings of compassion and fellowship. The professional rebels did not organize the revolution, but joined it after the fighting had started. Eventually they identified totally, and became the dominant figures, at least in the actual fighting.

The professional rebels were men with imagination and organizational abilities who had been barred from the regular channels of mobility in Dominican society. They never had a chance for an education or even for learning a trade or skill. They were self-made men who had achieved leadership within their own groups or local communities, who expected someday to achieve similar positions within the community as a whole. The professional rebels had often plotted to overthrow their country's established order, or had helped others do the same in their own countries.

The professional rebels were particularly valuable on the battlefield, especially during the early part of the revolution. They rallied the masses to the front, and with a great display of machismo led them first to resist and then to attack the loyalists and the Americans, both of whom had superior striking power. Because they were identified with the masses, they could command and lead the irregulars with much more authority than could the rebel officers.[17]

The most colorful professional rebel of the revolution was Jean Paul André de la Rivière, a Jesuit-educated Frenchman who had lived for years in Santo Domingo. He had fought as a paratrooper in Indochina and later in Algeria where he joined a right-wing organization in the French army to try to keep Algeria a French colony. After Algeria became independent, he established himself in Santo Domingo, where he organized groups of Haitian exiles for a revolution against the Haitian dictator, Duvalier.[18]

When the revolution erupted in Santo Domingo, la Rivière joined the rebels and soon became an advisor to Colonel Montes Arache. He was both courageous and efficient, and was credited with originating the technical aspects of the city's defense against the U.S. attack. At a conference I attended where rebel and civilian leaders were attempting to organize the distribution of food, la Rivière said to me in French, "You Spanish talk too much, waste too much time, and accomplish nothing." I agreed with him.

Around the first week in May, an OAS Special Committee arrived in the country to investigate, among other things, the accusation that the rebel forces had been infiltrated by communists. The committee's representatives were alarmed by the fact that a man with a marked foreign accent, evidently French, was near the conference table giving orders to rebel guards.[19] The man in question was la Rivière.[20]

---

17. These men are less valuable in the later stage of a revolution when it enters into the process of institutionalization. Perhaps at some point they even become an obstacle to the goals of the revolution, producing embarrassment for the idealista or acomplejado groups. This is why the professional rebel often moves from one country to another where revolutions are underway, and perhaps this is also why revolutions are said to devour their own children.

18. *Paris Match*, May 15, 1965, p. 63.

19. Organization of American States, *Tenth Meeting of Consultation of Ministers of Foreign Affairs, Official Documents*, no. 47, OEA Series F/11.10 (June 2, 1965), p. 7.

20. Philippe de Bausset, a French correspondent, wrote that la Rivière had been expelled from the French army for his right-wing tendencies (*Paris Match*, May 15, 1965). In another article the same correspondent wrote that la Rivière had also cooperated with the U.S. CIA (*Paris Match*, May 29, 1965, p. 65).

Catholic priests officiating at the funeral of rebel leader André de la Rivière, who was killed June 15, 1965, during the worst confrontation between rebel forces and the U.S. Marines

On June 15, while he was driving a black Pontiac on a reconnaissance mission near the U.S. corridor, the U.S. Marines opened fire on him. He tried to turn around, but the street was too narrow. Before he could finish the turn, a bullet hit him in the jugular vein. He died before I arrived to see him in the hospital. His car, being so close to the U.S. lines, remained on the street for several days before it could be removed.

A typical professional rebel was Ramón Mejía del Castillo, also known as Pichirilo. Dominican by birth, he had lived in Cuba for several years and, according to his own account, had been Fidel Castro's quartermaster in the original rebel expedition that invaded Cuba in 1956. For two years he had fought Batista in the mountains. The Cuban revolution had entered the process of institutionalization when Pichirilo left Cuba to return to Santo Domingo after the death of Trujillo. Although Pichirilo stated that he broke off with Castro when the latter embraced communism, he was often accused of being a Castro agent.

Busy on April 24 smuggling arms into Cuba for an anti-Castro group, Pichirilo returned to Santo Domingo as soon as he heard the news of the revolution. He became the comandante of more than one hundred men in Commando Pichirilo in the northeastern sector of the city and was respected by both civilian and military rebel leaders and greatly feared by the loyalists. His name became something of a myth in the rebel zone, since he was present wherever fighting broke out. Even though he was outspokenly anti-American and highly antagonistic toward the communists, he was accused of being a double agent for both the communists and the CIA. From long interviews with him, my impression was that he was no one's agent; he was simply a born rebel, had much machismo, was highly authoritarian, and highly independent. He had no formal education, but had the ability to lead men. After the revolution he was one of the few who dared to stay in his own barrio in downtown Santo Domingo. I visited him there several times, and he told me he had rejected a position the government offered him. In the summer of 1966, a year after the revolution had ended, Pichirilo was shot in the back as he was leaving his home. The assassin escaped through the customs warehouses which are usually heavily guarded by the Dominican police.

Type Four: Aprovechado (Opportunist)

A relatively small group of men joined the revolution for the thrill of carrying a gun and to take advantage of the disorganized first moments of the revolution. They had few ideological motives for joining the revolt, although a very high degree of alienation was common in this group. Many of them had criminal records for minor crimes such as petty theft, fighting, gambling, and prostitution. At the outbreak of the revolution many tigres and prostitutes joined the mobs and managed to secure weapons. But instead of going to the front to fight, they roamed the streets and indulged in arson and looting.[21] Occasionally

21. On April 26, El Listín Diario carried an article in which six cases of arson and looting were reported. The quarters of three political parties were destroyed and the offices of right-wing Prensa Libre set on fire.

groups of tigres skirmished with the police; since most of the tigres had often been in trouble with the law, they took great pleasure in chasing the police from their stations. Several police officers were killed by these hoodlums, and others escaped death only by dressing in civilian clothes.[22]

After the landing of the Marines, when the revolution entered a stabilizing phase, some of the tigres were incorporated into commando units. Some adapted themselves to the new discipline, but others dropped out after a while. Still others remained as "cowboys" in the rebel zone, where their presence posed some problems for the rebel leaders.

It would be unfair to suggest that all tigres behaved the same way. A number of these boys joined the revolution to make recompense for their pasts and fought with great courage, many dying in the front lines. These cases, however, are not grouped under this aprovechado type, but instead, under Type Two (acomplejado) or under Type Five.

It would also be inaccurate to suggest that the only people that fit the opportunist type were the tigres and cowboys. There were several aprovechado rebels from the middle and upper classes. For example, the man appointed by Caamaño as director of National Security—an aprovechado rebel—abused his position and had to be discharged for disorderly behavior.[23] There were other similar cases, but not enough evidence is available to name them.

The following two cases help to clarify what is understood by Type Four. The first case is that of Traboux, a cowboy from my barrio who was involved in the slaying of Oscar Santana, comandante of El Lido. Traboux was clearly an aprovechado who had joined the revolution for the thrill of carrying a gun. He was a thief, and spent most of his time drinking and gambling. Several times I heard the boys of San Miguel challenge him to come with them to the front. He never accepted, of course, since the revolution itself was of no concern to him. The boys of the June 14th Movement shot Traboux for Santana's murder and threw his ashes into the sea despite my efforts to get him

22. Although not justifiable, it is understandable that the tigres would harass the police. Before the revolution, cases of police brutality were reported every day in Santo Domingo.

23. *Gaceta oficial de la República Dominicana*, Doc. no. 52 (June 30, 1965). decreto 57, p. 41.

a fair trial. The punishment of Traboux was harsh and unjustifiable in a democratic situation, but the boys meant it as an example to all using the revolution for their own purposes.

A second case of aprovechado is that of Johnny Adams, a young Dominican with both American and Dominican police records. He apparently joined the rebels at the start of the revolution and became a leader of a group, but before the war ended he escaped from the rebel zone to the United States, where he testified before the U.S. Senate's Committee on the Judiciary on October 18, 1965.[24] After reading his testimony, I returned to Santo Domingo to determine how much of his testimony to believe. Several rebel leaders had the same reaction to the picture I had of him: "Yes, we know him; he is a thief and we had to put him in jail."[25]

Type Five: Hijo de Machepa[26] (Mass Rebel)

The fifth is a residual category which covers most rebels not included in the first four types. It is called the mass rebel type because it comprises the largest number of people. The characteristics attributed to this category are so general that they could be applied to any large random group of people.

These rebels were all from the lowest income groups; many were illiterate and chronically unemployed, and the majority were from the barrios altos, making them both geographically segregated and socially alienated from the rest of the Dominican Republic. It would not be inappropriate to say that they had a very elementary ideology. But since this minimal ideology was also shared by many in the same barrios who did not take any active part in the revolution, I was faced with the question of why some of these men had joined the rebels and others had not.

I found a clue to the answer only after many hours of discussion with the boys of San Miguel and many interviews with some of the

24. U.S., Congress, Senate, Committee on the Judiciary, *Testimony of Juan Isidro Tapia Adames,* 89th Cong., 1st sess., October 18, 1965.

25. The reliability of Adames' testimony is not necessarily impaired by the fact that he was a thief. The Committee on the Judiciary knew that the witness had criminal records in the United States. What the record does not say is whether the Committee knew that Adames had been jailed by the rebels for being a thief.

26. Expression coined by Bosch to indicate the man in the street, a kind of John Doe, without a job, uneducated, a social nobody.

informal leaders. The mass rebel did not join the revolution by making a personal decision, or because his strong convictions forced him to take sides. Each was simply a part of the small informal groups in the barrio or the community, and the decision to join or abstain from the revolution was made collectively. Whenever I asked a member of this category, "How did you make up your mind to join the rebels?" invariably the answer was, "Well, we all decided that the rebels were right and we joined them!" When I asked them to define "we," they invariably named a few friends in the barrio. When I then located these friends who formed the informal groups, the answers they gave me were quite similar. The groups were small: from three to eight persons each and in the same barrio different groups often mixed socially and exchanged information. The leader of the group was usually identifiable either by his position in the group, by the type of weapon he had, or sometimes by the formal rank he held in the commando post. In San Miguel, for example, I could distinguish six different informal groups, whose leaders were Tungo, Chiro, Francisco, Papito, Peralta, and Miguel el loco.

The next discovery concerning these groups was that, although the mass rebel did not have a clear-cut ideology of his own, he adhered so closely to the beliefs of the group leader that for all practical purposes the beliefs, desires, and norms of the group became his ideology. Of course, the leaders of the groups were not mass rebels, but belonged in other categories.

That the mass rebel was linked to the revolution by the ideology of his group leader was suggested by the fact that members of an informal group dropped out of a commando and even left the rebel zone after their leader had quit. This occurred in Commando San Miguel in the groups headed by Francisco and Chiro, and the same thing happened two months later in the group headed by Papito.

Thus, although a large majority of the masses living in the barrios altos favored the revolution, only a small minority took an active part in it for any length of time.[27] The differential participation of the

27. When I say "small minority," I refer to the participation of the masses during the second phase of the revolution, after the U.S. troops divided the city in three sectors. After Operation Clean-up, the barrios altos were taken over by Imbert's troops.

masses according to zones or districts appeared to be highly dependent on the actual participation and the ideological or political affiliation of the informal group leaders in those zones.

The mass rebel joined the revolution through the common decision of the informal group of which he was a member, but it was the group leader who was instrumental in making and maintaining this decision. The most important characteristic of this category is identification with the beliefs and goals of the informal groups.

Chapter 10

The Emergence of Leadership

The shift in the top leadership of the revolution, from Bosch to Molina Ureña and later from Molina Ureña to Caamaño, was described in Chapter 3. Chapters 4 and 5 briefly covered the reorganization of the civilian and military groups originally formed to cope with some specific aspects of the crisis. At the head of each of these groups, a leader coordinated the actions of group members in their pursuit of common goals. When one leader failed, another took his place. The group itself always seemed to be able to bring forth the type of leader it most needed in the circumstances.

Leadership emerged almost simultaneously from three different kinds of organization in the rebel zone: I have called these three organizations political, paramilitary, and civic. Different leadership levels existed within each organization, but all aimed at achieving the organization's general goals. The specific goals of each organization were different, although some very general goals may have been common to the three.

Because the three organizations were operating in the same geographical area, and because their actions were ultimately directed toward the same population, considerable communication and even interdependence was necessary. To avoid conflict, a certain degree of coordination was mandatory, although this did not imply subordination. The very nature of the political and paramilitary organizations made mutual interdependence unavoidable. The civic organization, however,

148

was in no way dependent on, or subordinate to, either the political or the paramilitary organizations.

My interest here is not to discuss the structure, goals, or composition of these organizations, but to describe how leadership emerged, what was its style, and what functions it performed. To understand the context of some instances, the reader should be familiar with the historical background of the Dominican Revolution much of which has been presented in the historical section of this study.

The Political Organization

Most original planners of the revolution may be included in this group. Bosch, Molina Ureña, Peña Gómez, Hernando Ramírez, Caamaño, Fernández Domínguez are among the scores of leaders who planned the uprising for months in advance. These men made the political decisions concerning the type of government and laws the country should have, and the means and strategies to achieve certain general goals of the Dominican people. They believed that their decisions reflected the will of the Dominican people as freely expressed in the elections of 1962.[1] It never occurred to them that their policies and decisions might be the product of their own middle-class frame of mind. On the contrary, they thought of themselves only as the interpreters of the mind and will of the people.[2]

The original leaders were recruited from the younger PRD members and from young officers of the armed forces. As indicated in Chapter 6, both politicians and officers scored high in political alienation and ideological conviction. The two groups also had in common the traits listed in Table 5.

When the revolution broke out on April 24, the original leaders were joined by a relatively large number of civilians and military officers who had similar social characteristics.[3] As mentioned in Chapter 3, some of

1. In 1962, Bosch was elected president by an overwhelming majority in the first free elections in Dominican history. Bosch's term was due to continue until February 1967.

2. Chalmers Johnson, *Revolution and the Social System* (Stanford, 1964), p. 52.

3. These men had never been approached by the original leaders, because the plot was maintained exclusively within the PRD ranks and among some sectors of the military. This secrecy was maintained for two reasons: (1) security: con-

TABLE 5

SOCIAL CHARACTERISTICS OF REBEL LEADERS

	Civilians	Military
Age Group	25–40	30–40
Social Class	Middle class	Middle class
Education	College graduates	Academy graduates
Experience abroad	Travel in the United States and Latin America	Training in the United States and Latin America
Alienation	High	High
Ideological conviction	Yes	Yes

these new recruits started to assume leadership roles within the first four days of the revolution. On the other hand, the unexpected eruption of the revolution forty-eight hours ahead of schedule confronted the original leaders with readjustments in their leadership cadres. Both Bosch and Colonel Domínguez, the masterminds of the revolt, were still abroad twenty-four hours after the revolt broke out, and their chances of returning to Santo Domingo grew progressively slimmer as the two major airports were seized by the loyalists.[4] In their absence, Molina Ureña and Colonel Ramírez took over as president and minister of defense, respectively. Both had long records of honesty, dedication, and commitment to democratic principles,[5] and there is no reason to believe that either had any ambition to remain in his temporary position.[6]

tacts were made only among relatively close friends who were expected to sympathize with the rebel cause; (2) ideology: the organizers of the plot did not want the Marxist parties to participate. When Colonel Caamaño was approached by Colonel Gutiérrez, the only condition laid down by the former was that "the communists are not to participate in the revolution." From private interviews with Molina Ureña.

4. In fact, Colonel Domínguez succeeded in returning to Santo Domingo on May 16, only to be killed on May 19. Bosch was unable to return until September 25, 1965.

5. In Chapter 9 they are classified under the idealista type.

6. It was made clear that Molina Ureña was only the "provisional president" until Bosch could return. A formula with Molina Ureña as president until elections

Since Molina Ureña and Colonel Ramírez were the chief organizers in the country, the rebels regarded the transfer of leadership from the absent Bosch and Domínguez to them as natural, and no one questioned their right to the new positions. Their leadership, however, was not to last long. The position taken by the loyalist generals at San Isidro and the U.S. Embassy against restoring the 1963 Constitution and Bosch as president[7] presented the rebel leaders with a new and serious threat. Molina and Ramírez made it quite clear in their talks with representatives of the generals that this issue was not negotiable. Moreover, the new leaders, thus far undeterred by the difficulties posed by their opponents, proceeded with the business of establishing their new order. They initiated contacts with the U.S. Embassy and the diplomatic corps, and practically all major garrisons in the country pledged loyalty to them. In the capital, General Despradel and Commodore Rivera assured them that the police and the navy were loyal to the new government.

On April 27, however, when negotiations with both the generals and the U.S. Embassy failed, Molina and Colonel Ramírez, thinking that the revolution had been defeated militarily, took asylum in foreign embassies.[8] Their desertion constituted a setback for the revolution's legitimacy claims and the rebel morale. The idea that their defection was followed by a vacuum of power soon to be filled by the extreme left is at variance with the evidence already presented, which indicates

---

could be held would probably have been acceptable at this point to the San Isidro group. The rebels, however, maintained their claims that Bosch was constitutional president and he was the only one with the right to the presidency. With regard to Colonel Ramírez's position, Molina Ureña told me that on April 27 he appointed Ramírez minister of defense, but Ramírez declined because Colonel Caamaño, with a higher rank in the armed forces, was supposed to fill the vacancy.

7. See Chapter 3.

8. To what degree their decision to withdraw from the fight was attributable to apparent military defeat or other reasons is hard to say. The fact of their taking asylum has been used to suggest that the revolution had evidently fallen into the hands of extreme leftists. (See President Johnson's statement on May 2, 1965, U.S., Department of State, *Bulletin,* 52, No. 1351 [May 17, 1965], p. 744.) In interviews with top rebel leaders, I was told that Colonel Ramírez was suffering severe hepatitis at the time, and thus could not exercise effective leadership. Molina, on the other hand, told me that the main reason for this decision was that the military leaders had begun negotiations at the U.S. Embassy without his consent, and "under such circumstances I could not stay as president any longer."

Colonel Ramón M. Montes Arache (center), minister of defense of the rebel government, with navy frogmen

that Molina and Ramírez entrusted the direction of military operations to Colonels Caamaño and Montes Arache as early as the morning of April 27. Later that evening while Molina and Ramírez sought asylum, the colonels went to the Duarte Bridge to direct the attack against the San Isidro forces. Before the evening's end, loyalist troops had withdrawn from the city and Caamaño and Montes Arache's rebel forces were in full control of the city.[9]

Several other men who had shown courage and organizational abilities at the battle by the bridge now gravitated toward Caamaño and Montes Arache. Some of these men—Peña Taveras, Lachapelle, Lora Fernández, and Nuñez Nogueras—had been among the original leaders. Others—Aristy, la Rivière, Capozi, Manolo González, Pichirilo, and Juan Miguel Román—were new recruits. These men found themselves in leadership roles without having been officially appointed. With their

9. See *El Caribe,* Apr. 28, 1965, p. 1. After the headlines of the paper had been printed containing the news that the rebels had been defeated, a bulletin was inserted in which the editor published a conversation with Caamaño, which showed that events had taken a new turn. What is particularly relevant here is that the bulletin credited Caamaño and Montes Arache with the top leadership of the movement.

above-average abilities, they found themselves performing essential tasks—providing arms and instruction on their use, locating food, or designing strategies for overcoming a militarily superior enemy. The groups began to obey the orders of those men who could best lead them toward their goals.

Caamaño's rise to supreme leadership of the revolution has been regarded with varying degrees of suspicion, with the frequent implication that he was a front man for the extreme left.[10] It is generally agreed that Caamaño was not a charismatic leader, but characterizing him as a front man seems to be based more on ideological prejudice than on factual evidence. In several interviews with civilian and military leaders, I asked, "Why did Caamaño emerge as the main leader?" The following are some of the reasons given:

1. At this particular moment in the revolution, a military solution was sought and Caamaño was the highest-ranking military officer in the rebel group.[11]
2. He had shown his patriotic nationalism at the U.S. Embassy and his courage in the battle of the Duarte Bridge.
3. Molina had already appointed Caamaño to conduct all military operations.[12]

In an interview, I asked Héctor Aristy why he had not become the leader instead of Caamaño. He replied, "In the early stages of the revolution I often found myself, a civilian, giving orders to military officers and you know how the military resent that. At the same time, I realized that the bulk of the rebel forces was still made up of army men. I discussed the problem with Caamaño, but he was reluctant to accept leadership solely, because he was only a military man and not a politician. When I finally persuaded him that the needs of the group at that moment were of a military rather than political nature, he agreed to lead the movement."[13]

10. See the episode related in J. B. Martin, *Overtaken by Events* (New York, 1966), p. 689: "I asked him [Caamaño] in a low voice: 'Are you a free agent?' He said, 'I am a free agent.'"
11. Although the title of "colonel" is given to several rebel officers in this and other studies, it must be pointed out that all these officers were lieutenant colonels; Caamaño was the only full colonel in the group.
12. See Chapter 3.
13. From a private interview with Héctor Aristy held on May 2, 1966. After the U.S. landing, it became apparent that Bosch could not return to Santo Do-

Caamaño's leadership seemed to have a catalytic effect on several other leaders whose groups appeared to be dissolving. Encouraged by the new turn of events under the combined leadership of Caamaño, Aristy, and Montes Arache, some of the original leaders who had gone into hiding, such as Peña Gómez, Colonel Bompensier, and Colonel Marte, once again assumed leadership. Some of the new leaders strengthened their position by integrating their groups with Caamaño's forces. After the successful military actions of April 28, 29, and 30, the catalytic effect of Caamaño's leadership apparently spread rapidly through the different levels of the political and military organizations of the revolution.

The landing of the U.S. Marines on the evening of April 28 posed a new threat to the rebels. From the beginning, they saw this intervention not only as an attempt to stop the revolution, but also as a physical threat to their own survival. It influenced many civilians and military personnel, particularly the enlisted men, to give up the fight and quit the rebel ranks. Others, however, stayed.

Until the Marine landing, the catalytic effect of Caamaño's leadership had been diffusive, enabling leaders on other levels to emerge or to reorganize their groups. When the various groups suddenly became aware of the external threat posed by the U.S. intervention, however, the diffusive process was reversed into an integrative and centralizing polarization of leadership. The process of polarization was accomplished by three different steps, with the first and second occurring almost simultaneously: (1) group members rallied around their politico-military leaders; (2) group leaders rallied around Caamaño; (3) group members and the masses at large rallied around Caamaño.[14]

When, on May 3, the Dominican Congress, elected in 1962 and

---

mingo. Finding a permanent substitute for Bosch was necessary. On May 2, Bosch told J. B. Martin that the Dominican Congress would elect either Colonel Fernández or Colonel Caamaño as constitutional president. See Martin, *Overtaken by Events*, p. 679.

14. Step 3 took place some time after steps 1 and 2, because Caamaño was not a national figure, but was in fact practically unknown to the population at large. He needed the support of other group leaders before he could count on the support of the masses. However, by the month of June, Caamaño's reputation as top leader was such that he could appeal directly to the masses for their support without the help of the group leaders.

overthrown in 1963, chose Colonel Caamaño as constitutional president,[15] the rebel leadership had crystallized into the political structure that was maintained until the end of the civil war.

The interaction and the direction of influence among the different levels of leadership shown in Figure 2 indicate that:

1. Although power seemed to emanate from Caamaño's central position, the flow of communication and mutual interdependence suggest a democratic rather than authoritarian type of leadership.
2. Division of power and jurisdiction existed among the higher echelons of civilian and military groups; but it was less clear in the lower echelons, such as the commando posts, which were subject to both military and civilian influences.
3. The degree of each group's influence is suggested by the number of lines from that group to others.[16]

Although Caamaño's leadership began primarily with the military purpose of pursuing the strategic aims of the rebel forces to defeat the loyalist generals, these aims became clearly unattainable after the U.S. intervention. Because the rebels' goal now had to be pursued by political rather than military strategies, the primary functions of Caamaño's leadership moved from the military to the political arena. The rebel groups assigned Caamaño three functions in his capacity as maximum leader: (1) executing the group's goals and policies, (2) representing the rebels to the outside world, and (3) controlling internal relations of the rebel organization.

The democratic aspirations of the revolution and the democratic structure of the rebel leadership indicate that policy making and establishing goals for the group were not the exclusive domain of one person, but concerned the whole structure.[17]

15. See Chapter 3.

16. The diagram suggests only the major organized groups and their approximate relative strength within the rebel government.

17. In his article in *Life,* May 28, 1965, and then in his book *Overtaken by Events,* J. B. Martin seemed to imply that Caamaño was not a free agent, but a puppet of the communists, because the ambassador noticed that Caamaño could not make final decisions without consulting his advisors. Also, the ambassador, not being fluent in Spanish, seems to have made a serious mistake by confusing the words *militares* with *militantes,* which, in Spanish, has a connotation of activism and is often used to describe subversive activities. See Martin, *Overtaken by Events,* p. 689.

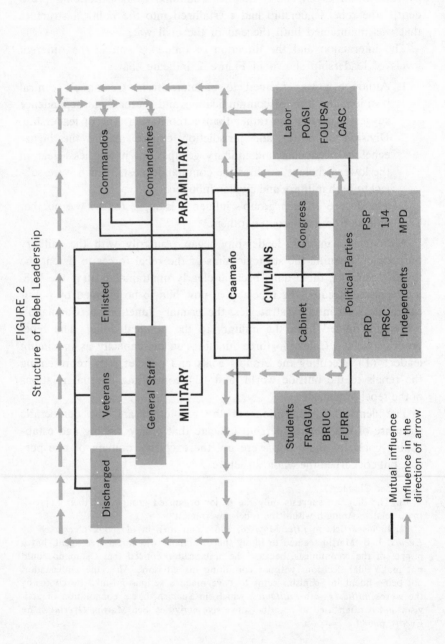

FIGURE 2
Structure of Rebel Leadership

Commandos

Comandantes

PARAMILITARY

Enlisted

Veterans

Discharged

General Staff

MILITARY

Caamaño

CIVILIANS

Congress

Cabinet

Political Parties

PRD   PSP
PRSC   1J4
Independents MPD

Labor
POASI
FOUPSA
CASC

Students
FRAGUA
BRUC
FURR

——— Mutual influence

⇢ Influence in the
   direction of arrow

Once decisions were made or policies formulated, Caamaño was responsible for overseeing their execution. He normally transmitted his orders through existing agencies, but where necessary, he created new ones. Caamaño always informed the public of major policy decisions, either by addressing the people in front of the Copello Building or in Indepencia Park, or explaining his decisions on the radio.[18]

Caamaño also represented the rebels at national and international levels. Caamaño was the spokesman for the rebels from April 30, when he met with Monsignor Clarizio to discuss the cease-fire, to September 3, when García-Godoy was inaugurated. For four months he discussed various agreements with twelve different negotiating teams, always advocating the views of the groups he represented rather than his personal views.

Another of Caamaño's functions was controlling the various revolutionary groups' internal relations. The rebel organization lacked the political homogeneity that the original leaders had attempted to maintain. Such heterogeneous groups as the military officers, the PRD, the PRSC, the PSP, the MPD, the June 14th Movement, the trade unions, and the students were not in agreement on all issues, although all supported the revolution and agreed on general ideology. Caamaño's function was to coordinate these diverse forces and make them cooperate in pursuing the revolution's immediate goals. Despite being a military man and a Catholic, Caamaño was able to control and work with civilians of different political ideologies, including the Marxists.

The Paramilitary Organization

The paramilitary, as used here, excludes the sectors of the Dominican armed forces that sided with the rebels, and includes those irregulars or civilian fighters who were organized into commandos and fought beside the regular rebel forces. I believe that the emergence of leadership among these groups was one of the most significant events of the revolution. The following information on the paramilitary organization is based on my observations while living and interacting with the commandos, and from personal interviews with many leaders and rank and file during and after the war.

18. See *La Nación,* July 9, 1965, for the speech delivered after the rebel leadership had decided to accept García-Godoy as president.

FIGURE 3
Military and Paramilitary Forces

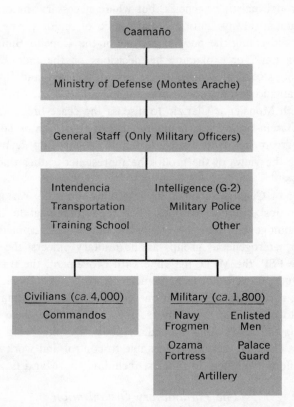

I will briefly analyze the emergence, functions, and types of leadership that existed in such organizations. Figure 3 depicts schematically the organization of Caamaño's military and paramilitary forces.

Appendix 5 lists 120 commando posts which operated in the rebel zone during the revolution. Not all were established on the same date; some were set up as early as April 27, others not until the middle of May.[19] As I suggested earlier, Caamaño's leadership had a catalytic effect on the restructuring of the politico-military organizations from

19. Manolo González set up a commando group with members of the PSP as early as April 26. This group later disintegrated, but Manolo helped to set up other groups, such as San Lázaro.

April 28 through April 30. The same social phenomenon—the catalytic effect of one man's leadership filtering down to bring out leadership qualities in other men—is operating here. In a highly disorganized situation[20] when law-enforcing agencies of the old establishment had crumbled,[21] four thousand civilians from various social origins succeeded in organizing into tightly knit defense units in less than a week.

The commando posts were not organized by Caamaño's officers, the Marxist parties, or any other specific group; they were organized by the people. They did, however, follow the lead of Caamaño's officers and other civilian leaders who had organized themselves into relatively small units. They were also encouraged by the military officers to stay in one sector of the city and defend that area against the enemy. After days of fighting, eating, and sleeping together, the group members developed some degree of solidarity.

Through conversations with several comandantes I was able to reconstruct the origins of several commando posts, including San Miguel, Pedro Mena, B-3, San Lázaro, Pichirilo, and Barahona. I found that the emergence of leadership was spontaneous as it had been in the political organization. It was often the case that a group of ten or fifteen men cooperated in attacking a police station, setting up a defense unit at some strategic point, or even finding a secure place to spend the night. Once a problem was defined as a group need, several members would offer solutions, and the most acceptable one would be chosen. A member suggesting the right solution several times would probably be selected as the group leader. As most of the problems were of a military nature, those with military training and organizational abilities often became the leaders. If those men also had great courage, their

20. There is no doubt that for some hours on April 27–28 confusion and disorganization prevailed. To say, however, that "looting was general" (Center for Strategic Studies, *Dominican Action—1965: Intervention or Cooperation?* Special Report Series, no. 2 [Washington, D.C., 1966], p. 19), that a "reign of terror began" (J. Mallin, *Caribbean Crisis: Subversion Fails in the Dominican Republic* [New York, 1965], p. 14), or that "the blood bath was being prepared" (Martin, *Overtaken by Events,* p. 647) is far from true, at least according to the events that I witnessed.

21. With the downfall of Donald Reid, all government agencies, including the police force, stopped functioning. However, it cannot be said that because those agencies stopped operating, all law and order ceased and chaos reigned in the city; the rebels enforced law and order.

chances of becoming leaders were even greater. Such was the case with Pichirilo and Barahona; the former had fought for two years with Castro in Cuba; the latter was a sharpshooter and former bodyguard of Juan Bosch. In Chapter 4 I mentioned how Francisco, Jaime, and Manolo González had used different strategies to become the leaders of the San Miguel, B-3, and San Lázaro commandos respectively. Santiago, a former sergeant in the army, and Oscar Santana, a student of engineering, were both idealistas, respected in their groups for their honesty and dedication to the goals of the revolution. Santiago organized his commando, Pedro Mena, in the "foxhole of Matthew," one of the poorest slums of the city. Santana commanded one of the largest units of the June 14th Movement and organized his group to protect the customs warehouses in the northeast sector of the city. When Santana's group was displaced from that part of the city by the U.S. Marines on June 15, they moved into the El Lido, a movie theater two blocks from where I was living.

The main functions of the comandantes were to represent their units before other groups, particularly Caamaño's General Staff, and to give their men military advice. At the beginning of the revolution, each group set its own goals, but as groups became coordinated by the General Staff, major goals and policies were determined at the top and communicated to the different levels. Almost every week the most important comandantes were called to the Copello Building for discussions with the General Staff and briefings on the negotiations.[22] Military strategies and rules for the enforcement of law and order were also discussed. At the same time, the comandantes represented the complaints, needs, or requests of their men, and appraised the combat readiness, morale, and striking capacity of their units.

In most cases, a group leader was supposed to be an expert in military skills who could give the boys technical knowledge relevant to the group's goals.[23] On visits to the commandos I often saw boys asking the comandante's advice on how to use or repair arms. However, the quality the boys seemed to most admire was their leader's machismo

22. A comandante's importance was determined by his political influence, the position he was defending, the sophistication of the weaponry he had, and the size of his unit.

23. This was one reason several armed forces veterans and young students who had received guerrilla training in Cuba achieved leadership positions.

in leading them in combat; if he showed courage, he could be sure his followers would obey his orders without hesitation.

Another function assigned to the leader of a commando group was providing food, lodging, clothes, and ammunition for his men. Towards the end of July when food was getting scarce, many boys asked me for food for their commandos. To avoid giving food two or three times to the same commando post, I asked them to bring a note signed by their comandante.

Although the leadership most frequently exercised in the commando groups was authoritarian, some semblance of democratic organization was maintained, inasmuch as every group member was supposed to have the same rights, and some issues were discussed at general meetings where decisions were reached by vote. I believe, however, that this procedure was common practice even in the most authoritarian commandos to avoid a "credibility gap" between the idealistic goals of the revolution and the means of achieving them at the commando level. I found that many commando boys would argue in favor of a democratic structure not only in government, but also in the commando post. They would often use such cliches as "We are tired of dictators," "We are all free and equal now," and "This is a democracy." In practice, however, when I asked them about decisions made in the commando, such as who should dig trenches, or who changed the hours for the military drills, or what punishment should be given to members who had committed crimes, the boys not only admitted that they took no part in making such decisions, but accepted the fact that this was the comandante's privilege.

I indicated in Chapter 4 that there were two different types of commandos, those organized on the structure of a previously existing formal organization and those based on an informal group and often organized by a charismatic leader. I suggested that the former seemed to enjoy a more stable and less personalistic type of leadership than the latter. Several members in leadership positions in a commando based on a formal organization gave the impression that the post was ruled in a more democratic manner than posts ruled by charismatic leaders. Purely on the basis of the relationship between rank and file and leadership, however, both types of organizations appeared equally authoritarian.

Decisions made by a charismatic leader were communicated to the rank and file of the group through his lieutenants; nobody dared to question or disagree with them, much less disobey them, simply because the decisions came from "the boss." In the commandos based on a formal organization such as a party or trade union, decisions made by the commando's leaders or perhaps by the party or union were communicated to the group members, who were not accustomed to being consulted. In both cases the outcome was the same; the leaders made the decisions, and the rank and file obeyed. At some point in my conversations with the rank and file, I concluded that, far from resenting this type of leadership, most welcomed it. Their attitude is summarized in the words of La Sombra, an army veteran enrolled in Commando San Miguel: "Our job is to fight for the revolution. The leaders' job is to show us how and give us orders."[24] I must add, however, that even with extreme authoritarian leadership, such as that of Manolo González and Barahona, relationships between the leader and group members were informal and friendly. Orders were not given in sharp, aggressive terms as in a military organization, but in a friendly tone. After seeing some of these leaders give orders to their followers, I realized that most Dominicans are more sensitive to the tone or inflection of the voice than to the actual content of the order.

The Civic Organization

Several social welfare organizations were started during the revolution exclusively to serve some urgent needs of the collectivity after most other agencies had ceased to operate. I refer here specifically to emergence of leadership from the medical services, public welfare agencies, the Church, and the educational system. My review is not comprehensive; it represents only the agencies and leaders I encountered. I cannot possibly do justice to all the leaders and organizations that were so deeply involved in this type of work.

The Medical Profession

I was able to observe closely the behavior of some forty-five physicians in three different sets of circumstances during the worst periods

24. My findings seem to confirm Peak's thesis that people under threat are inclined to accept authoritarian leadership. See Helen Peak, "Observations on the Characteristics and Distribution of German Nazis," *Psychological Monographs,* 59 (1945), p. 276.

of the revolution: the first was at the outbreak of the war in Morgan's Hospital by the Duarte Bridge; the second was at Moscoso Puello's Hospital during the first two weeks of May; and the third was in my own public health clinic in the rebel zone during the months of July and August. On these three occasions a group of doctors emerged as leaders of a civic collectivity facing extreme physical hardship. The directors of both hospitals, Dr. Cabral and Dr. Vicini, showed extraordinary professional dedication and responsibility in maintaining humanitarian and medical standards in their hospitals. Their medical staffs responded with equal dedication. Workers in these health centers came from different sectors of the city and from Santiago and often risked their lives travelling across a city under sniper-fire.[25]

When I started my public health clinic at the end of June, it had only one doctor; who came for a few hours three times a week. Two weeks later, the clinic's staff included thirteen doctors donating their time from 8:00 A.M. to 1:00 P.M. several days a week. Some came only for a few hours, since they were also working in other hospitals.

There is reason to believe that the leadership of these doctors had a catalytic effect not only on their colleagues, but also on the scores of medical students who came to help in the clinic and in the hospitals. This catalytic effect extended to the nurses and other hospital personnel, and their example stimulated me to help in whatever capacity I could.

The function of medical leaders was to provide expertise and high professional standards at a time when all facilities for providing minimal antiseptic conditions were lacking, to show professional commitment without expecting rewards, and to set examples for others. The many hours spent in the operating room and the equal attention to the wounded of either side clearly demonstrated their professionalism.

The leadership in my clinic was entirely democratic. Each doctor decided how many days he could work and how many patients he could take. When a minor incident developed concerning the order of appointments, I called together the doctors who had perhaps contributed to the trouble and explained the problem to them. One doctor did not like this policy and withdrew his services, but the clinic main-

25. It must be said that even the snipers showed deference to the doctors. Several times they stopped my car, and when I told them I was working in the hospital they would shout, "He is a doctor! Let him go! Open the barricades for him, quick!"

tained its standards of equality for all. While helping in the hospitals, however, I observed that leadership was rather authoritarian. The director set up the work schedule, leaves, and shifts, which the doctors had to follow without discussion. Certain drugs were kept in the director's office and every time a doctor prescribed one of those, he had to come for it personally. Perhaps in a highly confused situation such policies were wise, although I heard frequent complaints from the doctors about the authoritarian control.

The Church of San Miguel

Soon after our arrival in San Miguel, Father Tomás and I set up a food distribution center for the hungry people of the barrio. We also established a vaccination center to meet the danger of an epidemic from the unsanitary conditions. We later became aware of a problem of missing persons, so we organized a human rights center. After the danger of epidemic was over, it became apparent that no doctors or drugs were available to treat chronic infant ailments such as colds, worms, and vitamin deficiency, so we started a public health clinic. Because schools had been closed for over a month, we also opened a catechetical school and a language school where English would be taught. Finally, Father Tomás started the Tigres Club. In less than two months we had organized the barrios as illustrated in Figure 4.

The organizations shown in Figure 4 were not the result of a calculated plan to influence the community. On the contrary, community pressures moved us. The community discovered that because Father Tomás and I were not political, we enjoyed a mobility through the city that others did not. The community trusted us because we had moved into their zone when others had fled the dangers of the war; we had become part of their community and considerable solidarity developed among us.

Father Tomás and I could not have set up all these organizations in less than two months without the help of dedicated leaders who emerged at the community level. First, a group of boys and girls of Lebanese extraction from the white middle class offered us unselfish cooperation: they helped with the distribution of thousands of pounds of food and then went home empty-handed, even though their families

FIGURE 4

Organization of San Miguel's Community

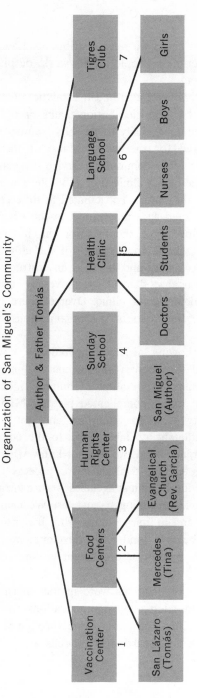

Recipients in the Community:

1. Over 2000 adults and children received the three shots against typhoid and para-typhoid fever (June 1 to June 25).

2. Our census figures show that we provided one-third of the weekly diet for 15,000 people (May 24 to Sept. 15).

3. A total of 230 rights cases were dealt with (June 1 to Sept. 3).

4. About 125 children attended our Sunday school daily for three weeks (June 20 to July 15).

5. The clinic cared for 2,200 patients. Drugs were given to nearly 3,000 people (July 1 to Sept. 3).

6. English was taught every evening from 6-7:30 p.m. to forty boys and girls (Aug. 19 to Sept. 16).

7. The club started with twenty-five boys, ages 13 to 19. This figure later rose to seventy members (Aug. 15, 1965).

could have used some of the rice and beans we were distributing. Later, we were able to use some dark lower-class people in this work, despite some initial difficulties in selecting them.

The emergence of leadership at this level also had a catalytic effect, inasmuch as the boys and girls on the food distribution teams brought in some friends and relatives who adapted easily to the high standards of dedication and efficiency required for the work. Many of these young people began to participate in other community service projects, such as the vaccination center and the health clinic. For example, David Matos, a high-school graduate from the barrio, participated at different times in all seven organizations; he acted as a male nurse in the vaccination center, distributed food, helped type the lists for the human rights center, taught at the Sunday school, took charge of the clinic's drug department, attended English classes, and became an instructor in the Tigres Club. His sister, a medical student at the university, also helped in several organizations, particularly the clinic. Over 60 percent of the leaders participated in more than two of the organizations at some time or other.

To discuss organizations without showing, at least schematically, how we obtained food and drugs, found the doctors and teachers to help in our projects, or proceeded in cases of violation of human rights, would be to describe only half of a rather complicated picture. Many human problems in the community required attention, and yet no means for solving them were immediately available. New to the community and not supported by any organization, we did not know where to go for help. We started a long, tedious, trial-and-error process of applying to all of the national and international agencies or organizations for any help they would be able or willing to give us. We came in contact with all kinds of civilian and military groups who, by virtue of their positions in society, coud help or hinder the development of our different projects. Some of the groups or organizations we contacted are shown in Figure 5.

All but two of these groups and organizations were in the international zone, which meant that when telephone communications were out of order, we had to make the time-consuming drive through the rebel, loyalist, and U.S. lines, with a slow search for weapons at every checkpoint.[26] Recourse was made to international agencies for food and medical supplies and for requesting investigations or protection in cases of violation of human rights. Frequent contacts were also made with intermediary groups for medical supplies or, in certain cases, technical help. We also approached national agencies, to request help in expediting transportation of goods from one zone to another, to file claims on behalf of the community, or to protest violations of human rights. Finally, a routine part of life was the communication with law enforcement agents, which was not always pleasant.

Once leaders had emerged in the community, we had no problem running the seven projects. If I had to go to the international zone, Josephine, a medical student, would open the clinic and arrange the appointments. When the trucks brought food, Father Tomás and the Tigres would unload and store it. If someone came to complain of violation of human rights, Catalina Navarro, the secretary, would take the information and send it to the Papal Nuncio or to the OAS.

Our main function was to provide material help and moral or spiritual support to the community. This spiritual support was sometimes religious, such as the Mass we held on Sundays which part of the community attended and the provision for burial rites for the dead. But moral support generally took the form of human solidarity in times of crisis, for instance, when the city was under heavy mortar fire. During the fighting we tended to the wounded in the barrio and sheltered people in the old church.

Another function we assumed was representing the community before all the agencies and groups shown in Figure 5. By the end of June, whenever I had to go to see an official of the Caamaño government, I was admitted before scores of people waiting outside. An aide to Caamaño explained this privilege: "We do this for you because you represent a quarter of the people in our zone!"

Our leadership was a curious blend of authority and democracy.

26. I estimate that in the four months I spent in the rebel zone, 120 hours of my time were lost being searched for weapons by the U.S. Marines. I averaged three trips a day across the lines. Each time ten minutes were lost waiting and being searched. Coming back into the rebel zone, I had to go through the same process.

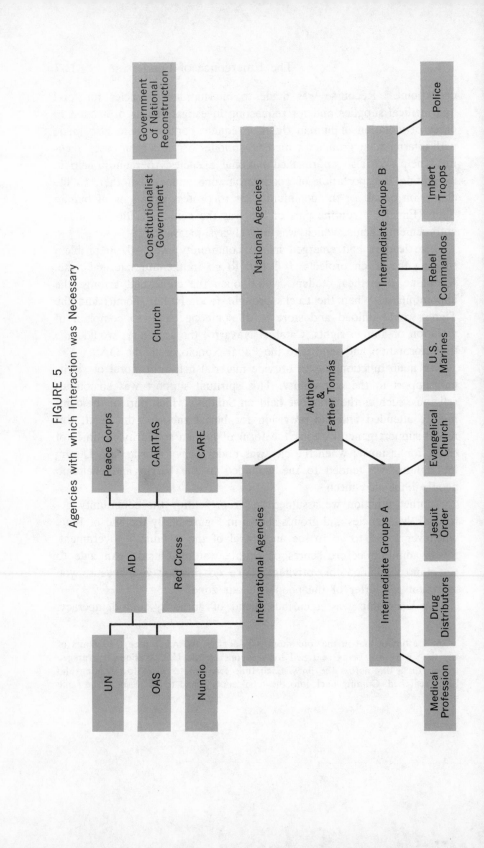

FIGURE 5
Agencies with which Interaction was Necessary

In setting initial patterns for action within the organization, we were authoritarian because urgency did not allow experimentation with alternative methods. Once the group members had acquired some skills in what they were doing, however, they were allowed to change roles and organize the group the way they wished. Our main emphasis was on justice; group members had to treat community members equally, with no favoritism permitted. The same principle was enforced within the leadership group: no special privileges allowed. The leaders made a special effort to help with the less pleasant tasks such as sweeping the floors after the food distributions or unloading the heavy bags from the trucks. The standards of cleanliness we enforced were far above the barrio norm. The only way to show the boys the value of cleanliness was to pick up the broom and sweep the floor as we wanted it swept. We could then hope that the next time they might sweep it that way themselves.

Perhaps the most interesting case of a barrio leader emerging from the community was that of Doña Clementina García, a middle-class Spanish woman we called Doña Tina. She organized a food distribution center in her home and also cared for three hundred barrio families. She worked at the city hospital as a volunteer nurse in the mornings and in the afternoon organized the activities of her center or performed other community services. One day I saw her walking toward San Miguel followed by a garbage truck. When I asked her why she had the truck, she told me that the garbage in the barrio had not been collected for two weeks, so she had asked the mayor for a truck. He had given it to her and now she was conducting a trash removal operation.

Summary

The similarities and dissimilarities of leadership in the three different kinds of organizations are shown in Table 6. It is interesting to note that these three organizations, despite their interrelations, were more or less independent of each other, although in such matters as military strategy the political and the military organizations were of necessity dependent on each other.

The emergence of leaders was spontaneous in each of the three organizations. Group leaders did not emerge because they chose to be

TABLE 6

LEADERSHIP IN THE REBEL ZONE

Organization	Emergence	Functions	Type	Representatives
Political	Spontaneous To satisfy urgent needs of group Diffusive process followed by polarization Catalytic effect on others	Executive of group's policies and decisions Group representative Coordinator of group's internal relations	Democratic	Caamaño Aristy Montes Arache Lachapelle Peña Gómez Jottín Cury Guzmán
Paramilitary	Spontaneous To implement group's tasks Catalytic effect on others	Expert in group's most needed skills Group representative Group provider	Authoritarian (with semblance of democracy)	Pichirilo Manolo González Oscar Santana Carbuccia Santiago
Civic	Spontaneous To satisfy urgent needs of group Catalytic effect on others	Expert help for group's needs Provider of material and moral support Group representative	Democratic (with some authoritarian methods)	Physicians Priests in San Miguel Lebanese boys and girls Doña Tina

leaders, or even because the group decided to appoint them; they became leaders by showing ability during the process of finding solutions
to common problems. In all three organizations, leaders seemed to
emerge in response to the group's needs in a given set of circumstances
or to the immediate goals the group wanted to achieve. In all three
cases, the emergence of leaders seemed to have had some kind of catalytic effect which caused leadership formation to spread not only among
the members of the group, but also to other similar groups.

In all three organizations, a major function of the group leader was
representing the group before other groups. In the political organization, because of the democratic structure of its groups, leaders were
assigned the function of executing rather than planning group policies.
The political group leader was not necessarily looked upon merely as
an expert, but as a coordinator of the internal activities of the group
and as the group's representative to the outside world. The leaders of
the paramilitary and civic organizations, however, were often regarded
as experts in providing solutions to the group's needs. Both organizations saw their leaders as providers of material and in some cases, moral
support.

The leadership practiced in each organization corresponded not only
to the structure, goals, and tasks of the group, but also to the composition of membership. The leadership in the political organization was
democratic because the power for setting policies and making decisions
was shared by several members and subgroups. In the paramilitary
organization the leadership was more authoritarian than democratic,
although a semblance of democracy was maintained. In the civic organization, on the other hand, leadership was more democratic than authoritarian, although of necessity a certain degree of authoritarianism
was occasionally maintained.

The structure, goals, and tasks as well as membership composition of
the political organization clearly demanded a more democratic leadership than did those of the paramilitary.[27] It is not so clear why the
political organization should have been more democratic than the civic
organization. Perhaps it was not: my perception of the civic organiza-

---

27. Several investigators have pointed out that workers may resist democratic
leadership. See David Krech et al., *Individual and Society* (New York, 1962),
p. 437.

tion as less democratic may be a distortion caused by my close observation. It may also be that differences in membership composition were greater in the civic organization than in the political organization. No doubt the social gap between a doctor and a nurse in my clinic, or between Father Tomás and one of the tigres, was greater than that between Caamaño and Aristy or between Montes Arache and Lachapelle. I am inclined to believe that the greater the social gap between leader and group members in an organization, the slighter the chance for a democratic leadership in its many manifestations.

Chapter 11

The Role of Informal Organizations

📌 Previously I emphasized that the commando groups were not organized by the leaders, but by the revolutionaries themselves—the people who were fighting, eating, and sleeping together. When I asked who the original members of several commandos were, I consistently found that the original group consisted of a core of friends or relatives.[1] During the confusion of the revolution's first week, the rebels started to protect themselves by gathering in primary groups of varying forms, from which the commandos grew. In tracing the origins of forty-eight commandos through written documents I arrived at the categories shown in Table 7.

By the time the anxieties and insecurities of the first week were over, the commandos were established and enough solidarity had developed among the members to keep them together. The membership of the commandos did not remain the same, however, throughout the period of the war. I estimate that less than 50 percent of the original revolutionaries stayed until the end. In most commandos, membership was maintained by new recruits from the province, pueblo, or barrio, who

1. From the secret files of the rebels in Santo Domingo, I verified that it was common to find several relatives in the same commando. In Commando San Antón, Zone 4, father and son were comandante and subcomandante of thirty-five men. In Commando Grupo Bravo, of a total of thirteen men, seven were brothers and another one was their cousin. In Caamaño's presidential bodyguard, the leader was Caamaño's own uncle, and three of Caamaño's cousins were in the same group.

173

TABLE 7

ORIGINS OF 48 COMMANDOS

Primary Groups		Formal Organizations	
Family	4	Trade union	7
Barrio	9	Military unit	5
Pueblo	8	Profession	4
Province	3	Political party	5
Nationality	3		
Total	27	Total	21

replaced the dropouts. It was natural for the new recruits to go first to a commando where their friends or relatives were. Thus, a boy coming from towns of La Vega, Mao, or San Juan would naturally go first to Commando La Vega, Mao, or San Juan. Sometimes new recruits came only out of curiosity, but after a day or two with friends in the commando posts decided to stay. The role of primary groups in the revolution would appear to have been, first, to set up many commandos in the early stages of the revolution and, second, to maintain group membership by attracting new recruits.

Primary groups also helped the commandos to achieve an internal unity and aided in their integration into the surrounding community. Most commandos were not homogeneous groups. They included people with various educational and social backgrounds, political affiliations, and regional origins. Some had never seen one another before and many, especially those from the provinces, were away from their relatives and might have felt like strangers in the capital. Instead, they were able to feel very much at home because they had joined commandos with friends from the same region or barrio. Some were from the same neighborhood and some were even relatives. When off duty, the boys went around the city with their compañeros, and the comandante often put them on duty together for the night shift to lessen the tedium and anxiety of sentry duty. An old member would unofficially instruct the new recruit from his barrio, telling him what he was allowed to do, what things he should avoid, and how he should treat other men in the commando. Each of these primary groups normally had a group leader who was the liaison between the group and the comandante.

Often the comandante did not have adequate room in one building for all the members of his commando. Schools, warehouses, movie theaters, and other buildings were used as headquarters, and overcrowding often forced small groups of six to eight boys to sleep in abandoned apartments or houses. In these cases, the primary group set the behaviorial norms for the membership in practically all aspects of everyday life; the small units were incorporated into the larger unit only for common drills, day and night duties, and to receive their food. The members of the small unit arranged their own cooking; often they simply asked a girl from the barrio to do it. By the end of July, each group's food allocation was little more than half of what it needed. Consequently, the comandante in places such as San Miguel did away with their common kitchen. By dividing the available food among the different groups at the beginning of each week, he freed himself from these responsibilities and instead placed them either on general headquarters or the small unit.

Because food was so scarce, the members of most small units had to pool whatever commodities or cash they could get. This placed a considerable burden on the community, particularly the food distribution centers and small businesses. Some boys began to ask for contributions from their area's small businessmen and shopkeepers. Although the boys did not often threaten the merchants, considerable pressure was felt, since the boys carried guns and the merchants knew that some stores in the area had been broken into during the night. This bullying by the rebels aroused considerable ill feeling among the middle class, whose businesses, after three months of crisis, were bankrupt. The food distribution centers were also bothered by the boys' frequent requests for food. As I said, my center gave food only to the comandante; it was his responsibility to distribute it to the boys. At the height of the food shortage, however, this rule did not work. The boys came without notes from their comandante, and they took up so much time that I decided to change one of the center's basic policies. Originally, if any food was left over after the official distribution, it was stored for emergencies during the week or to balance off the quota of the next distribution. Because the boys knew there was food in storage, they would come and sit in the park all morning, waiting for me to arrive. When I showed up, they would not demand food immediately, but would tell me they had to speak with me. Since they used this approach,

I never knew whether they had come to beg food or to see me about some other problem. When I finally ushered them in, they would tell me that they needed food. Never discouraged, the boys would repeat this procedure five or ten times every day. I finally decided that all food would be given away the same day and none stored. The empty storage room was left open for everyone to see. From that day on we had more time to run the other six projects.

However, the fact that this practice of asking for food became a burden on the community does not diminish the fact that the membership of the primary groups had to provide for the group. Considering that the commando provided the boys with only half of their diet and that cash was distributed to the membership only twice during the four-and-a-half months of the war,[2] it is apparent that the number of cases of looting, as well as the number of complaints filed by store owners threatened by the boys, was relatively small. This relative orderliness may be attributed to the efforts of many civilian and military officers to maintain law and order, and to the integration of the commandos with the surrounding community through the interplay of informal relations.

In some cases this integration with the community was no problem since the commando boys were largely from the community. Such was the case of Commando San Miguel. The commando members knew everyone in the barrio, and it was only natural for them to protect the property and interests of the community.[3] The boys from the barrio often ate and slept in their own homes. Sometimes they took home one or two commando friends from other parts of the city. If the guests liked a friend's home, they returned to play cards, drink, listen to the radio, or visit the girls of the barrio.

In commandos where most members were from another area of the city, integration with the resident community, particularly the middle class, was more difficult. If some members of the commando were university students, then some integration was possible along class lines. Integration was relatively easy when the commando members and the surrounding community belonged to the same social class. Thus, the members of the June 14th Movement who made up Commando José

2. From the official list of the rebel government, the amount given to each man was about three dollars on each occasion. A copy of the document is in my files.
3. See Chapter 4.

G. García had no problem integrating with the residents of Ciudad Nueva, a middle-class area. On the other hand, the dock workers of POASI, after being displaced from their area by the Marines and settling in a middle-class sector of San Miguel, were unable to integrate with the community. According to a local girl, "They were too tough and aggressive to mix with our group."

Integration of lower-class commandos with middle-class communities became more difficult when ideological or racial prejudices existed between the two groups. The lower-class commando boys said that the middle-class people were *tutumpotes*[4] or bourgeois. Middle-class housewives complained that the commando members were all tigres, or that they drank and fought among themseves, or that they were communists. However, the same housewives would not mind having a white middle-class student member of the same commando in their homes. Working together in the food distribution center, the clinic, or the center of human rights helped both the commando boys and community members to overcome some prejudices. Although we had decided to separate these groups for efficiency and task specialization, cooperation on a common task helped to establish informal contacts which were later continued outside. Several times early in the evening I visited some of the middle-class families who helped with the food distribution and often found one or two boys from Commando San Lázaro in the living room playing the accordion for the girls or watching television with the family. Sometimes, seeing me in front of a house talking with a family, the boys would approach and start watching television through the window. Normally, after the ice was broken, the family would invite him in if he seemed "a nice boy," and from then on, he might feel free to return.

It was suggested in Chapter 9 that the so-called mass rebel did not have an ideology of his own and that his decision to join the revolution was made by the informal group of which he was a member. Along the same line of thought, I would add that perhaps as many as 50 percent of the commando members belonged in this mass rebel category. Most of the rank and file of the commandos joined the revolution because their compañeros in the primary group decided to do so. They

4. Word coined by Bosch to describe the rich who can afford whatever they want.

also stayed despite the hardships and boredom of the four months of negotiations, again because their friends stayed. Once a young member of the PRSC discussed with me whether or not he should leave his commando, since his parents were pressuring him to return home. He finally said, "I cannot leave unless my brother also leaves."[5]

Finally, to maintain group stability and morale under the difficult conditions of the revolution, some ideological sustenance was necessary. Both the political and paramilitary organizations were aware of this need and took pains to communicate group goals to their memberships, emphasizing the progress being made. Radio and television,[6] newspapers, posters, mass rallies, and political indoctrination were used to instill the message of the revolution in the minds of the rank and file. How much ideology was really communicated directly to the masses is difficult to estimate. I am inclined to think that the comandantes and some of the informal leaders of the primary groups frequently acted as opinion leaders for the rank and file.[7] The role of the opinion leader was to process information related to the revolution from communication media and pass it on in simplified form to the rank and file. However, the leader did not have to pass it on to each and every member. Once the information was digested in a concentrated form, the members of the different primary groups would communicate it to others. I often found myself acting as opinion leader. For example, when a boy asked me, after a speech by Caamaño, "What did he say?" I answered, "The negotiations failed." I had not forgotten the rest of the speech, but I knew that that was what he wanted to know or as much as he could understand.

5. The two brothers finally decided to leave the rebel zone, and I arranged their safe departure through the International Security Zone. Weeks later they started to come back periodically to receive military instruction in the School of Commandos run by Colonel Montes Arache.

6. Radio and television were perhaps the most powerful weapons used by the rebels in the first three weeks of the revolution. After Operation Clean-up, the main station was taken over by Imbert's troops. As mentioned earlier, *La Nación* and *Patria* were published in the rebel zone and distributed all over the city.

7. See E. Katz and P. Lazarsfeld, *Personal Influence* (New York, 1964), p. 31.

Chapter 12

Conflict and Conflict Resolution

✍ The rebel social structure, as I indicated earlier, was heterogeneous in terms of its members, groups, organizations, and ideologies. The suddenness with which these individuals, groups, and organizations found themselves not only living together, but trying to maintain a relatively complex structure, was a natural source of social conflict. The rebels were not only holding a city in which all social, political, and economic mechanisms had crumbled, but were also trying to establish a nationally and internationally recognized government to deal with the overall conflict that had brought the rebel groups together. The solution of the overall conflict between rebels and loyalists was the primary concern of the rebel leadership. Consequently, the top leaders spent most of their time and energy in these negotiations.

There were, however, other types of conflicts which originated within the rebel structure. While Caamaño, Aristy, or Jottín Cury were negotiating with Colombo, Mora, or Bunker, several minor conflicts arose between commando posts or other rebel groups. Although these conflicts had to be resolved, solving the overall crisis was more urgent. Nevertheless, it was imperative that the rebel structure minimize internal conflict to maintain the cohesiveness needed to present a common front to the enemy.

Conflict is defined here as actions involving tension, antagonistic

179

competition, disputes, and perhaps open clashes.[1] A social structure created by a sudden and violent change must experience some manifestations of conflict, if only because the roles, norms, and rules defining the individual's behavior and the new organization's sphere of action have not yet been clearly determined.

A study of the different conflicts within the rebel structure will facilitate understanding of the internal workings of the revolutionary process. I observed several conflicts, and was personally involved in a few. Here I examine some conflictual situations at group, organizational, and ideological levels, the way they were handled, the agencies created to deal with them, and their solutions.

Conflict at the Group Level

Several commandos had developed from informal groups which remained the main integrative mechanism. Each commando included thirty to two hundred men, some of whom belonged to primary groups, some not. Conflicts developed not only within these groups, but also between them.

Common tasks had to be performed, and rewards were very scarce. If the tasks and rewards were not distributed equally, tensions between different primary groups were likely to mount. If the leaders failed to provide an appropriate solution, these tensions often mounted to open conflict. In such a case in San Miguel, the conflict resulted in a coup d'etat by the local boys against Francisco's group. On other occasions, conflict resulted in an open fight and brought about the disintegration of the unit; the leaders of one small commando located in Mella Avenue killed each other in a fight over personal matters, and Caamaño ordered the whole unit disbanded.

Usually, however, internal group conflict was successfully handled by the group leaders, particularly the comandante, who was regarded as the representative of the General Staff. "Discipline and justice," several comandantes insisted, "is the key to avoiding conflict in our groups." By discipline they meant enforcement of the laws against drinking or women visiting the boys' living quarters. By justice they meant equal

1. Ralf Dahrendorf, *Class and Class Conflict in Industrial Society* (Stanford, 1965), p. 135.

participation in the common tasks and equal sharing of whatever goods were obtained. Another comandante told me, "No favoritism is the best rule for keeping the boys happy."

Interaction between commandos was another source of conflict. The boys of one commando, usually carrying their guns, might walk into another commando's sector and for no apparent reason a fight might develop. Since only those on actual military duty in that area were permitted to carry weapons, the intruding boys were often jailed until the comandante could study the case. Thus, a fight which may have started as a personal affair became an intergroup conflict. These cases were usually settled amicably by the comandantes of both groups, but sometimes a case was taken up by the General Staff, especially if someone had been wounded during the fight. Even then, the General Staff usually supported the decision of the comandante in whose territory the conflict had occurred. Thus the concept of territoriality became important in the lives and organization of the commandos. In his territory, the comandante was the legal authority and the boys under him were the law-enforcing agents, but outside that territory they were merely ordinary citizens.

For several months I closely observed the boys of San Miguel, and noticed that they rarely left the San Miguel area except to attend a political rally or a show. Even then, they went in groups of three or four. I also found that in cases of territorial overlapping, the boys of one commando did not normally interact with members of another. After the battle of June 15 several commandos (Pedro Mena, Pedro Cadena, and Poasi) were displaced from their own territories in the northeast and established themselves near San Miguel. Seldom did members of these three groups interact with the San Miguel commando or even among themselves; each group remained relatively aloof from the others. When I asked a boy from San Miguel why he and his friends did not mix with others, he said, "It is better to stick to your own group. There are fewer problems that way!"

In some areas of the rebel zone, particularly in the north, the night patrol became a serious problem by the end of July when food was scarce. Often small groups of armed rebels broke into stores to steal groceries or liquor. Although the comandantes had strict orders from the General Staff to curb such actions, they found them difficult to enforce, because gunfights could easily develop on the excuse that the two groups were unknown to each other. To solve the problem, three of the comandantes, Pichirilo, Barahona, and Pujols, established a joint patrol, with one man from each commando in every night-patrol vehicle. A looter from any of the three commandos would be dealt with by a comrade from his commando who would have the full support of the other two guards. This pattern of intergroup cooperation greatly helped to reduce conflicts among three of the most aggressive commandos.

Conflict at the Organization Level

Organization refers here to the political, paramilitary and civic organizations. Although their functions were different, considerable interaction existed and their activities overlapped to a certain degree. Consequently, some conflict was unavoidable.

I have shown how areas of conflict were likely to develop in Figure 6. The three organizations are represented by three overlapping circles, with the political organization represented by circle A, the paramilitary by circle B, and the civic by circle C. Areas of conflict are represented by Roman numerals.

FIGURE 6

Overlapping of the Three Organizations

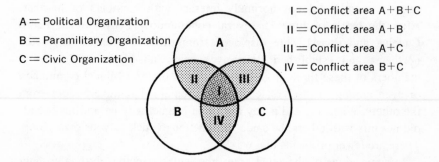

A = Political Organization
B = Paramilitary Organization
C = Civic Organization

I = Conflict area A+B+C
II = Conflict area A+B
III = Conflict area A+C
IV = Conflict area B+C

The most sensitive area of conflict is that represented by Area I, where all three organizations operated. The crime and punishment of Traboux provides an example of this three-way conflict.[2] When Tra-

2. See pp. 55–57.

boux sought refuge in the San Miguel's Human Rights Center, Father Tomás, aware of the seriousness of Traboux's crime, personally handed him over to a representative of the Caamaño government (*C* recognizes the jurisdiction of *A*). The June 14th Movement members, wanting to avenge the murder of one of their leaders (*B* pressures *A*), managed to get Traboux to their headquarters (*A* yields to *B*). When we discovered this had happened, we protested to Caamaño (*C* pressures *A*). Caamaño sent Lachapelle to investigate the situation (*A* pressures *B*). The leaders of the June 14th Movement and Lachapelle assured us that the prisoner would have a fair trial (*B* yields to *C*). When we heard that the June 14th boys had executed Traboux, we protested to the leaders of the June 14th Movement (*C* protests the actions of *B*), as well as to Caamaño, who ordered an investigation (*C* protests to *A* and *A* takes action against *B*). This conflict ended with the government apologizing formally to us "for the irregularities of the process" and the leaders of the June 14th Movement excusing themselves saying "the death of Traboux was the result of an accident."

An example of conflict between two organizations occurred when we organized the distribution of food by giving punch cards to each family in the barrio.[3] We discovered later that some elements of the government were issuing similar cards and sending people to our center without consulting us (*A* pressures *C*). Since we had a limited amount of food and because we did not want to be an instrument of the political organization, we refused these people food (*C* confronts *A*). The mayor tried to persuade us to honor the government cards (*A* pressures *C*). We refused on the grounds that we did not have sufficient food for all the hungry people of the city and we could not favor any one political party (*C* maintains independence of *A*). The mayor and his aides agreed to let us organize our centers according to our own plans, so the conflict was solved on the basis of justice rather than subordination.

Conflict between *A* and *B* was rare because of the interdependence of the two organizations and the subordination of *B* to *A*. Only at the end of the revolution was there a concerted effort by *B*'s general structure to exert pressure on *A* for a cash reward for the commandos before they were disbanded. The grass-roots movement, known as Los

3. See p. 76.

Hijos de Machepa, demanded $300 for each man in the commandos. The Caamaño government did not have that kind of money, and the comandantes were advised to discourage such activity. After a few days the movement died out, and public rallies held on its behalf were discontinued.

Caamaño's government created several agencies—the military police, the transportation center, the commando school, the tailor shop, the food supply center, and the gun repair shop—to deal with some of the commandos' problems. These agencies represented the government and supplied the commandos with services. If the commandos had any further complaint or requirement, they could still appeal to the General Staff. Most agencies, however, were able to handle the day-to-day problems. For example, most commando posts had one or two vehicles for transportation and patrol. After U.S. troops sealed off the rebel zone, no fuel, food, or medicine was allowed into the zone.[4] The rebels soon ran out of gasoline, and the transportation center organized some boys to request contributions of gas from all cars entering the rebel zone. This group of nine boys, known as Commando Euclides Morillo, set up a post near the U.S. entrance to the rebel zone. Each had a bucket and a piece of hose for siphoning one or two gallons of gas from cars after the owners had consented. Eventually they managed to fill big drums, which were then transported to headquarters and distributed among the 250 vehicles used by the rebels.[5]

Interaction between *B* and *C* was maintained without much conflict once they understood each other's functions. At the beginning of the revolution before the role of the commandos had been defined, our food trucks were often stopped at different places in the rebel zone and a "contribution" of one hundred pounds of rice requested. Some of my assistants were afraid of the commando boys and gave them what they requested. One day two boys from San Miguel took a bag of rice from the truck parked in front of the church. When I noticed

4. The shipment of food and drugs was allowed only through international welfare agencies.

5. My own experience will verify the fact that as a rule the boys did not compel owners to give gas. When requested to contribute, I often excused myself by saying, "I am sorry, I am low on gas today." The boys were not pleased, but they always let me go without further pressure or threat.

the rice was missing, I followed the two boys to their commando post, found the bag of rice, and told them to return it. They did so and from that day on there were no more "requests" for contributions (although we continued to give the commandos a share of the surplus from the food distributions).

Preferential treatment requested by some commando boys was another source of conflict. Some came to the food distribution center or to the clinic with their guns to "request" what they needed. I always declined to give them anything, saying I was too busy. When they realized they could not force me to do anything, their attitudes generally changed. No rebel leader ever tried to compel me to do anything. Rather, the higher the rank and importance of the leader, the more deference and understanding he showed for our work. For example, Colonel Montes Arache supplied us with several trucks of food for the hungry people of San Miguel. A clear definition of each organization's functions helped avoid and resolve conflict between them.

Conflict at the Ideological Level

The various groups supporting the revolution—the PRD, PRSC, PSP, and June 14th Movement—shared their opposition to the government of Donald Reid and their support of a return to constitutional democracy, but they did not necessarily share a common ideology.[6] A consensus on certain immediate goals and means bound the groups together and the morale and cohesiveness of these groups was strengthened by the external threat of adversaries who sought their destruction.[7] Centralization was achieved because the military threat from outside demanded a unified response. The groups' individualities and their ideological differences were maintained, however, as is evident from the

6. "When a social structure is no longer considered legitimate, individuals with similar objective positions will come, through conflict, to constitute themselves into self-conscious groups with common interests." Lewis Coser, *The Functions of Social Conflict* (New York, 1964), p. 37. See also p. 140.

7. This basic ideological consensus and the external threat coincide with the principle that "a sensed outside threat to the group will result in heightened internal cohesion." See Robin M. Williams, Jr., "The Reduction of Intergroup Tensions," *SSRC Bulletin*, 57 (1947), p. 58.

documents published by the different groups.[8] Each group tried to maintain its own image before the government and the populace by being represented in high-level conferences and public rallies.

During the four months of negotiations, the outside threat to the groups seemed to diminish. However, the threat to ideological consensus persisted. The continuing external threat was enough to maintain some solidarity among the groups, but it was no longer sufficient to eliminate internal conflict. As negotiations proceeded, each group approached the various issues according to its ideological position. The radical MPD was at one extreme and the moderate PRD at the other—the former rejecting negotiations, the latter accepting them as the only solution to the political impasse. The powerful June 14th Movement tended to support the radical position, whereas the PSP and the PRSC were inclined to accept the solution offered by the moderates.

Tensions between these two positions grew as the negotiations progressed, wtih the MPD and June 14th Movement accusing the other groups "of selling out the revolution to the bourgeois moderates."[9] The PSP was not excluded from these accusations, and its members were accused of being revisionists. These tensions, sometimes latent, often overt, generated conflict on several occasions among these groups, particularly the more powerful ones. The June 14th Movement, which had succeeded in building a powerful paramilitary structure, was particularly dissatisfied with its lesser influence in the political negotiations. Its members resented the moderates of the PRD and the military, and took every opportunity to show their strength and quasi-autonomy from Caamaño's governmental structure. The punishment of Traboux could be interpreted along these lines.[10]

In another case some boys from Commando El Lido (June 14th

8. *La Nación* was the mouthpiece of Caamaño's government, which represented the moderates and the military groups. *Patria* was published by the June 14th Movement, in addition to a weekly bulletin *14 June*. The PSP published a weekly bulletin, *El Popular*, the MPD published *Libertad*, and the PRSC published *Pueblo*.

9. See *Libertad*, Sept. 3, 1965, pp. 6–7.

10. See p. 57. I asked the opinion of a high ranking officer of the rebel army about the way the June 14th Movement had handled the case. He was very upset and said, "If they do something like that again, I'll call a press conference and expose them in public. I think that time for a showdown is running short."

Movement) refused to honor a permit given to a merchant by Manolo González (PSP). This show of aggressiveness was directed not only against the Caamaño government for allowing a middle-class business- man to take his goods out of the rebel zone, but against the members of the PSP for implementing the order and supporting Caamaño.

At the end of the revolution the June 14th Movement and the MPD attempted to create an "anti-imperialist front." The PSP supported the idea, but the PRD and the PRSC refused to join. This refusal was another sign of the growing ideological divergence among the groups that had been united previously in their fight to return to the 1963 Constitution.

In Table 8 I have summed up the sources of conflict and the way they were handled at different levels. At the beginning of the revolution most situations of conflict originated on the group or organizational level; at the end of the revolution most conflicts originated on the ideological level.

TABLE 8

CONFLICT IN THE REBEL STRUCTURE

Levels	Source of Conflict	Solutions
1. Group	Scarcity of goods Unequal task allotment Overlapping of zones	Group discipline Justice in allocation of tasks and rewards Territoriality

2. Organization	Unclear definition of
	    group roles
	Lack of norms
	Overlapping of action areas
		Definition of group roles
		Delineation of action areas
		    through establishment of
		    norms
		Creation of agencies

3. Ideological	Ideological stand Decline in external threat	Realization of larger group goals Threat to survival

The conflict on level 1 was caused primarily by the scarcity of mate- rial goods in a situation of physical and psychological stress.[11] It was also caused by the failure of some leaders to understand the principle,

11. See Chalmers Johnson, *Revolutionary Change* (Boston, 1966), pp. 36–37.

"We are all equal" for which they were fighting. In distributing group tasks unequally, the leaders violated this tacit rule. Once they accepted the principle of equality in the allocation of tasks and rewards, most of the conflict at the group level disappeared. The concept of territoriality was enforced to avoid intergroup conflict.

At the organization level, conflict arose mainly before areas of action and organization roles and norms had been clearly defined. Once these areas were delineated and agencies created to deal with problems, fewer conflicts arose between organizations. The Traboux case probably created conflict because the rebel government never had an effective judiciary system.

Finally, the ideological level had very few open conflicts at the beginning of the revolution when imminent threat to physical survival was a binding factor which tended to minimize ideological differences. When the physical threat was totally or partially eliminated, however, ideological differences and conflicts reappeared. The only factor uniting the different groups was the realization that unity was the only way to attain, either in full or in part, the basic goals of the revolution.

Chapter 13

Conclusions

It is evident that from the type of data and the analysis used in this study that its conclusions cannot be presented under the form of precise propositions but purely as broad general orientations. In describing and attempting to analyze some aspects of such a complex process of change as a revolution, I have been forced to use only qualitative data. Yet, I would like to stress that in presenting such qualitative data, it has not been my intention merely to illustrate a certain number of concepts. These qualitative data represent real events, which, even if they cannot offer a rigorous proof in any statistical sense, can contribute according to their numbers to the formation and corroboration of so-called trend-theories, or to a more systematic examination of case material. It is my hope that the present study, together with other similar case works on similar processes of violent social change in Latin America and other countries of the underdeveloped world, will be used one day in a larger study that will approximate more closely the classical canons of proof. However, until we have a sufficiently large number of cases to support the statistical analysis, the present type of study seems to be not only necessary, but for the time being, the best approximation we can offer.

In studying the revolution, the first thing that struck my mind was how a peaceful people of "noble and resigned character"[1] placed in a

1. Dominican authors used to refer to their own people as "el noble y sufrido pueblo dominicano."

given set of circumstances can react violently and produce a chain of events which departs entirely from expected social and political patterns. About 3,000 persons were killed in the revolution, most of them civilians, including women and children.[2] The historical background was described from which the present social structure developed. Special emphasis was paid to the thirty years of Trujillo's dictatorship and its outgrowth, the Trujillista aristocracy and the military structure. The unsuccessful experiment in constitutional democracy under Juan Bosch was also suggested as an antecedent to the present crisis.

Focusing attention on the social situation previous to the revolutionary outburst, two social traits were found to be widely present among the rebels, which basically differentiated them from the loyalists—a high degree of alienation and a certain ideological frame. Alienation or feelings of powerlessness to influence the course of social events was experienced by politicians, students, and organized labor. In other groups, such as the young military and the professionals, alienation was evidenced by feelings of meaninglessness or estrangement from the roles they thought they could play in their own society. The ideological frame was described as a sort of a map that guided the minds of the rebels, drawing them together regardless of other ideological specifications and differentiating them from the loyalists. There was nothing new or extraordinary in the ideological frame. It advocated social change in the form of greater participation of all classes of people in the cultural, economic, and political life of the country. This type of change has been implemented both by Western democracies and by socialist countries since the turn of the century. However, what in most modern countries is taken for granted, regardless of the ideological bias of the system implementing it, in Santo Domingo, and probably in most Latin American countries, is not only *not* taken for granted, but condemned and opposed as specifically linked with one kind of ideology.

Fundamentally, the ideological frame of the rebels was designed by the PRD and supported by a group of young officers in the armed forces. As a product of two groups of moderates, it received the support of all those groups which advocated change in the same direction.

---

2. Most of these casualties were not produced by an enraged populace, but by the Dominican armed forces, particularly by the strafing of the loyalist air force over the civilian population.

The Dominican case seems to point out that structural change of the social system, particularly in its violent form (revolution) will be supported by groups with a so-called left-of-center ideology, including among them the democratic left, the Social Christians and the Marxist parties. These groups will be violently opposed by the so-called right-of-center groups including the oligarchy, the military, the U.S. Embassy, and possibly the Church in its upper echelons.

If the process of change reaches the stage of open armed conflict, the different groups will tend to polarize around the moderates of left and right at first, and then polarization will tend to sharpen toward more radical groups if the intensity of the conflict increases. If the conflict between rebels and loyalists means a positive threat to the physical survival of the members of either group, the group which is losing will seek help and support (foreign or national) otherwise considered undesirable.[3]

The existence of a threat to the survival of the members will tend to level off ideological differences among the members of the same group and will tend to increase internal cohesiveness among them. The adversary will often use this apparent identity of the opposite groups for its own purposes, either to destroy them or to negotiate with them as a group. When the outside threat decreases, internal ideological differences tend to reappear. Internal ideological conflict poses a threat to the revolution—a threat which at times might prove more difficult to overcome than the external threat of the enemy. This new threat presents the revolution with danger of internal disintegration. The only real solution to this type of conflict is the realization by the leaders of the ideological factions that the goals of the revolution are common to all of them, but not to their common enemy and that achieving these goals now is a step forward on the way to reaching the final goals of their own specific ideologies. Weak and temporary as this coalition might appear, it is, in my opinion, the only way to avoid, or to postpone

---

3. The help of the Marxists was only accepted by the Dominican rebels when the air force and the navy opened fire on the city, and the military rebels thought they could not face the far superior equipment of the loyalists. On the other hand, the U.S. intervention was requested only when the loyalists thought that the rebels would march on San Isidro. (From private interview with high ranking loyalist officer.)

at any rate, a conflict that could bring disintegration to the revolution. Convinced that realization of these facts is not enough to avoid the problem entirely, rebel leaders often try to maintain or help create a threat from the external enemy that will divert the attention of their members from their own internal conflicts.

Some other types of less important conflicts existed in the rebel structure among its different organizations, groups, or individuals. They were less important because they represented a threat only to the existence of a particular group or to the functioning of some organization and not to the revolutionary process itself. Conflicts between groups and organizations were less frequent once the areas of the organizations' activities, the territory belonging to the groups, and the norms regulating individuals and collective behavior were established.

An attempt was made to understand in detail who were these people we call "rebels." Five different types of rebels were found who had a number of common traits among themselves within each type and at the same time were quite different from those in all other types. The first three groups encompass the types that are essential to the revolutionary process in its different stages, while the last two are more of a residual category. Of the first three groups, the *Idealista* plans the revolution, the *Acomplejado* puts it into practice, and the Professional rebel fights for it. Each of these types plays an important role in the different stages of the revolutionary process, and leadership roles might shift from one type to another according to the exigencies of each stage. Type 4 (the Opportunist) can be highly deletereous to the revolution, but can hardly be avoided in its beginnings. Type 5 (the Mass rebel), however, is highly useful and it will depend on the first three types to what degree he becomes not only physically but ideologically integrated within the revolution.

Three main organizations were found to be involved in the revolutionary process: the political, the paramilitary, and the civic organizations. Their areas of action were different although there was some degree of overlapping among them. Each of these organizations was called upon to fulfill certain functions of the revolutionary process, which would not have been able to subsist without them. They interacted among themselves and a certain degree of coordination was necessary, but this did not necessarily imply subordination. Naturally, a high degree of dependence existed between the political and paramilitary organizations.

The emergence of new leaders was studied in the context of these three organizations. It was suggested that once the revolutionary process was underway, changes in leadership and the emergence of new leaders was a rather spontaneous phenomenon conditioned only by the needs of the group and by the availability of someone capable of minimally satisfying them. Leadership was thought to have a catalytic effect in such context, inasmuch as the emergence of leaders in one group would help other leaders to emerge in such similar groups. The functions of the leaders were different in each organization, but in all cases, the leader was looked upon as the representative of the group in contacts with other groups. The type of leadership seemed to have been rather democratic in the top echelons with a tendency to become more authoritarian at the lower levels within each organization.

Probably the most significant social event of the revolution was the formation of civilians from different social origins into tightly knit units. These units were called commandos and their function was to assist the rebel military in the defense of the city against the attacks of the loyalists and the U.S. troops. The origins of the commandos were traced back to formal or informal organizations which existed previous to the outbreak of the revolt. These two kinds of organizations also helped in recruiting new members for the commandos to replace those who had dropped out. They also were instrumental in maintaining the morale of the organization and were used as integrative mechanisms particularly in times of stress because of either the external threat of the enemy or the scarcity of goods available to the rebels.

Conflict within the group or between different commando groups could not be entirely avoided, particularly at the start when areas of action or norms of behavior had not been clearly defined. The concept of distributive justice in the allocation of tasks and rewards by the leaders seemed to have helped greatly in solving and preventing a number of conflicts between the members of the same commando. On the other hand, the concept of territoriality favored by the General Staff also helped to prevent dissension between the different armed groups.

The same concepts of distributive justice and territoriality were applied successfully to avoid discontent and even riots in the distribution of food to the hungry crowds.

A final conclusion summarizes or indicates the direction toward which many of the suggestions seem to lead us. The violent process of change that began to develop in the Dominican Republic seemed to have been powerful enough to bring about a number of structural changes in the system, changes that many national and foreign observers now believe to have been unavoidable. It seems to be commonly accepted that every revolution undergoes, roughly speaking, two stages: one in which the mechanisms of control of the old order are eliminated; and another in which the structure of the new order is built. In the Dominican case, it was quite obvious that by April 28 the most powerful instrument of the old order, the armed forces, had practically crumbled. To avoid its total destruction, a landing of U.S. troops was necessary. By protecting the old order and by surrounding the rebel forces in a small sector of the city, the United States succeeded in halting the revolutionary process.

Inside the rebel zone, however, the process was not totally halted, despite the fact that the efforts of the rebels were now focused on the negotiations rather than on the structural reforms they had contemplated. A number of social processes, however, took place that may be used as indicators of what could have happened if no foreign intervention had taken place. Such processes as the emergence of new leaders and the formation of new organizations indicate that the same processes could have occurred on a national scale if the rate of change had been maintained and extended over the whole system. With a relatively small number of men and with very outdated and inefficient military equipment, the rebels managed to keep the enemy away from their zone. Further, they built a government to handle internal and external problems; agencies were created to deal with situations of conflict; new leaders emerged to direct the actions of groups and organizations and to satisfy the needs of the group in a situation of relative deprivation. All this, in my opinion, seems to point out that once the process of change is initiated, the system itself will provide, in its own frame of reference, adequate solutions to the problems created by the new situation.

These solutions will probably be considered inadequate if measured by our own norms, but not by theirs. The problem of whether or not we can impose our norms on other systems is an ethical one, and as such, lies beyond the scope of this study.

Appendixes
Bibliography
Index

Appendix 1

Chronology of Events

1961

May 30   Generalissimo Trujillo is assassinated after thirty years in power.

1962

January 1   The Council of State is sworn in to prepare the climate for democratic elections to be held under the OAS.

December 20   Juan Bosch is elected with 59.5 percent of the electoral votes in the first free elections since 1924.

1963

February 26   Juan Bosch is inaugurated as constitutional president.

April 29   After three months in session, the National Assembly approves a new constitution.

September 25 Juan Bosch is ousted by a group of army officers headed by Colonel Wessin y Wessin. Allegations are made that Bosch is weak on the communists. A three-man civilian junta known as the Triumvirate is inaugurated.

December 21   Manolo Tavárez Justo and fifteen other members of the nationalistic organization, "June 14th," are killed in the mountains by army patrols.

December 22   Emilio de los Santos, head of the Triumvirate, resigns to

197

protest the repressive measures of the army against the guerrillas. Donald J. Reid Cabral is appointed head of the
Triumvirate.

1965

April 24   A group of young army officers revolt against the generals
and their civilian Triumvirate; they demand the return of
Juan Bosch and the 1963 Constitution.

April 25   Donald Reid resigns and negotiations begin between the generals and the rebels. General Wessin and General Santos do
not agree with the rebels and order the air force to strafe the
Presidential Palace, where the rebels have set up a "Constitutional Government" under the former Speaker of the House
Rafael Molina Ureña.

April 26   Acting President Molina Ureña seems to have consolidated
the rebel government with the support of most military garrisons from the provinces and in the capital, with the exception of the air force and the San Isidro Camp. Commodore
Rivera Caminero and General Despradel pledge loyalty to
the new regime, offering it the support of the navy and the
national police. The air force continues to attack the city.
Arms are distributed to civilians.

April 27   Heavy fighting breaks out between rebels and loyalists when
the latter start a major operation in an attempt to take the
city by land, sea, and air. The navy and police seem to have
changed their minds, and now side with the loyalists of San
Isidro, who seem to be getting increasing moral support from
the military attaches of the U.S. Embassy. Over two thousand
people are reported dead, mainly from the air force strafing
of the Duarte Bridge. Late in the afternoon the tanks from
San Isidro are said to be entering the city, and a group of
rebel officers appeal to U.S. Ambassador W. T. Bennett
to mediate in the fight. The U.S. Ambassador refuses and
suggests that total surrender is in order. Molina Ureña and
other civilian leaders seek refuge in foreign embassies, while
most military leaders go back to the battlefield. Later that
evening the entire city is reported under the control of rebel
leaders Colonel Francisco Caamaño and Colonel Ramón
Montes Arache.

April 28   Rebel leaders take the initiative and stage a number of operations against the Ozama Fortress and other loyalist posts in
the city. Loyalist troops in San Isidro are highly demoralized
by their failure to capture the city and request military support from the United States through its embassy in Santo
Domingo. A military junta is created to deal officially with
the United States. Late in the afternoon Colonel Benoit, head
of the new junta, requests an urgent landing of the U.S.
Marines to cope with the situation. By 7:00 P.M. the first
platoon of U.S. troops lands on Dominican soil. (By May 7,
there were thirty thousand U.S. troops in the country.)

April 29   U.S. troops reinforce the positions held by the loyalists at
the bridge and in the outskirts of the city. Rebel leaders begin
a complex network of defense units—the "commandos"—to
defend the city from U.S. and loyalist attacks.

April 30   The Papal Nuncio, Emmanuele Clarizio, succeeds in convinc-
ing the contending factions to sign a cease-fire. U.S. troops
create the International Security Zone (ISZ) around the
U.S. and other foreign embassies. John B. Martin arrives in
Santo Domingo as special envoy of President Johnson to
open contact with the rebels.

May 1   Martin meets with Imbert and Caamaño separately to begin
negotiations toward a settlement. An independent group of
Dominican public figures start conversations to help solve the
crisis. OAS Secretary General José A. Mora arrives in Santo
Domingo.

May 2   Martin declares in a press conference that the revolution has
been taken over by the communists. In Washington, President Johnson repeats the charge. Martin goes to Puerto Rico
to meet Bosch. A five-man OAS commission arrives in the
country. After midnight U.S. troops move into the city to
open up a line of communications between the ISZ and the
international airport near San Isidro. The city, which is still
under rebel control, is thus divided by a U.S. line.

May 3   Caamaño is elected by the 1963 Congress as constitutional
president. Martin continues conversations with Imbert in an
attempt to create a "loyalist government."

May 5   The OAS commission succeeds in ratifying the cease-fire
worked out by the Papal Nuncio. Both contending factions

agree to sign the Act of Santo Domingo, by which the ISZ is recognized. Several Dominican leaders decline Martin's invitation to participate in a junta with General Imbert.

May 6   The OAS approves a U.S.–sponsored resolution to establish an international peace force to help restore order in Santo Domingo.

May 7   Ambassador Martin succeeds in setting up a five-man junta under General Imbert to replace the military junta of San Isidro. There are now two governments in the country: the Constitutionalist Government headed by Colonel Caamaño, and the Government of National Reconstruction headed by General Imbert.

May 9   General Imbert removes nine high-ranking officers from their posts and sends them abroad. However, Navy Chief Rivera Caminero, Air Force Commander General Santos, and San Isidro's General Wessin stay.

May 10   Ambassador Martin goes to see Colonel Caamaño for the second time since his arrival to open contact with rebel leaders. Colonel Caamaño refuses to negotiate with Imbert.

May 13   Imbert troops, with logistical and strategic support from U.S. troops stationed in Santo Domingo, begin a major operation against rebels, despite the cease-fire signed by all concerned —including the U.S.—and now ratified by the OAS.

May 14   Caamaño appeals to the United Nations Security Council. UN Secretary General U Thant is empowered to send a mission to observe the events.

May 15   President Johnson sends a new mission headed by McGeorge Bundy and Thomas C. Mann. Heavy fighting continues in Santo Domingo.

May 18   UN Special Representative José A. Mayobre begins conversations toward a new cease-fire. U.S. envoys Bundy and Mann hold conversations with rebel and loyalist leaders.

May 19   Rebel leader Colonel Fernández Domínguez stages a suicidal attempt to recover the Presidential Palace from loyalist troops and is killed by U.S. troops. Bundy's negotiations seem almost completed; the rebels agree to a formula presented by Bundy, in which Antonio Guzmán, a rich landowner and former Minister of Agriculture under Bosch, would become provisional president. General Imbert, however, does not agree to this formula.

May 20   A twelve-hour humanitarian truce is agreed upon by General Imbert.

May 26   Negotiations are suddenly stopped and Bundy returns to Washington.

May 31   The OAS ratifies a U.S.–sponsored resolution to send a three-man Ad Hoc Committee to Santo Domingo. U.S. Ambassador Ellsworth Bunker is appointed head of the three-man team.

June 3   The OAS Ad Hoc Committee arrives in Santo Domingo. Conversations toward a settlement are immediately resumed.

June 15   Heavy fighting breaks out between U.S. and rebel troops. U.S. troops advance into rebel zone and forty city blocks are taken from rebel control.

June 18   The Ad Hoc Committee makes public the proposals for a permanent settlement.

July 8   Rebel leaders agree to accept Héctor García-Godoy, the candidate presented by the Ad Hoc Committee, as provisional president.

August 30   The Imbert junta resigns in open disapproval of the negotiations of the Ad Hoc Committee. Sixty mortar rounds are fired into the rebel zone during the night.

August 31   The Constitutionalist Government and the loyalist armed forces sign the Institutional and Reconciliation Acts.

September 3   Héctor García-Godoy is inaugurated as provisional president to rule the country for one year and to hold elections on June 1, 1966. The city of Santo Domingo is still divided into three different zones, and U.S. troops are still in the country. The rebels agree to surrender their weapons to the provisional president, but not to the OAS. The war is over.

Appendix 2

Main Actors in the Dominican Crisis

ALVAREZ HOLGUIN, P. A. — Army colonel, commander of army barracks, *"27 de Febrero."* One of the organizers of the revolt. Appointed undersecretary of defense in the rebel government.

AMIAMA TIO, LUIS — Influential politician and one of the two survivors of the five-man group that killed Trujillo. Head of PLE. Started the negotiations with Dr. Despradel to set up a negotiating group to find a solution to the crisis. Gave asylum in his house to many refugees from both sides at different times.

ARISTY, HECTOR — Former associate of Imbert and Amiama Tió. Sided with the rebels at the outbreak of the revolt and soon became one of its most important leaders. Appointed by Caamaño as minister of the presidency. Highly influential. Later ambassador to UNESCO.

BAEZ ACOSTA, JOSE — Helped in the hospitals in the rebel zone during the revolution. Later mayor of Santo Domingo.

BALAGUER, JOAQUIN — Scholar and politician. Served as president under Trujillo and the Council of State in 1962. Ousted from the presidency. Lived in exile in New York. His Reformista Party has large support in the countryside. Some of his followers organized a coup against the Triumvirate. His party won the 1966 elections, and he became president.

BENITEZ, JAIME — President of the University of Puerto Rico. Helped the negotiations between Bosch and Martin. Later came to Santo Domingo for the same purpose.

BENNETT, W. T. — U.S. Ambassador to the Dominican Republic since

202

March 1964. Friend of Donald Reid. Absent from Santo Domingo when revolution broke out on April 24. Returned on April 27 and requested a U.S. landing on April 28.

BENOIT, PEDRO B. — Air force colonel. Became head of the military junta created in San Isidro on April 28. Requested the U.S. landing. On May 7, he became part of Imbert's Government of National Reconstruction.

BONILLA AYBAR, RAFAEL — Radio commentator and publisher of extreme right-wing newspaper, *Prensa Libre*. Chased by rebels on April 27, causing incident at El Embajador. Managed to escape with U.S. refugees.

BONNELLY, RAFAEL — Right-wing politician. Minister of the interior under Trujillo. President of the Council of State in 1962. Supported the *golpe* against Bosch in 1963.

BORDAS, MANOLO — Brother of Diego Bordas, former minister of finance in Bosch cabinet. In charge of administering the supplies for the rebels.

BOSCH, JUAN — Mastermind of the revolution. Could not return to Santo Domingo until the end of the revolution. Presidential candidate in the 1966 elections. Presently in self-imposed exile in Spain.

BREISKY, ARTHUR — Second Secretary in the U.S. Embassy. Took a very active role in the first days of the crisis.

BROSSA, JORDI — Conservative politician of the UCN. Rejected J. B. Martin's offer to participate in the Government of National Reconstruction.

BUNDY, MCGEORGE — Special Assistant to President Johnson. Sent to Santo Domingo on a special mission to negotiate a new Dominican government.

BUNKER, ELLSWORTH — U.S. ambassador to the OAS. Became head of the OAS Ad Hoc Committee which negotiated the settlement.

CAAMANO DENO, FRANCISCO — Army colonel who became the leader of the rebel forces and was elected constitutional president on May 3, 1965.

CAPOZI, ILIO — Italian by birth, former SS officer. Instructor of the navy frogmen. Sided with rebels. Killed on May 19.

CAMPAGNA, ANIBAL — Former UCN deputy. Sided with the rebels to defend the return to a constitutional government. Appointed president of the Senate.

CASALS, P. MANUEL — Young politician from Santiago. Participated in the government of the Triumvirate, but later resigned. Sided with rebels and tried to stir the revolt in Santiago.

CEDENO VALDES, AREVALO — UCN deputy who became independent after the overthrow of Bosch. Sided with rebels. Appointed president of the Congress. Died of a heart attack during the revolution.

CLARIZIO, MSGR. EMMANUELE — Papal Nuncio in Santo Domingo. Managed to have rebels and loyalists sign the first cease-fire agreement. Became the target of the extreme right, whose members accused him of being a communist.

COLOMBO, RICARDO — Special envoy of the OAS. Headed a five-man commission to ratify the Act of Santo Domingo. Left Santo Domingo to protest before the OAS the role of the UN in the Dominican case and the unilateral negotiations undertaken by the U.S.

CONNETT, WILLIAM — Chargé d' affaires taking the place of the U.S. ambassador during the first four days of the revolt. Sent the first reports of the revolution to Washington.

CUELLO, JULIO — Minister of justice under Bosch. President of the Supreme Court under Reid Cabral. Selected by Dr. Despradel as member of mediating group.

CURY, JOTTIN — UCN deputy who proclaimed himself independent after the coup against Bosch. Sided with rebels. Appointed minister of foreign affairs in the rebel government.

DE LA RIVIERE, JEAN P. ANDRE — French paratrooper who helped the rebels organize the defense of Santo Domingo. Died on June 15, 1965.

DEL ROSARIO, ANTONIO — President of the Social Christians. Signed the Pacto de Río Piedras with Bosch. Sided with rebels, whom he represented before the OAS.

DEL ROSARIO, ENRIQUILLO — Politician and diplomat who tried to negotiate for the rebels in the first days. Became ambassador to OAS in Washington.

DE LOS SANTOS CESPEDES, JUAN — Chief of the air force. Ordered the strafing of the Presidential Palace on April 25 and following days.

DESPRADEL, ARTURO — Conservative politician. Secretary of foreign affairs under Trujillo. Adviser to General Imbert. Made attempt to set up independent group to start negotiations between rebels and loyalists.

DESPRADEL, FIDELIO — Son of Arturo Despradel. Leader of the powerful June 14th Movement. Became involved in the revolution after April 24.

DESPRADEL BRACHE, HERMAN — Chief of Police. Promised loyalty to Molina Ureña, but later sided with loyalists.

ESPAILLAT NANITA, LEOPOLDO — Leader of group of intellectuals who protested against status quo on February 27, 1965. Sided with rebels. Special adviser to Provisional President Molina Ureña.

ESPINAL, MANUEL — PRD member who organized revolt among civilian groups. Now deputy to the Dominican Congress.

FERNANDEZ DOMINGUEZ, RAFAEL — Air force colonel who helped to restore the Council of State in power. Mastermind of the revolt from abroad. Returned to Santo Domingo during the revolt and died on May 19, 1965.

FIALLO, VIRIATO — Right-wing politician. Head of UCN. Presidential candidate against Bosch in 1962. Supported the *golpe* against Bosch in 1963.

FISHBURN, COL. THOMAS — Air attaché of the U.S. Embassy in Santo Domingo. Played an important role in the crisis, helping to establish loyalist stronghold in Santo Domingo.

GARCIA-GODOY, HECTOR — Foreign minister under Juan Bosch, and vice-president of Balaguer's Reformista Party. Favorite candidate of the group of entrepreneurs from Santiago for provisional president. Became provisional president on September 3, 1965.

GAUTREAU, BONAPARTE — Young intellectual of the PRD. Vice-minister of the presidency and secretary to Caamaño.

GOICO, FELIX — Highly respected physician who refused to participate in the Government of National Reconstruction set up by J. B. Martin.

GONZALEZ, MANOLO — Middle-class businessman, originally from Spain. Member of the PSP. Helped to organize commando posts to enroll civilian fighters.

GRISOLIA POLONEY, CARLOS — UCN deputy to the Congress of 1962. Member of the Government of National Reconstruction.

GUTIERREZ, GIOVANNI — Army colonel who helped organize the revolt, but later went into asylum. Managed to join the rebels again at the end of the revolution.

GUZMAN, S. ANTONIO — Rich landowner. Minister of agriculture in Bosch cabinet. Rebel candidate for provisional president.

HERRERA, RAFAEL — Editor of the independent newspaper *El Listín Diario*. Refused to participate in Government of National Reconstruction.

HEYWOOD, COL. RALPH — Naval attaché of the U.S. Embassy. Played an important role in the Dominican crisis, helping to establish loyalist stronghold in Santo Domingo.

IMBERT BARRERA, ANTONIO — Honorary general of the army for having participated in the killing of Trujillo. Powerful political figure. Chosen by J. B. Martin to head the Government of National Reconstruction. Resigned on August 30, 1965.

ISA CONDE, ANTONIO — Young middle-class student, member of the PSP. Took active part in the revolution.

JAVIER CASTILLO, CAONABO — Secretary general of the Social Christian Party. Signed the Pacto de Río Piedras with Bosch. Sided with rebels, but could not come to the country until the end of the revolution.

JORGE BLANCO, SALVADOR — Young intellectual and independent politician who sided with rebels. Attorney general for the rebel government.

LACHAPELLE DIAZ, HECTOR — Army captain. Rebel chief of operations.

LOCKWARD, ANDRES — Young lawyer of the PRSC. Represented that party in the negotiations.

LORA FERNANDEZ, J. M. — Army major. One of the original organizers of the revolution. Chief of staff of rebel forces. Killed after the revolution in the battle of the Matun Hotel in Santiago in December 1965.

MAINARDI REYNA, VIRGILIO — Former governor of Santiago. Opponent of Bosch. Sided with rebels from the start of the revolution.

MANN, THOMAS C. — U.S. undersecretary of state. Went to Santo Domingo with McGeorge Bundy to report to President Johnson on the state of affairs in the Dominican Republic.

MARTIN, JOHN BARTLOW — Former U.S. ambassador to the Dominican Republic. Went to Santo Domingo as special envoy of President Johnson. Formed the Government of National Reconstruction with Antonio Imbert as president.

MARTINEZ FRANCISCO, ANTONIO — Wealthy businessman. PRD secretary general after the *golpe* against Bosch. Later minister of finance in the Balaguer government.

MAYOBRE, J. A. — Special UN representative sent by Secretary General U Thant to observe and report on the Dominican situation. Managed to have both factions agree to a second cease-fire.

MEJIA DEL CASTILLO, E. R. (a.k.a. PICHIRILO) — Former quartermaster of Fidel Castro, with whom he fought in Cuba against Batista. One of the most important civilian fighters of the Dominican revolution. Shot in the back one year after the revolution. He was an outspoken "anticommunist."

MEJIA, JUAN B. — Middle-class lawyer who represented the interests of the June 14th Movement before the Caamaño government.

MOLINA URENA, RAFAEL — Former president of the House of Representatives under Bosch. Main organizer of the revolt. Became provisional president on April 25, but went into asylum on April 27. Later he went back to the rebel zone. Later Dominican ambassador to the UN.

MONTES ARACHE, MANUEL RAMON — Navy colonel and former director of the navy school of frogmen, the elite fighters of the Dominican armed forces. Played an important role as commander of the rebel forces. Appointed minister of defense in the rebel government.

MORA, JOSE A. — Secretary general of the OAS. Took an active role in the negotiations. Became the target of both factions, who accused him of being biased.

MORILLO, LOPEZ JOSE — Colonel in the air force and friend of Colonel Caamaño, with whom he had forced the resignation of corrupt General Peguero from the police force a few months earlier. Did not join the rebels, but reported to San Isidro. After the revolution he was appointed chief of police for one year.

NUNEZ NOGUERAS, MANUEL A. — Leader of the group of officers who joined the revolt after being discharged from service by the government. Helped organize the revolt and stayed with rebels until the end.

PASTORIZA, TOMAS (JIMMY) — Influential leader of the Santiago group of entrepreneurs tied to the oligarchy.

PEGUERO, BELISARIO — Chief of police ousted by Donald Reid for openly corrupt behavior. Tried unsuccessfully to participate in the revolution.

PEGUERO, LEMBERT F. — PRD leader and minister of justice under Bosch. Maintained his position in the rebel side until the end. Appointed minister of justice by Caamaño.

PENA GOMEZ, FRANCISCO — Radio speaker and youth organizer of the PRD. Remained with the rebels. Secretary general of the PRD in 1966.

PENA TAVERAS, MARIO — Army captain who organized the revolt among non-commissioned officers and the rank and file. Was instrumental in rescuing the group of officers put in jail by the loyalist Chief of Staff General Cuesta.

PEREZ, JULIAN J. — Lawyer and economist who rejected Martin's offer to participate in the Government of National Reconstruction. Became special advisor to President Balaguer after the 1966 elections.

PICHARDO, NICOLAS — Physician and conservative politician. Vice-president of the Council of State after Trujillo. Declined to participate in the Government of National Reconstruction.

PITTALUGA, S. LOVATON — Foreign minister of the Provisional Government of Molina Ureña. Went into asylum on April 27 after several attempts to negotiate.

POSTIGO, JULIO — Bookseller. Member of the Government of National Reconstruction. Resigned post in August 1965.

RAMIREZ, HERNANDO — Army colonel who was the main military organizer of the revolution. Took asylum on April 27, 1965, apparently for reasons of health. Later returned to the rebel zone, but had to leave a second time.

REID BARRERAS, EDUARDO — Dominican ambassador in Rome. Presented to the OAS Ad Hoc Committee as the rebel candidate for president or vice-president. Came back to Santo Domingo in July 1965, but did not accept the job of vice-president offered to him.

REID CABRAL, DONALD — President of the Triumvirate or civilian junta set up by the military in 1963 after the coup against Bosch. Overthrown by the rebels on April 24, 1965.

RICART, GUSTAVO — One of the main leaders of the violent MPD.

RIVERA CAMINERO, FRANCISCO — Commodore of the navy who finally sided with the loyalist troops. Secretary of defense in the Government of National Reconstruction and in the Provisional Government. Ordered to leave the country in 1966.

RIVERA CUESTA, MARCOS — General of the army, Head of the loyalist chiefs of staff. Put in jail by the rebels but later freed.

ROMAN, DR. JUAN MIGUEL — Top leader of the June 14th Movement. Died on May 19, 1965.

SEIJAS, NEIT NIVAR — Colonel in the army with ties to the so-called San Cristobal Group. Follower of Balaguer.

SHLAUDEMANN, HARRY — U.S. diplomat who had worked in Santo Domingo in 1963. Went to Santo Domingo with Martin and stayed there until the end of the crisis.

TAVERAS, FAFA — Top leader of the June 14th Movement. One of the main organizers of the civilian fighters.

TAVAREZ JUSTO, MANOLO — Maximum leader of the June 14th Movement. Killed fighting in the hills against the military after the *golpe* against Bosch in 1963.

VINAS ROMAN, ELBY — General of the army and secretary of defense. Ousted by Donald Reid, allegedly for corruption.

WESSIN Y WESSIN, ELIAS — General of the army and commander of the loyalist stronghold at San Isidro. Became the center of resistance to the demands of the rebels to reinstate Bosch, whom he had ousted eighteen months earlier.

YEARA NASSER, JORGE — Young PRD politician. Organizer of the fight in its early stages.

ZELLER COCCO, ALEJANDRO — Engineer who became member of the Government of National Reconstruction.

Appendix 3

Rebel Military Officers

Army

Col. Francisco Caamaño
†Col. Hernando Ramírez
Col. Pedro A. Alvarez Holguín
Col. Servando A. Buompensiere
†Col. Giovanni Gutiérrez
Col. José M. Fernández
‡Col. Ludovino Fernández
    Domínguez
§Col. Rafael Fernández Domínguez
Col. Jose Caonabo Fernández
Col. Armando Sosa Leyba
Col. Rogelio A. Jiménez Herrera
Maj. Juan M. Lora Fernández
Maj. Ramon Grullón Gallardo
Maj. Manuel A. Núñez Nogueras
Maj. César A. Caamaño
Cpt. Mario Peña Taveras

Cpt. Héctor Lachapelle Díaz
Cpt. Rafael A. Quirós Pérez
Cpt. José A. Noboa Garnés
Cpt. Luis Androcles Arias
Cpt. Miguel A. Calderón Cepeda
Cpt. Luis Mélquiades Suero
Cpt. José M. Beras Porrata
Maj. Eladio Ramírez

Air Force

Col. Luis C. Tejeda
‡Col. Carlos Tejedas González
Maj. Antonio Marte Rodríguez
Cpt. Odalis Cruz Ventura
Cpt. Alfredo Alcibíades Hernández
Cpt. Jorge Percival Peña
Cpt. Rafael Yegues Arismendi
Cpt. Hermán Franklin Imbert

The list includes only officers with ranks of captain, major, or colonel, or their equivalent. All of these officers, except those specifically mentioned by the symbols § (dead), † (took refuge on April 27), or ‡ (put in jail by the loyalists), remained in the rebel zone until the end of the revolution. The list has been taken from the official document of the rebel government (Gaceta Oficial #4, September 2, 1965). In the same document are the names and ranks of 135 other officers of the Dominican armed forces who were promoted by the rebel government for their actions during the revolution.

Navy[1]

Col. Ramón M. Montes Arache
Col. Tomas Poter Titre
Maj. Agustín Liberato Morrobel
Maj. Porfirio Amador Ruíz
Maj. Porfirio Torres Tejeda
Cpt. José Silberberg Suárez
Cpt. Juan A. Montalvo
Cpt. José N. López Lantigua
Cpt. Rafael E. Ubiera

Police

Col. Jorge Gerardo Marte
  Hernández
Col. José Francisco García
Col. Dante Rafael Canela
Col. Fausto Pantaleón Delgado
Cpt. Alejandso Derro Suero
Cpt. Domingo A. Vargas
Cpt. Sergio Félix Paredes
Cpt. Manuel E. Rivera

Appendix 4

Dominican Leaders and Other Observers Interviewed

Amiama Tió, Luis
Aristy, Héctor
Aybar Nicolás, Andrés
Báez Acosta, José R.
Barahona, Andújar
Bennett, William T.
Benoit, Pedro Bartolomé
Beras, Octavio (Msgr.)

Bernard, Leonte
Bosch, Juan
Botello, Norge W.
Brossa, Jordi
Bunker, Ellsworth
Caro, José A.
Castaños Espaillat, J. C.
Clarizio, Emmanuele (Msgr.)

The list does not include the names of persons whom the author was in contact with during the revolution, but who were not in Santo Domingo on his second visit to the country. Some of the interviews were made in Canada or in the United States.

1. The name of Ilio Capozi, instructor of the navy frogmen, should be added to this list. He was killed on May 19, 1965.

Cuello, J. I.
Deschamps, Miguel Angel
Despradel, Arturo
Espinal, Emmanuel
Estrella, Julio C.
Fernández, Spencer, Tomás
Figueredo, Sergio
Gautreau, Bonaparte
González, Manolo
Gasso y Gasso, M.
Gutiérrez, Giovanni
Herrera, Rafael
Imbert Barrera, Antonio
Inchaústegui Cabral, Héctor
Isa Conde, Antonio
Isa Conde, Narciso
Javier Castillo, Caonabo
Lockward, Andrés
Martínez Francisco, A.
Martínez, Rafael
Mejía del Castillo, E. R. (Pichirilo)
Molina, Henry

Molina Ureña, Rafael
Molina Morillo, Rafael
Montes Arache, M. Ramón
Morillo Lopez, José
Morrobel, Liberato
Moreno, Ernesto
Peña Gómez, Francisco
Pérez y Pérez, Enrique
Postigo, Julio
Puentes, Pablo
Reid Cabral, Donald
Reyes Cerda, Rafael
Ricart y Ricart, Gustavo
Sánchez, Carlos
Shlaudemann, Harry
Santos Céspedes, Juan
Tavares, Froilán, R. J.
Taveras, Rafael (Fafa)
Ubiera, Rafael E.
U.S. Embassy Official
Wessin y Wessin, Elías
Yeara Nasser, Jorge

Appendix 5

Commandos and Other Military Posts

Official Name	Number of Men
1 Commando "A," Zona no. 1 (Palacio de Justicia)	42
2 Policía Militar (Cuerpo de Vigilancia)	154
3 Commando San Miguel "Luis Chez Javier"	54
4 Guardia interior del Palacio Presidencial	98
5 Commando del PRD	37
6 Commando Operaciones U-2 Zona 4 (San Antón)	35
7 Personal Escolta del Presidente	29
8 Personal Oficina del G-1	10
9 Dirección nacional de Seguridad	43
10 Commando Luperón	48
11 Commando "Villa Juana"	26
12 Commando No. 2	30
13 Commando B-2	67
14 Commando Rafael A. Velázquez (Cibao)	33
15 Commando H	28
16 Commando Enrique Jiménez Moya	30
17 Commando General Benito Monción	39
18 Commando Ilio Capozi	73
19 Commando José Horacio Rodríguez	45
20 Personal Fortaleza Ozama	312
	(Continued)

The information furnished here was provided by the official record of financial aid given to these groups by the Constitutionalist Government around the month of July.

	Official Name	*Number of Men*
21	Oficiales Fortaleza Ozama	23
22	Commando Capri	47
23	Commando San Cristobal	49
24	Avanzada del Commando Duarte #1	15
25	Commando Móvil #2	8
26	Cuartel General Zona 2	6
27	Commando Zona No. 4	20
28	Oficiales Zona No. 3	7
29	Commando de la Aduana	39
30	Commando El Conde	18
31	Personal Ministerio Fuerzas Armadas	15
32	Commando A-B-C No. 3	31
33	Commando Duarte No. 1	34
34	Commando Duarte No. 2	26
35	Commando La Vega	80
36	Commando Veterano No. 2	22
37	Personal Intendencia General	53
38	Cuartel General Zona No. 1	29
39	Commando José Gabriel García (Grupo B)	71
40	Commando Euclides Morillo (Recolector de gasolina)	9
41	Commando Rafael Fernández Domínguez	27
42	Commando Libertad	33
43	Commando As Negro	36
44	Commando Julio Lluberes, hijo	16
45	Commando A Espaillat (Zona No. 2)	14
46	Commando Elías Bisonó Mera	43
47	Commando Villa Consuelo	30
48	Commando Nacionalista	33
49	Commando Pedro Mena	51
50	Commando Padre las Casas	36
51	Personal Sub-direccion de Seguridad	60
52	Commando B-3	183
53	Commando G-2 (registro de entradas)	36
54	Commando Valverde (Mao)	17
55	Commando de Artillería	9
56	Commando 30 de Marzo	59
57	Commando Armeria (Centro Sirio)	46
58	Commando Pasito Polanco	41

(Continued)

	Official Name	Number of Men
59	Commando Tony Barreiro No. 1	19
60	Commando Tony Barreiro No. 2	29
61	Commando San Juan	17
62	Commando Puerto Plata	46
63	Commando Constitución No. 1	33
64	Commando General Bordas Valdés	46
65	Commando Batallón Blindado	26
66	Commando Independencia 15	37
67	Commando Manolo A. Tavárez Justo	46
68	Commando La Esperilla	19
69	Commando Cucaracha 20	30
70	Commando Central Ciudad Nueva (unidad móvil)	30
71	Commando Barahona	41
72	Commando Poasi	67
73	Personal Intendencia General (Almacen No. 2)	59
74	Commando Ibarra Ríos No. 2	13
75	Personal de Investigaciones	12
76	Commando Manolo Mena	26
77	Commando San Antón	73
78	Organizacion de Foupsa-Cesitrado	30
79	Personal de la Policía Militar	49
80	Commando Juan Pablo Duarte	41
81	Commando Polo Rodríguez	20
82	Commando José M. Marte	13
83	Commando El Lobo (San Carlos)	25
84	Commando Rafael Fernández Domínguez No. 2	90
85	Commando Patrulla móvil de aduana	7
86	Commando Pedro Cadena	61
87	Commando Beller	32
88	Commando Juan Miguel Román	51
89	Commando Luis Ibarra Ríos #1	32
90	Commando Miguel López (Zona No. 2)	24
91	Commando General San Martín	26
92	Commando Zarpadores (José M. Reyes Araujo)	42
93	Personal de Transportacion Const.	88
94	Commando La Romana-B	42
95	Commando Francisco del Rosario Sánchez (S. Carlos)	97
96	Commando Jima-abajo (La Vega)	21

(Continued)

Official Name	Number of Men
97 Commando Nelson Duarte	24
98 Commando Santa Bárbara	21
99 Commando La Romaña-A	29
100 Commando de Instrucciones (Sección AA central)	92
101 Commando Armando Aybar	36
102 Commando Jacques Viau	34
103 Commando Carlos Gómez Ruíz	9
104 Commando Santiago	21
105 Commando San Lázaro	53
106 Commando Euclides Morillo (El Lido)	60
107 Commando Manuel de J. Liriano	23
108 Commando C-A (Seccion Arti.)	27
109 Commando Grupo Bravo	13
110 Commando Central San Carlos	40
111 Commando San Carlos (Avanzada A)	77
112 Commando Libertador	53
113 Commando Arturo Jiminián	43
114 Commando de Instrucción	10
115 Commando Rubén Díaz Moreno	15
116 Commando Euclides Morillo (Zona No. 2)	26
117 Commando Enriquillo No. 2	45
118 Commando José Jiménez R.	12
119 Commando Adolfo Pérez Sánchez	30
120 Commando Miguel el Loco	30
121 Commando Cabeza de León	45
122 Commando Pedregal	24
123 Commando Argentina	140
124 Commando San Diego	69
125 Commando Juan Miguel Román-B	18
126 Personal presta servicio Palacio Presidencial	13
127 Personal del Edificio Copello	61
128 Personal sastrería militar	28
129 Personal Jefatura de Estado Mayor	26
130 Personal Ministerio della Fuerzas Armadas	20

Appendix 6

Organizations Referred to in the Text

ASOCHOIN   *Asociación de Choferes Independientes* (Association of Independent Drivers). Trade union of taxi drivers affiliated with FOUPSA.

BRUC   *Bloque Revolucionario Universitario Cristiano* (Association of Christian University Students). Student union quite active in university affairs with Social Christian orientation.

CASC   *Confederación Autónoma de Sindicatos Cristianos* (Autonomous Confederation of Christian Trade Unions). A very powerful federation of unions of industrial and farm workers with orientation of Christian Democracy. Associated with the regional CLASC.

CEFA   *Centro de Enseñanza de las Fuerzas Armadas* (Armed Forces Training Center). A military school at the San Isidro military camp, and elite corps of the army under the direction of powerful Brigadier General Elías Wessin y Wessin, who was instrumental in ousting Bosch.

CLASC   *Confederación Latino Americana de Sindicatos Cristianos* (Latin Confederation of Christian Trade Unions). Quite active organization with orientation of Christian Democracy.

FOUPSA   *Frente de Obreros Unidos Pro Sindicatos Autónomos* (Workers United Front of Autonomous Trade Unions). Originally organized by the UCN, but later threw their support for Bosch.

FRAGUA   Revolutionary Federation of University Students with Marxist Orientation. Quite powerful in student affairs. Connected with

217

both PSP and June 14th Movement. Very popular with students.

FURR

Radical student movement with relatively small following in the student body.

JRC

Juventud Revolucionaria Cristiana (Revolutionary Christian Youth). Association of high school students with orientation of Christian Democracy.

June 14th Movement (1J4)

Agrupación Política 14 de Junio. Political movement with strong nationalistic ideology, organized as an underground movement against Trujillo in 1959. Its leader Manolo Tavárez Justo was killed by the army after Bosch was ousted in 1963. Oriented toward Castro's interpretation of Marxism.

MPD

Movimiento Popular Dominicano (Popular Dominican Movement). Marxist-Leninist group founded in 1956 with strong orientation toward Mao Tse-tung's brand of communism.

POASI

Longshoremen's trade union organization. Quite strong and well organized. Oriented toward the PRD.

PRD

Partido Revolucionario Dominicano (Dominican Revolutionary Party). Founded by Bosch and other Dominican exiles with broad Aprista orientation of the Democratic Left. Won elections of 1962 by a large popular majority.

PRSC

Partido Revolucionario Social Cristiano (Social Christian Revolutionary Party). Small party with great political potential. Orientation of Christian Democracy like similar parties in Chile and Venezuela.

PR

Partido Reformista (Reformist Party). Founded by Joaquín Balaguer and quite popular among the peasants. Won the elections of 1966 against Bosch.

PSP

Partido Socialista Popular (Popular Socialist Party). Official Communist Party in the country. Founded during Trujillo's regime. Orientation toward Moscow line of communism. Relatively small but well established in some intellectual and industrial sectors.

UCN

Unión Cívica Nacional (National Civic Union). Political group founded as a resistance movement against Trujillo. Became a political party in the 1962 campaign and appealed to upper and middle classes. Lost elections against Bosch. Instrumental in coup of 1963 against Bosch.

Selected Bibliography

Books

Bosch, Juan. *Crisis de la democracia de América en la República Dominicana.* Mexico City: Centro de Estudios y Documentación sociales, 1964.
———. *Partido Revolucionario Dominicano: tesis sindical.* Santo Domingo: Private Edition, 1966.
———. *Trujillo: causas de una tiranía sin ejemplos.* Santo Domingo: Impresora Arte y Cine, 1962.
Brugal Alfau, Danilo. *Tragedia en Santo Domingo: Documentos para le Historia.* Santo Domingo: Editorial El Caribe, 1966.
CEFA. *Libro blanco de las fuerzas armadas y de la policía nacional de la República Dominicana.* Santo Domingo: Editorial El Caribe, 1964.
Clark, James A. *The Church and the Crisis in the Dominican Republic.* Westminster, Md., 1966.
Crassweller, Robert D. *Trujillo, The Life and Times of a Caribbean Dictator.* New York: Macmillan, 1966.
Draper, Theodore. *The Dominican Revolt: A Case Study in American Policy.* New York: Commentary Reports, 1968.
de Galíndez, Jesús. *La era de Trujillo.* Buenos Aires: Editorial Americana, 1962.
Estrella, Julio César. *La revolución dominicana y la crisis de la OEA.* Santo Domingo: Editorial Ahora, 1965.
Franco, Franklin I. *República Dominicana: clases, crisis y comandos.* Havana: Casas de las Américas, 1966.
Jiménez Grullón, J. I. *La República Dominicana: una ficción.* Mérida, Venezuela: Talleres Gráficos Universitarios, 1965.
Kurzman, Dan. *Santo Domingo: The Revolt of the Damned.* New York: Putnam Publishing Co., 1965.
Mallin, Jay. *Carribbean Crisis: Subversion Fails in the Dominican Republic.* New York: Doubleday, 1965.
Martin, John Bartlow. *Overtaken by Events.* New York: Doubleday, 1966.
Martínez, Julio César. *Santo Domingo: desde Trujillo hasta la revolución de Abril.* Caracas, Venezuela: Impreso en "Rotolito," 1966.
Szulc, Tad. *Dominican Diary.* New York: Delacorte Press, 1965.
Thomas, Norman, ed. *Dominican Republic: A Study in the New Imperialism.* New York: Institute for International Labor Research, 1966.
Volman, Sacha. *Quién impondrá la democracia?* Mexico City: Centro de Estudios y Documentación sociales, 1965.

Articles

Bosch, Juan. "Communism and Democracy in the Dominican Republic." *War and Peace Report*, 5 (July 1965). (This same article may also be found in *Saturday Review*, 48 (August 7, 1965), p. 13.)

————. "The Dominican Revolution." *The New Republic*, 153 (July 24, 1965), pp. 19–21.

————. "El Pentagonismo sustituto del imperialismo." *Ahora* (1967).

————. "A Tale of Two Nations." *The New Leader*, 48 (June 21, 1965), pp. 3–7.

Cuello, J. I., and Isa Conde, N. "Revolutionary Struggle in the Dominican Republic and its Lessons." *World Marxist Review*, 8 (December 1965), pp. 71–81.

Cuello, Julio A. "Memorias de una tentativa frustrada de mediación por la paz." *Ahora* (1966).

Draper, Theodore. "A Case of Defamation: U.S. Intelligence vs. Juan Bosch." *The New Republic*, 154 (February 26, 1966), pp. 15–18.

————. "A Case of Political Obscenity." *The New Leader*, 49 (May 9, 1966), pp. 3–7.

————. "The Dominican Crisis: A Case Study in American Policy." *Commentary*, 40 (December 1965), pp. 33–68.

————. "The New Dominican Crisis." *The New Leader*, 49 (January 31, 1966), pp. 3–8.

————. "The Roots of the Dominican Crisis." *The New Leader*, 48 (May 24, 1965), pp. 3–18.

Gerassi, John. "Intervention in Santo Domingo." *Liberation*, 10 (June–July 1965), pp. 3–7.

Lowenthal, Abraham F. "The Dominican Republic: The Politics of Chaos." In *Reform and Revolution*, edited by A. von Lazar and R. R. Kaufman, pp. 34–58. Boston: Allyn and Bacon, 1969.

————. "Foreign Aid as a Political Instrument: The Case of the Dominican Republic." *Public Policy*, 14 (1965), pp. 141–60.

Martin, John B. "Struggle to Bring Together Two Sides Torn by Killing." *Life*, 58 (May 28, 1965), p. 28.

Slater, Jerome. "The Limits of Legitimation in International Organizations: The OAS and the Dominican Crisis." *International Organization*, 23 (Winter 1969), pp. 48–72.

————. "The United States, the Organization of American States, and the Dominican Republic, 1961–63." *International Organization*, 18 (Spring 1964), pp. 268–91.

Wedge, Bryant. "The Case Study of Student Political Violence: Brazil 1964 and Dominican Republic 1965." *World Politics*, 21 (January 1969), pp. 183–206.

Wiarda, Howard J. "Contemporary Constitutions and Constitutionalism:

The Dominican Republic." *Law and Society Review,* 2 (June 1968), pp. 385–405.

————. "The Development of the Labor Movement in the Dominican Republic." *Interamerican Economic Affairs,* 20 (Summer 1966), pp. 41–63.

————. "The Politics of Civic Military Relations in the Dominican Republic." *Journal of Interamerican Studies,* 7 (October 1965), pp. 465–84.

Wilson, Larman. "The Dominican Policy of the United States: The Illusions of Economic Development and Elections." *World Affairs,* 128 (July–September 1965), pp. 93–101.

Santo Domingo Newspapers

Ahora, May 1, May 16, September 18, 1965.
El Caribe, April 25, 26, 27, 28, 1965.
La Información, April 24 to July 27, 1965.
El Listín Diario, April 25, 26, 27, 28, 1965.
La Nación, May 6 to September 16, 1965.
Patria, May 14 to September 16, 1965.

Documents

Center for Strategic Studies. *Dominican Action—1965: Intervention or Cooperation?* Special Report Series, no. 2. Washington, D.C.: Georgetown University, 1966.

Constitutionalist Government. *Gaceta oficial de la República Dominicana.* Nos. 1, 2, 3, 4. Santo Domingo, May–September, 1965.

Clarizio, Emmanuele (Msgr.). "Chronología de las gestiones para conseguir el cese de fuego." Santo Domingo, 1965. (Mimeographed.)

Government of National Reconstruction. *Gaceta oficial de la República Dominicana.* No. 8944. Santo Domingo, June, 1965.

Mensajes del Santo Padre Paulo VI a los dominicanos, Abril 1965—Abril 1966. San Juan, Puerto Rico: Talleres Gráficos Interamericanos.

Organization of American States. *Tenth Meeting of Consultation of Ministers of Foreign Affairs, Official Documents.* Nos. 47, 81, 374, 430, 433, 435, 436, 437, 445, 447, 452, 454, 463. OEA Series F/11.10. Washington, D.C.: Pan American Union, 1965.

U.S., Congress, Senate, Committee on Foreign Relations, *Background Information Relating to the Dominican Republic,* 89th Cong., 1st sess., October 18, 1965.

U.S., Congress, Senate, Committee on the Judiciary, *Testimony of Brigadier General Elías Wessin y Wessin,* 89th Cong., 1st sess., October 1, 1965.

U.S., Congress, Senate, Committee on the Judiciary, *Testimony of Juan Isidro Tapia Adames,* 89th Cong., 1st sess., October 18, 1965.

U.S., Congress, Senate, *Congressional Record,* 89th Cong., 1st sess., 1965, 111, pt. 18:23855. (Senator William Fulbright's speech before the Senate, September 15, 1965.)

Index

Abuse, "tolerable" vs. "intolerable," 103
Acomplejado (rebel type), 137–40, 192
Adams, Johnny, 145
Ad Hoc Committee, 38, 53
Alienation of rebels, 90–97, 190
Aprovechado (rebel type), 143–45
Aristy, Héctor, 30, 40, 139–40, 153
Armed Forces: and Bosch, 19; and Trujillo, 19; young officers' revolt, 25–31 passim; San Cristobal group, 26; San Isidro group, 26, 27; disintegration, 194
Auténtico Party, 18

Balaguer, Joaquín, 16, 26, 87*n*
Barrio, 5*n. See also* San Miguel, San Lázaro
Barrios altos, 28, 88, 92, 93, 94
Batista, 3
Bennett, W. T., 33
Benoit, Col. Pedro B., 32, 37
Betancourt, Rómulo, 16
Bonnelly, Rafael, 16
Bosch, Juan: exile, 15, 16, 26, 28, 35; PRD, 16; opposition to, 18, 19, 20, 21, 88, 126; elections 1962, 17, 18; coup against, 20, 22, 24, 124; and communism, 21; and Marxist parties, 24, 122; and democracy, 97, 110, 136; government of, 102; elections 1966, 117; relations with J. B. Martin, 135–36

Bundy, McGeorge, 37, 38
Bunker, Ellsworth, 35, 38, 44

Caamaño: information about, 9, 10; leadership of, 30, 35, 38, 41, 44, 52, 53, 56, 138, 152–59 passim; cabinet of, 40; *acomplejado* type, 138; agencies created by, 184
Capitalism, 123, 126
Capozi, Ilio, 139
CASC, 117
Castro, Fidel, 3
Casualties, 29, 66, 190*n*
Catholic Charities, 68, 69, 74, 75
Catholic church, 15, 24, 37, 70, 127–28, 131
Cayo Confites, 15
Cefa troops, 66, 67, 82
CIA, 10, 33, 121
Ciudad Nueva, 35, 71
Civilian troops, 30, 31, 46, 47
Civic organization, 11, 162–69
Clarizio, Msgr. Emmanuele. *See* Papal Nuncio
Clergy, 128
Comandante, 160
Comando médico, 79, 82
Commando school, 55
Commandos: information from, 10; characteristics of, 42, 47, 63, 174, 176; leaders of, 42, 64, 75, 159, 160, 161, 162; organization of, 42, 46, 47,

223